Dedication
For John Magan of Kill

Acknowledgements

To Marianne Gunn O'Connor, for encouraging me to find what I really wanted to say.

To Paddy McMahon and Billy Connell for their belief and encouragement.

To Simon Carty, David Handy, Ruán Magan, Eoin Mooney for the unsavoury task of reading early drafts. To Anne Haverty for her generosity. To Mary Conneely and the guardians of wisdom at Pembroke Library, Dublin.

To Mark Geary, Josh Ritter and Michael Stipe for the soundtrack to my writing.

To Steve MacDonogh for his belief.

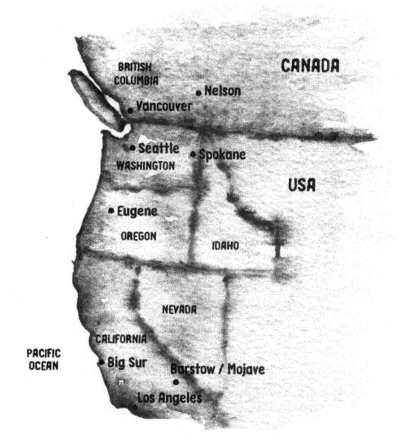

ANGELS AND RABIES

MANCHÁN MAGAN

ANGELS AND RABIES

A JOURNEY THROUGH THE AMERICAS

BRANDON

A Brandon Original Paperback

First published in 2006 by Brandon
an imprint of Mount Eagle Publications
Dingle, Co. Kerry, Ireland, and
Unit 3, Olympia Trading Estate, Coburg Road, London N22 6TZ, England

ISBN 0 86322 349 4

2 4 6 8 10 9 7 5 3 1

Mount Eagle Publications/Sliabh an Fhiolair Teoranta receives support from the
Arts Council/An Chomhairle Ealaíon.

Cover design: www.designsuite.ie
Cover photos: Ruán Magan
Typesetting by Red Barn Publishing, Skeagh, Skibbereen
Printed in the UK

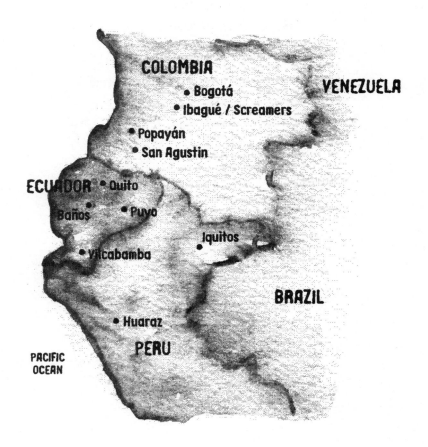

I'd tell you that I'm suffering
from the worst kind of loneliness,
The loneliness of being misunderstood,
or more poignantly
the loneliness of being afraid
to allow myself to be understood.

The Disposable Heroes of Hiphoprisy

Chapter 1

AFTER DINNER, THE Welshman lit candles and we all sat around in a circle. Fiona turned to me, welcoming me to the farm and thanking me for all the work I had been doing over the last two days.

"Mocha says he has come here to change," she announced to the group, "and we're going to help him."

I could hear Rabbit murmuring, *Oh no.*

She got me to sit in the centre of the circle, asking, "How does that feel?"

"Okay," I said.

"You really hate us, don't you?" she said. "You wanted to screw me and the girls in the forest today. But you were too scared. Right?"

No.

This was all a big misunderstanding. Earlier in the day, Fiona and some of the girls had brought me to a pool in the forest for a swim, and I had quickly stripped off and dived in. Of course, I wouldn't have done it if I had known, but I figured that since it was a commune, not stripping off would have caused more offence. I was wrong. The girls had kept their bras and shorts on and had looked worryingly at me.

I didn't really know how to answer Fiona now. Of course I didn't hate them; I had only met them the previous day. And I certainly didn't want to *screw* them. I had never screwed anyone and didn't want to start now, halfway up the Andes among these strange, voracious people. Rabbit chuckled.

Finally, I said, "Well, no, actually, I didn't."

"Admit it," she said. "For once in your life own up to yourself. See what you are – a weed, completely out of touch with your own sexuality, tied to your mammy's apron strings."

"Well," I said, trying to be as polite as I could, "I don't see how that's got anything to do with . . ."

"Shut up, you ponce. Shut up!" she screamed.

She was really shouting now.

"Admit it, you're shackled to the tabernacle and all the black priests back in Ireland. Admit it!"

I could tell Rabbit was impressed by her perceptiveness.

"Look," I said, "I'm probably not the most liberated man in the world, but what's that got to do with . . ."

"Spit it out! Tell us who you hate."

"Well, I'm not exactly sure I . . ." I dithered.

I could hear Rabbit. *Who are you kidding?* he was saying.

"You faggot!" she cried. "Go on, keep on denying it. Keep up your sick honeymoon existence. What do you think, Moore?"

Moore, a middle-aged man with a beard that extended into a coat of fur down his midriff, said with a delighted glint in his eye, "I think he's a slimy faggot."

"Yeah," piped up one of the children. "He's a frightened, little-boy faggot who wants to run home to his mammy. Little mammy's boy."

The child was fourteen at the very most. I had helped him fly his kite earlier that day.

"To be honest," I said, "with all of you shouting at me, I don't feel like I'm in the safest place. I feel a bit vulnerable actually."

"Vulnerable," Moore mimicked. "Do you hear him? He doesn't even know what a feeling is. He's a walking anal sphincter. He hasn't felt anything all his life."

Tracy looked me in the eye and said, "I'll fuck you, then you'll know what feeling is."

She wasn't a day over fifteen.

Fiona interrupted, "Okay, that's okay. We're getting nowhere. That's enough for tonight."

And she sent us off to bed.

How the hell did I get here?

I had written in my diary a few weeks earlier, *Hey Rabbit, I want to change. I really want to change. I want to like people. Be happy.*

Rabbit told me to go to America and when I asked him why, he said, *Because of what it means.*

I didn't understand, so he said, *Ame Rica – look it up.*

I did. *Rica* meant sweet and *ame* meant soul or love, but that didn't help much. He hadn't said North or South, so I chose South, thinking it would be cheaper. When I told people the plan, they said I was crazy, I was sure to be robbed, and not only robbed, but have my throat slit too. I didn't much mind having my throat slit. I've never been too worried by death – I liked the freedom of it, the sense of infinity. But I didn't like the idea of being robbed: I owned so little anyway that I couldn't stand losing any of it. I know it's tight-fisted of me, and not very Zen, but what the hell. So I decided to bring just two shopping bags with me, with some shorts, T-shirts and a toothbrush; that way it wouldn't matter.

There was another Irish bloke on the plane. He was scared too. I could feel him ten seats back, so I kept away. When we were refuelling in the Dominican Republic, he somehow sniffed me out, saying he had heard of a good hotel in Bogotá, and did I want to share a cab there? I accepted.

What did you do that for, you spa?

What's the harm? I whined. *I'm a little scared. I'd like the company.*

It was a fine hotel, the Platypus; it's in all the books. I went straight to bed, dead: flights really kill me – but not in a good way. In the middle of the night, I woke lost and I could hear voices through a door below me and Rabbit whispering that maybe the answers lay down there. The door led to a basement, and in it was a long table speckled with tiny

11

mounds of dirty white powder, like woodworm dust, which backpackers were cutting and sniffing on little mirrors. I ran away again.

Very funny, I snarled.

Drugs weren't what I was looking for. Every other disillusioned dreamer I knew was losing themselves in drink or dope back home in Ireland, or in the States if they had a Green Card – it was the one thing I was sure I didn't want. What was I looking for? The absence of hate? More than that, maybe. I was looking for love and I hated everything and anything that stood in my way – including Rabbit. The Screamers had been pretty perceptive about that.

It rained on my first morning in South America, and since I didn't feel like getting wet I spent the day drinking *café con leches* and reading the Platypus guest book, which was full of recommendations for good *empanada* joints and ways to avoid getting your throat slit: basically don't go up Monserrate at dusk and don't walk about the city but stride or even run, as if you were on military manoeuvres. Scanning through the pages, I came across a long rant by a Swede about a really awful commune up in the Andes. She had spent time with them and claimed they were crazy, backstabbing freaks. I could just imagine. Reading on, I found that they were called the Screamers.

No way! The Screamers. I knew them!

It was this bunch from Donegal who had built a boat and sailed to South America a few years before. I was ten when I first heard of them, sitting with my mum and dad watching *The Late Late Show*, and they came on talking about organic farming and letting their kids run around naked.

"No, Gay, we don't grow pot," they had said, and I remember asking my dad what pot was. I was transfixed. Children didn't run around naked in Ireland back then. They still don't. That was the eighties and only Germans knew about organic farming.

The Screamers, I said to Rabbit, *who would have thought?*

He didn't say anything, but I knew what had to be done.

I went down to the Terminal Terrestre and took the next Expresso Boliviano to Ibagué. There was a riot going on when I arrived, and the *collectivo* refused to bring me into town. In fact, it was the driver who called it a riot; it was actually just a fracas with gunfire and burnt-out cars. Since he wouldn't bring me, I had to book into the Terminal Hotel, which seemed more extra-Terrestre than anything; run by a dwarf and her huge hermaphrodite husband who slunk through the corridors clinging to an old broom, craning his neck to look into the bedrooms.

I could hear Rabbit chuckle, *God that's so clichéd, it's like bad fiction.* The place reeked of tea and tar and it was hard to keep in mind what I was looking for, that I wanted to live in love – was that too much to ask? I mean, a leaf or a bird does that, doesn't it? It's infused with life. But also with truth and love too. It never pretends to be anything else. It never holds back. That's all I wanted. To presume abundance. To not hold back. I knew that if I tried it at home they might lock me up, so I ran away. Rabbit had said *Ame Rica,* and after I had thought about it a while, I knew exactly where to go. In the *Observer,* I had read about a shaman who claimed there were three places you could find pure love: the first rush after swallowing Ayahuasca; as deep inside your own heart as you can get; and in the eyes of some prehistoric statues in San Agustin in south Colombia. I had been working on a farm in Wicklow at the time and decided that as soon as I had enough money I would go see those statues.

At the Terminal Hotel early the following morning, I paid the dwarf and took a wooden bus with no doors or windows up into the mountains. It left me on the side of the road in the rain, and a woman in a local shack pointed up into the rainforest, suggesting the Screamers lived somewhere up beyond the cloud line. She looked at me with that odd look reserved for tax collectors and reformed alcoholic uncles, and warned me there had been landslides and that the route would be treacherous, then gave me a pair of her own boots, because she thought I'd kill myself in my sandals.

Maybe I didn't want to die, after all.

I walked for hours up through the jungle. Like hours and hours. I couldn't believe how far away it was. The landslide had wiped out the path in parts, but most of the time I was able to walk around it. By nightfall I was so tired I couldn't go on. The boots had filled with mud, and my shopping bag luggage gouged into my hands. Normally when you reach the end of your endurance, an inner strength comes to guide you forward and goad you on, but for some reason I didn't have that mechanism, that turbo booster. I have always lacked the motivation to keep living, to keep focused on reality. And so it was no great surprise when I just collapsed on the ground, to sleep or die or whatever. I had nearly died a few times in Africa, and ever since then I had lost my fear of it. Part of me was only too willing to let go. It wasn't so much a death wish or anything, just that I didn't much care either way. I understood that humans were meant to go on living, and I did, of course, try to honour the commitment. I never planned suicide or anything, but it was just that I always had an inkling that life was a temporary intermission between somewhere else and that the love I was looking for was probably to be found in infinite amounts over there. I was pretty certain of that. So why not head there straight away? At the same time, I figured that, seeing as I was here, I might as well hang around for a while.

I dozed off and the rain continued to gush past me down the track. I'm not sure how long I was out for, but I doubt it was very long. Something shivered through me, and I awoke. Maybe it was Rabbit, or the thought of how much I wanted love in this life and how I had come all this way to find it. Whatever, the fight picked up in me again, and I scrambled to my feet. To be honest, I doubt it was Rabbit; he was being pretty useless at the time. You'd think if you have an angel, that's exactly the kind of time he'll kick in. Uh-uh. The thing is, I'm not so sure if Rabbit is even an angel at all . . . how can you tell?

More than anyone else, it was the old woman I met an hour later who saved me. Around midnight, I came across her squatting having a pee on the track in front of me. She wouldn't speak, but she led me through the trees to a cabin and gave me a cup of hot sugar-cane juice. I was fine after that, and I walked on, reaching the Screamers finally at dawn.

The place wasn't at all what I had imagined. There were no rainbow flags or pretty, hand-carved signs. It was just a farm like any other *campesino* farm in the area, with three wooden shacks and a few fields hacked out of the forest. But it bustled with life. The Screamers were all up and about, milking cows, lighting fires, making porridge. A few of them glanced at me but didn't seem too surprised or interested. I told a young girl washing pots that I had come to visit them, and she mumbled something about having to talk to Fiona, the leader, and then fell silent and returned to her scouring. I asked her where I might find Fiona, and she gestured towards one of the shacks.

Sure enough, she was there, sitting proudly on a large American quilt brushing her hair. She was a stocky Irish countrywoman in her early forties with strong eyes and fair skin. I told her that I too was a refugee from the West and that I had known about the Screamers from when they were on television twelve years before.

"We're not called the Screamers," she said testily. "That was a slur invented by the media. We have a new name now."

"Oh," I said. "Well, can I stay?"

"Are you prepared to work?" she asked.

"Sure."

Fiona showed me around the three huts. One was a kitchen, with a big adobe stove and a long refectory table, another doubled as a sewing room and Fiona's bedroom/office, and the third, which was as big as a shed, served as a dormitory divided into cells by curtains. On the far side of the rabbit coop was another log house where the children lived. It reminded me most of the opium/cocaine processing camps that Rambo or Agent Jack Ryan aerial bombed in Hollywood movies. After pointing out my bed, Fiona told me to leave my bags down and follow her outside to plant cabbages.

The cabbage field was in a clearing in the jungle, maybe half a mile from the farm, and as we worked Fiona grilled me about why I had come. I told her about wanting to change and to start liking people. I didn't tell her about love. She said I was angry and I admitted that maybe I was.

"It's weird you're here," she said. "We haven't had visitors in a while."

We must have planted half an acre of cabbage and only got back in time for dinner; that was when I first got to meet the rest of them properly. There were four adults, a couple of adolescents and countless children. Everyone looked a bit ragged and surly, but they were full of life. Moore, the middle-aged man with the fur, was from Longford. He was sleeping with Gina, a nineteen-year-old girl from Utah who was using him as therapy to try and overcome her fixation with good-looking men. She had come to the farm seven months earlier with her boyfriend, and within days the group had shown them how much they hated each other and convinced them to split up. He had run away, but she stayed on because she was pregnant and wanted to give birth outside in the open air and Fiona had agreed to help. Gina now had a beautiful two-month-old baby, but the group had convinced her she hated him too and her milk had dried up. I got the sense no one was feeding him and he cried all day. There was talk about selling him to bring in extra money, but I was sure it was just a sick joke. Of the rest of them, Tony was a quiet Welshman who had been with the Screamers for over twenty years, Tracy was fifteen, and her cousin Matthew was just turning eighteen. We didn't do very much that night; I told them a bit about myself and they in turn told me about life on the farm; then, as they had no electricity, we all went to bed after dinner.

It was the following day that they asked me to come swimming with them, and I had taken off my clothes and all the trouble began. Now I was in the thick of it. It had suddenly become shockingly apparent to me precisely what Fiona had meant when she talked about problems being aired openly in the group. I hadn't realised it involved being reviled, flayed of every scrap of dignity. When she spoke of group therapy, I imagined something safe and nurturing. Now here I was sent to bed in shame, desperately trying to work out what I should do next. I wanted to run away, of course, but some masochistic element urged me to see it through. The place was too bizarre to just walk away from, and anyway I admired their zeal, their idealism, their simple, Spartan life. They claimed to be after the truth, which was what I was looking for too. I needed to find out if they were serious. And if so, I ought to hang around and swallow the medicine.

The morning after the therapy session, it was as if nothing had happened. Everyone was sweet and charming again. Fiona gave me a machete and sent me off up the mountains with instructions where to find a cornfield that needed weeding. I hacked my way through the undergrowth following her directions until I found the place. It had been a heroin poppy field until the previous year when a FARC guerrilla commander murdered the *campesino* who owned it and gave the land to the Screamers. It was great soil – the same rich mahogany colour as the trees that had once stood there. I swung and hacked my way through the weeds and vines that were choking the corn until I was stopped dead in mid-swing by Moore, who came springing up out of the weeds like a pheasant, waving his hands in terror.

"What the fuck do you think you're doing?" he roared.

"Fiona told me to clear the weeds," I squealed.

"Well, not here, you're not. Fuck off down the hill and clear the bottom field."

I turned down the hill and Moore settled back to sleep in the grass. The bottom field was crawling with snakes – or at least I saw one tiny one – and since I was only wearing sandals, I was either going to have to slay every one of them or suffer the bites. It just wasn't worth it. I knew the Screamers were entirely dependent on the food they grew, and that they had no money to buy anything else; nevertheless I wasn't going to risk my life to save a few corn–cobs. After a few tenuous swings, I abandoned the field to the weeds and headed back to the farm. I didn't dare return to Fiona without the job done, so instead I went off to the children's house. It was separate from the main farm because one of their core principles, I remembered from the television programme, was that the children should rear themselves. The children were expected to work from dawn till noon and then were free for the rest of the day. They came to the main house for meals and could come to the therapy sessions in the evenings if they wished, but they were not encouraged to hang around at other times. There were about six children in all, most of them half-brothers or half-sisters, but some of them didn't really know who their parents were. The child-parent bond was not encouraged as it was thought to weaken the collective.

The oldest boy, Rory, was out cutting down a tree, while the younger ones were peeling manioc root from a large bucket. Two of the children were painting, while another two were snuggled up in bed together. I got the impression that they were all pretty sexually active; either with each other or with the local *campesino* neighbours. Fiona had told me that expressing yourself in a sexual way was encouraged from an early age. The walls of the house were covered with their paintings, which were all environmental in theme. The youngest girl, Níamh, showed me some of their poems and songs about green issues, which were shocking in their rage and ruthlessness, suggesting frightening scenarios to combat families who didn't recycle and imagining horrifying punishments for industrial polluters. She asked me to teach her an Irish song, and we got out a tin whistle and played until lunchtime.

I spent the rest of the day shovelling manure out of the guinea pig pen and wheeling it to the herb garden. Fiona said we'd have another therapy session after dinner, but in the end a rich couple from Ibagué, the local magistrate and his wife, came to buy Gina's baby, and they forgot all about me. The couple had heard rumours that a white baby was for sale and had come with a case crammed full of *pesos*. The

Screamers were furious. They cursed and roared at the couple, and refused to give them even a cup of tea before banishing them back where they'd come from – this, despite the fact that the couple had walked all day to get here. I felt genuinely worried for them and snuck them a couple of stalks of sugarcane while no one was looking, just to keep them going on the long march back down.

I didn't understand – I was sure I had heard talk of selling the baby. Gina certainly didn't seem to want him, and no one else appeared to care. It was an unimaginable situation that a mother could be made to hate her own baby, but somehow in the warped hothouse of the commune it made sense. If Gina wasn't prepared to look after him and if she wasn't going to give him away, I feared what would happen. It was one thing to watch on idly as a mother suffered through post-natal depression, but what would I do if it looked like they were determined to let him weaken and die? I sensed there were things going on behind the scenes that I had no idea about and that if I challenged anything I would live to regret it. The best thing was just to keep an eye on the situation and say nothing for the moment. I hoped that maybe the realisation that the couple was prepared to take her baby away from her for ever might have jolted Gina out of her depression. Maybe that's why she and the rest of them had reacted as they did. Perhaps all would be okay from now on. I had to hope it would.

Looking back I realise that I should have confronted her, but at the time it was not so easy. I didn't dare. I was too scared. Whatever primal therapy they had done to Gina since she arrived had opened up every raw nerve in her body. She was an angry, voracious, walking wound, who in a split second could lash out in any direction. I was terrified. One day when I was chopping wood, she came out and asked me to hold the hose while she had a shower. There was a perfectly good hook to hang the nozzle on, but she wanted someone to direct the water at her. First she told me not to look. And then she said, "I know you're watching. You want to fuck me, don't you? You've never seen anything like me."

She was right, of course, I hadn't. Her body was more nubile than anything my post-adolescent mind could have imagined. Any sign of stretch marks had already disappeared. She laughed heartily, which I took as a subtle come on, until she turned suddenly, hissing, "You creep! You're raping me with your eyes. I should blind you, you freak."

And she burst out crying and ran off. Later, when I went to apologise, she spat in my face. After that I kept away.

The longer I spent with the Screamers, the more I questioned why I was there at all. Part of me wanted to be back home working on the farm again. I knew I was running away. That much was obvious. I had done it too often before. The first time was eight months in Africa after my dad died, and I had been running ever since. At least this time I had a goal: I wanted to be happy. I *was* going to find love. But already I was becoming doubtful I would find it here; yet I wasn't prepared to leave just yet. The Screamers intrigued me, and besides, I didn't have anywhere else to go. I was in no rush to head back out into the turmoil of South America again.

Although I didn't fit in here, there was nowhere else that I did. It was fine in school – at least I had a legal obligation to be there and a little status too. The 'loner boy' mightn't be up there with class prefect, but he matters. I had super powers, you see, and they gave me an air of mystery. A weirdo chic. I knew things: I could tell what people were feeling; I could feel their fear, and, instinctively, know how much life was in them. It wasn't much use in exams and stuff, and I never really talked about it, but it was cool. I knew things and the rest of them sensed that.

Who am I kidding? It wasn't cool at all. It was lonely and a curse. Imagine how sad it is to be able to sense how little passion people have running through their veins? Seeing everyone drowning in fears and anger and inadequacies, and the older they got the worse it got. Imagine watching as their life-force ebbed away year on year? Up until age five, everyone had been the same as me: all bundles of effervescence, of ebullience, all tuned to the same frequency. Then they began to move on. They made the shift from my world into reality, and I just couldn't keep up. I wanted to make the leap, I really did. And, God, I tried. My parents and teachers coaxed and bullied me, but part of me just wasn't willing. I got sicker and sicker until they had to let me stay where I was. I started playing with younger kids and even stayed back a few years in school, but it was like running backwards on a conveyor belt: everyone kept on moving on. I was left alone. And in fact, it got to be that I preferred it that way. I started sensing things – trees mainly – hearing and feeling them, and I preferred their company. I could be freer with them. I had a favourite tree stump, and I would just sit there on my own until a teacher came and forced me back to play. Play? As far as I was concerned, the others weren't playing. All those sports and doll games were forms of warfare, and I refused to allow myself be corrupted by them, by their nefarious politics of competing, managing, marshalling and fighting.

Chapter 2

AFTER ABOUT A week, Fiona got me to plant cabbages with her again – the first lot had been eaten by leaf-cutter ants. When we were alone, she was far more relaxed and reasonable; she seemed to value having someone from outside to talk to. The commune was in a bad way, she said. Its founder and guru had run away a few months before, chasing a young backpacker she had fallen in love with. The rest of them didn't really have the heart to go on. They were getting older – in their forties and fifties. Some of them had been together for over twenty years. Fiona said she was the only one who did any work any more. The rest just lazed around. They had planted very little last season, and most of what was planted was never watered or weeded. For the last six months, they had been living on green cabbage and yucca, and the children were showing signs of malnutrition. Famine was an ever-increasing possibility. The local FARC guerrilla command seemed to sense their enervation and had grown increasingly menacing. A patrol of rebels had held them up at gunpoint a few weeks earlier and stolen whatever amount of money was left. The only way they had been able to afford the yucca was by a judicious arrangement between one of their daughters and a local farmer. Now they faced the harsh decision of whether or not to arm themselves for protection. The prospect of it sickened them more than anything.

Just your luck, Rabbit murmured, *to find people more messed up than you.*

Fiona told me about the idyllic early days on their island off the west coast of Ireland: the daily primal screaming sessions that had made them feel so alive; the raw, uninhibited sex that made their bodies pulsate with life; the hope, the idealism, and the over-arching belief that if mankind vented its deep-seated anger, we could reach a state of peace. She explained their initial conviction that the penile nuclear warheads and rapacious capitalist systems were all results of our repressed anger – a cancer devouring us. The Screamers had the cure. They would make Ireland a primal therapy centre for the world. Just as we had saved Christianity after the collapse of the Roman Empire, now this new tribe of Celtic warriors would reconnect the people of the developed world to their bodies and their feelings. There was no shortage of angry, raw recruits, keen to liberate themselves from the repression of the church and their frightened parents.

It was messy work, Fiona told me. People turned into insane, befanged monsters during therapy, their eyes hideous and venomous. The depth of darkness that emerged from inside horrified everyone. They had never dreamt that such evil existed beyond the pages of Tolkien or the nadirs of Nazism. These were abysses never before charted by psychology, and the Screamers thrived on it for a time. Referrals came from local health authorities, and positive articles appeared in medical journals: it was the tail end of the electro-convulsion era, and people were casting blindly about for alternative solutions. But it wasn't long before parents of children whose brains had been broken down and crushed by the Screamers started to ask questions. They wrote to the newspapers and to the government. Questions were asked in the Dáil, and these in turn sparked police raids. The tabloids had a field day. But the Screamers weren't deterred: they thrived on the controversy and continued fighting on gallantly until the early nineties when the authorities in the West of Ireland tried to take one of the Screamers' children from her. They had no choice but to flee. After looking at the Canaries, Cape Verde and the

Caribbean, they finally settled in Colombia, where the adventure began all over again.

Fiona told me how great life was here in the beginning. The forest soil was so rich it gave three crops a year, and they feasted on papayas, bananas, peppers, beans, aubergines and walnuts. It was paradise. But it wasn't long before they noticed the relentless logging all around them: acres and acres of old-growth mahogany and ebony being chain-sawed and shipped downriver so that opium farmers could move in and grow something more valuable. These new crops were so precious that the farmers patrolled them day and night with submachine guns, and this unsettled the local guerrilla army, who moved in, allegedly to establish control and clean up the drug trade, but in reality they wanted to get a piece of the action. The Screamers found themselves in the line of fire, and whatever anger they had managed to overcome in Ireland was replaced with unbridled fury at the loggers, the opium farmers and the guerrillas. They came to the decision that environmental campaigning would have to take precedence over their therapy sessions, and they were now gradually phasing out the screaming sessions altogether. They had made an exception for me only because they were so touched by all the work I was doing and because they could see how badly I needed it. I was meant to feel honoured. Little did they know that the only reason I was working so hard was to hide from them.

I enjoyed talking to Fiona. If nothing else, it made the planting less laborious. Towards the end of the day, she tried again to convince me to take advantage of what they were offering and to open myself up and release control during the therapy session that evening.

"No offence," I said, "but you guys have been doing it for over a decade, and you're the angriest people I've ever met."

The minute the remark was out, I regretted it. I knew I would suffer later, but Fiona brushed it aside with a few stabs of her trowel in the ground and said that secretly everyone was as angry as they were; we just repressed it. If I opened up and released my fears, she said, eventually I would be left with absolute love. We continued planting in silence, and after a long time a thought came that seemed to explain the situation. I mulled it over, worrying whether I should say it or not. Eventually, thinking I'd explode if I didn't, I began, with as much compassion as I could.

"Fiona?"

"Yeah?" She looked up.

I laid my handful of seedlings on the soil. I could hear Rabbit warning me to stay quiet.

"Do you think that, maybe, instead of finding love, all the releasing of anger you did might have just brought up more anger, and that now you're addicted to it?"

Fiona didn't reply. She looked straight at the soil as if frozen, with her shoulders so tense I was sure I'd hear them crack.

"Fiona?" I said, reaching over to touch her, but she shrugged me off and stood up brusquely. She stood there looking around for a long time, finally wiping her eyes roughly on her sleeve, and barked, "Come on, you ponce, it's time for dinner."

After dinner I was put straight into the centre of the circle again, and Fiona was on her feet as inquisitor. Without any preliminaries or niceties, she came straight out with, "You're gay, aren't you?"

Oh, not this one again. My attitude was simple: girls were angels, heroines, and should be cherished, not fucked up. If there was some way of fucking them without fucking them up, I might have tried. But, that would have required love, and since I didn't even love myself . . .

I didn't know how best to reply to Fiona's question. Denying I was gay might be worse than admitting it, although I had already gathered they despised homosexuality. Girls screwing old men was fine. Children screwing children was fine. Tracy, who was fifteen, had three different boyfriends, each older than her; and from what I gathered some of the adults had slept with her more than once. I got the distinct impression Fiona was sleeping with her best friend's eighteen-year-old son. All that was fine, but sex between men was depraved. The only thing worse in their eyes was drugs, because drugs hid you from your emotions, as well as leading to the destruction of the forest through the planting of poppies and coca bushes.

In the end, I said I wasn't gay.

"Jesus Christ," Moore said, "can you not see it? Are you really that blind? You have completely shut off your masculinity because you hate your father."

I thanked him for the insight, and said I would consider it. But he carried on: "What's to consider? You know it's true. How long can you keep denying it, you faggot?"

Tracy had asked me really sweetly for my birth date earlier, and now she launched in. "I did his astrology chart – he's a classic case of denial. Non-physical, non-sexual, non-feeling. He lives in a bubble, choking on New Age bullshit. Listen to us, Mocha, we only want to help you, but first you've got to get in touch with yourself. You're a walking haemorrhoid."

Again, I thanked Tracy for her observation and assured her she was most likely correct, but that unfortunately I didn't feel like exploring these issues right now.

The night went on like that – their telling me, with heartfelt and venomous honesty, how they saw me, and my politely refusing to engage. I could see how infuriating I was being. I even felt sympathy for them at times.

To put them out of their misery, finally, I said, "Look . . . maybe I'm just a lost cause. Can't you just strike me off as a failure?"

I hated to think that their own therapy was being held up on my account. They seemed so much more in need of it than I was. I suggested they put me down as irredeemable and let me go on working on the farm. I was enjoying the work, the communal aspect of it and all, and living in the forest was a treat. Could we not just agree to differ and be friends?

A silence descended on the room and Rabbit murmured, *Hold on tight, here we go.* My remark had been like an open welt to a flagellator, and they flayed me bare for my hypocrisy, my sanctimoniousness.

Whatever respect my previous obstinacy had earned me was now forgotten as they laid into me incessantly for over an hour.

I would be lying to say that it didn't begin to wear me down. My self-esteem was dropping ever lower. It was all I could do to hold back the tears, but there was no way I was going to cry in front of them. These people were dangerous; they wanted to feed on my weakness.

For the next few days the same pattern continued: I would work hard during the day, and at night they would set about liberating me from myself. I became ever more unassailable as they grew more ruthless. Things continued like that for a week, until something happened that turned everything upside down and forced them to deal with far more pressing issues.

One of the core precepts of the Screamers was to make you acknowledge your repressed hatred for your parents, which in turn was thought to unleash further floodgates deeper within you. The method was foolproof since everyone at some stage has hated their parents – all they had to do was stir up these feelings until they provoked a reaction. Fiona had set to work on Gina and her boyfriend the minute they arrived, and it had been one of the reasons her boyfriend had fled. He was one of those people who claim their parents are their best friends and, as such, was repulsed by their ideas. Gina, on the other hand, had found the process liberating. She had dug up every childhood memory of abandonment and alienation (starting with the time her parents had laughed at her when she threatened to run away aged three) and had hung them like chains around her parents' necks. She went over this litany of incidents again and again, worrying them like a rosary until Fiona convinced her that the only way to move on was to confront her parents, force them to apologise and make amends. Initially something inside her baulked at the idea. But after more therapy she summoned up the courage to call her parents in Colorado and scream down the phone at them. Her parents had reacted with concern, of course, but they refused to apologise or even to admit that they had been living a lie and had, in fact, never loved her. With the help of Fiona and the rest, she wrote letters to them outlining their crimes and demanding an apology, a form of textual screaming. When no apology came, the Screamers suggested she seek amends in more direct ways. They told her to ask for compensation. This had worked for others, they explained; in fact it was how the Screamers had funded themselves from time to time. So Gina rang her parents and demanded a few thousand dollars, threatening that unless it was sent to a local PO box within a month, they would never get to see their grandchild. It was at this point the Screamers had often got themselves into trouble in the past.

I could understand Gina's situation to an extent. We all have that sense of victimhood, of being the aggrieved party – if only there was a court of psychological hurt we could go to for retribution. I remember how, when I left school, after all those elevenses and lunchtimes sitting on my tree stump, I felt the germinating rancour of the long-term loner, and if I hadn't gone off to Africa, who knows what would have happened. It would have been me ringing my mum from a farm up in the Andes demanding money. As it was, Africa kicked some sense into me. Travelling there on the back of an ex-army truck with twenty others and no purpose except to drive from London to Nairobi overland for the sheer hell of it. Twenty thrill-seeking Westerners in the back of a Bedford truck driving through some of the most war-torn areas on earth. I found myself cast amidst 650 million people, most of them struggling to survive from day to day.

After eight months I returned to Dublin shell-shocked. I started college, strapping myself onto the conveyor belt until I got a degree. My degree in cretinhood. A bachelor of mediocrity. All I could think about was the bigger picture: the millions of worshippers at the Kubla Mela; the mathematicians at MIT working on four-line equations to define all life; the Tarahumara Indians chasing prey with spears in the Sierra Madres; the Voyager Space Probe racing out of the solar system at 38,000 miles an hour into the wilds of inter-stellar space with the music of Chuck Berry and an image of a Filipino woman breastfeeding her baby on board.

By the end I was so frantic to get away I didn't even hang around to collect the degree. Instead I took a job on a farm in County Wicklow. It was there that I had my first encounter with common sense: Diarmuid, a tough, garrulous farm labourer who was the most honest man I'd ever met. He taught me what really mattered: that digging was the best thing a man could do; turning a sod was like talking to God.

"Good morning," I used say to him each day, and he'd growl, "What's so fucking good about it?"

He taught me to abhor banality. One's primary objective was to hunt down the marrow of life, he used to say, and suck from it deeply.

"And when you have it, know that you have it. Keep a hold of it without crushing it until it wants to go. And when it wants to go, let it go, for God's sake."

It was on the farm I met Rabbit. He turned up inside my head one day, saying we had known each other in the past and not to worry if I couldn't remember. It's hard to explain Rabbit. He's more than just an imaginary friend, but that said, I know for sure he doesn't exist in the real world, not any more at least. He used to be a furry toy I had as a child. Nowadays, he is mainly just a voice, and although he used to be very sweet and loving, over time he's become more and more cynical. I don't know what that's about.

When Diarmuid got gout and things got complicated with the farmer, I decided it was time to leave. So here I was, halfway up the Andes in a primal therapy commune, among half-starved Western dropouts who had just learnt that some brutish-looking Americans had turned up in the Platypus hostel in Bogotá asking about Gina. Rumour had it that they were cult-busters sent to fetch Gina and her baby home. It shouldn't have been a surprise; her parents had been threatening to send in the cavalry for a while, but so far they couldn't find her. We knew things were hotting up when CIA helicopters (which accompanied local crop-dusting planes as they flew over the forest spraying glyphosate on the poppies and coca bushes) began to fly so low that we could actually see the narcs spying down on us through binoculars. And although the CIA were using coded radio communications in the chopper, the children could easily pick up the local frequency used by the crop-duster on their short wave radio. We heard the local pilot pointing us out to the CIA blokes. It was only a matter of time before there was a raid, either by the CIA or the cult-busters.

This mess had nothing to do with me and anyway, I was beginning to get cravings for chocolate and coffee. There was only so much yucca and cabbage I could stomach.

This isn't what I brought you here for.

I decided to take a bus south towards Ecuador the following day. Fiona said she'd be sad to see me go, and she asked Tracy to bake a carrot pudding for my farewell dinner. I was chuffed. In honour of my departure, we didn't have any therapy session that night, and instead opened a bottle of rhubarb wine and had a singsong. It was a great night. Moore got out his guitar, and we all danced around the kitchen until well past midnight.

Early the following morning I was awoken by glimmers of light playing on my eyelids. In my exhaustion and grogginess, I thought it might be the first rays of sun streaming in through the curtain, but on looking around I realised it was well before dawn. Deciding that it must be the embers in the kitchen stove glinting off a mirror, I turned back to sleep again, but something wasn't right. Turning it over in my mind, I realised there was no way I could see the kitchen fire from my bed. I heard some rustling from over by Gina's side of the dorm and the unmistakable crackling sound of flame. Suddenly, with chilling horror, I realised what was happening. Fire! Gina had started a fire near her bed. She was trying to kill her baby!

Oh, Christ.

I could either get up and investigate or turn around, put my head back under the pillow and pretend nothing was happening.

It's none of your business, I heard Rabbit say.

You have to remember, I had just endured a whole week of mental harassment. On top of that my brain was suffering the effects of the paint-stripper wine: I was nowhere near my usual frame of mind. The effort of maintaining a strong front against the Screamers had left me weakened – on the verge of cracking, to be honest. Also I was petrified of Gina. She was just too raw, too unpredictable, too alive. An Incubus.

That's all I have in my defence, I'm afraid. I know it doesn't amount to much, but it's the truth. It's why I turned to face the wall again and closed my eyes. It's why I made no effort to save the baby. I just didn't have what it takes. Unless you've been through it, you can't know. And you can say I'm just avoiding responsibility by blaming it on Rabbit, but he really did whisper to me that I shouldn't interfere. *She is free to make her own choices*, he said. I had to respect that, and not judge her.

What about the baby, Rabbit? I remonstrated. *He can't choose; he's helpless.*

He chose her, Rabbit shot back. *He knew what he was doing. This is between the two of them. There's no way you can understand.*

I was asleep again before I knew it.

I'm not sure how long after it was that I heard the screams. Possibly just a few minutes. Suddenly it was hot, extremely hot, and people were running everywhere. I leapt out of bed to find Gina, her hair in flames, screaming at me.

Soon everyone was in the room, Tony and Moore racing through with buckets of water. Gina's bed was a mini inferno, and the walls were cracking and splintering in the heat. We formed a human chain which got longer and quicker as the children raced up from their house. An almost continuous supply of water was being carried in, but it still took maybe half an hour to douse the flames, to carry the mattress out and cool the roasting walls and floor. We worked well together, like nuns in a convent.

We were all too buzzed afterwards to go back to sleep, and Fiona called an impromptu therapy session in her room. A bunch of us clambered up on to her high spring bed with damp pyjamas and our faces smeared with soot. Fiona asked Gina did she want to talk about it, and at first she just shook her head, wrapping her arms tightly around her knees and swaying back and forth sullenly. She was wearing only her bra and panties – her nightgown lay in a heap of plasticized polyester on the floor. The baby was cooing softly in Tracy's arms. How both of them escaped without burns is a miracle. Gina's hair was badly singed – she thought it must have been the smell that had woken her. We all sat dead quiet, numbed by shock, until Gina softly and haltingly began to explain how she had woken to feed the baby and lit a candle, but then must have fallen back to sleep, knocking the candle over on to the mosquito net.

Subconsciously she wanted to kill the baby, she said. That was why she had left the candle burning. Tony offered some garbled Jungian analysis, and there followed a long drawn-out debate about Gina's feelings towards the baby and whether she should keep him or not. Finally, Fiona was about to call an end to the meeting when she spotted me and remembered I was leaving in a couple of hours.

"Mocha," she said, "we can never fully thank you for all you've done here. The gardens are in better order than they've been in a long time. Hopefully your efforts have shamed some of the others into doing a bit more. We have the cabbage planted and almost enough sugar-cane cut that we can barter for oil and tea. Now give us one more chance to help you. Once you leave us, you'll never find anyone as open or honest again. Trust us. What harm will it do? Open your heart. Let go for once in your life. We don't promise to love you, but we'll be truthful, and that's way more important. If you leave now, your rage will end up eating you alive. You'll by ravaged by cancer, I promise."

A few of the children joined her pleas. We had grown fond of each other; I was the only one who gave them any attention, and they genuinely wanted to help. I was really moved, but I told them that I just didn't feel this was the place to work through stuff. As usual they wouldn't give up. Fiona begged and cajoled me, but I was resolute.

Finally Gina, who was sitting up against the bedstead between Tony and Moore, lunged across at me, shouting, "Go on, please! Let yourself go, Mocha! For me! For all of us. For the sake of the cancer eating you inside. Fuck me here and now. Please! For God's sake, save yourself. Fuck me! Come on, you know you want to, you know you can do it."

Ripping off her bra, she threw her naked body against me and began tearing my clothes off. The others, impressed by her selflessness, egged me on, telling me to unshackle myself from the bindings of my fear. And for a second I did consider it. Gina was heartbreakingly ripe and was slamming up against my body, panting and ramming at me. But I was hopeless. I hugged her tightly so that she couldn't take her panties fully off and whispered into her ear how grateful I was to her, but that I really didn't feel this was the time or place.

I felt wretched. Once again I had failed them all. Gina had to pull herself dejectedly off me and fetch back her bra. She was languid with disappointment and snuggled back up against Tony for solace. There was disgust etched in Fiona's eyes. They were all disappointed in me, and we got up off the bed and had our breakfast in silence. I had let them down.

Later, as I left the farm to head back through the jungle to the outside world, only Fiona came to say goodbye. She looked terrible. I thought again about how she had hoped to find love beneath all her anger, and I cursed whatever snake-oil merchant had first sold her on the therapy. Fiona had now become as addicted to anger as I was to dreams.

She led me arm in arm down the track, saying, "It's obvious you're looking for something, Mocha. I can smell it off you a mile away. You're looking for love, aren't you, you dumb dreamer?"

How did she know? I hadn't even told Rabbit that.

"You won't find it," she continued. "No one will ever be as honest with you as us, just remember that. We may be moody old crocks, and smell and fart, but at least we're living the truth. Everything out there is a façade – a pretty bubblegum charade. Go out and get lost in it if you want, have a ball. But remember, you can't hoodwink yourself for ever. You'll be back."

Chapter 3

THE BUS SOUTH to Popayán was stopped once by FARC guerrillas and twice more by the Colombian army. The army made us all get out and stand with our hands above our heads against the aluminium siding, the other passengers knowing to get their identity cards out first. When I was asked for mine, I reached down to my bag and they almost shot me. I threw my hands back up, but they kept shouting for my passport. I don't know how they expected me to get it. The FARC were a lot kinder. They allowed women and *gringos*, except Americans, to stay on the bus. Americans were generally being shot on sight at the time, so there weren't many of them around. There was a particularly violent Jean-Claude Van Damme video playing on the bus television which segued nicely with the military harassment.

Popayán was glorious – a ravishing Colonial town with elegant colonnaded arcades and fountain-gushing courtyards. My hotel room overlooked the palm-lined central square and was just like the one Robert De Niro went to seed in in *The Mission*. After my fortnight of deprivation, the outside world had never tasted so sweet. One of the reasons I like communes and ashrams and other New Age gulags is the intense relief one feels on getting out again. That first cup of good coffee with a little biscuit and piece of chocolate: it makes all the mind-messing and deprivation worthwhile. Stupidly, with dinner on the first night I drank tap water and got dysentery, which knocked me out for three days. I was trapped in the hotel room with a roaring fever, too enervated to even reach a chemist for drugs.

Fevers, for me, are invariably rough. They soar to 103 degrees, which fries my brain to a mush. And this was no exception: weird hatchings of light appeared in lattices on the periphery of my vision, and I knew I was slipping away into yet another intense purgation. I had little enough control of my mind at the best of times, but push it even a degree or two above body temperature and it detonates. It's always scariest at the start – you don't know how long it'll last or how bad it'll be. Luckily, I had a twelve-litre pack of mineral water already bought, so all I needed to do was lie back and ride out the storm. I knew from Africa that one always comes out the other side. One just has to somehow starve the bacteria to death without succumbing to malnourishment oneself.

Stretched flat on my back in the dark, I tried to hang on to reality as long as I could, but it was only a matter of time before I cut loose. In the meantime, I grew hypersensitive to my surroundings, and it became obvious that the place was more a brothel than a hotel. This really pissed me off, as it was just another cliché. The piped music blaring through each room only half hid the sound of sex.

By the second day I was really cooking and had long since lost my bearings. Gina kept appearing – she had the letters S-P-U-R-N-E-D filed into her front teeth. She promised me wonderful things but did really horrible things instead. On and on she went, until I finally found that if I didn't wish her away she would leave on her own accord. That was a great relief. I was left with just Rabbit and me. We were by the seaside in France, and everyone was going through puberty, and there was sand in my shorts. But then he brought me to a forest, and I was hanging from the top of a pine tree, and I could hear muffled cries of orgasm coming from somewhere in the leaves. I jumped into the surrounding canopy and fell through it to an eighty-storey atrium lined with bookshelves. Rabbit was holding my hands, and we could fly up and down to any of the shelves just by wishing it so. He kept on whooshing me this way and that, picking out volumes which all seemed to correspond to some weakness or hurt in me. In each one I was always the victim. One was about me during my dad's final illness. Another featured the boy who had terrorised me at school and another a failed attempt at love.

Before I had much of a chance to read any of them, Rabbit drove me straight through the mosaic floor to another eighty-storey underground atrium which was again surrounded by books. It was dark and damp. The volumes, Rabbit told me, were agreements I had signed with everyone I hated. If I wished to, I could read them and find out why they had done the things they had; to understand them, so that I could forget and move on. But before I even picked up one, I found myself in a monotony of brilliant white near the North Pole, sitting at a fire with a bunch of Inuit who were eating roots chopped up and mixed with blubber. Around me, children wearing antlers that arched to the sky were playing in the churned-up sea ice. The smell of musk-ox was overpowering. Each Inuit man and woman stood up in turn and told me I hated them and why. Their skin was stretched too tight across their features, and larvae caked their nostrils. I looked to the ground and noticed their shoes were crawling in nematode worms, and when I looked back, their faces had changed into people I knew: my dad, my mum, my sister, my best friend, the bully from school and a girl I knew long ago. They all said I hated them. Someone said something about the Northern Lights, and I looked up and saw a spider the size of a whale looming over us, its belly hanging directly above the fire and its legs arched out like flying buttresses around us. When I looked down again, I realised that each leg was joined to one of the people. The spider picked up each one in turn and covered them in some sort of mucus, then stuck them like eggs to its underbelly.

Suddenly my world became an octagonal matrix, and I realised I was looking out through the spider's eyes. I had become the spider! All these hated friends and family had become my eggs.

I was outraged. Turning to Rabbit, I cried, *That's not fair! These people victimised me. They're not my eggs. They are not my creations. It was they who made me what I am, not the other way around!*

37

Whatever, Rabbit said resignedly. *You're just as responsible as they are. It was a partnership. Accept it. Stop hating them.*

But I don't hate them, I said.

Well the Screamers thought you did, he said.

I don't, I love them, I insisted. *They're my family, my friends.*

You can hate someone and love them at the same time, Rabbit said. *Stop it. Stop the victim game. They made you who you are . . . love them for it. Do you think the pearl hates the grain of sand that made it?*

It all became so absorbing that I hated it when my stomach would spasm and I'd have to shake myself awake and crawl to the lavatory. As the days passed and the fever raged on, I grew closer to Rabbit than I had been in a long time. He was his old self again, the friend I was beginning to remember from childhood – always looking out for me, always taking care. It was good to have him back.

When Rabbit was still only a toy, he wasn't called Rabbit at all, but Níní, short for *coinín*, which means rabbit in Irish. He was a wooden block pasted with fake fur, with those wire eyes that rip the lining of children's throats when they swallow them and make them bleed internally. I had two of them. The first one got so much love for so long it had no fur left. I even went on loving the wooden block until it got vomited on one too many times and my mother threw it away. Níní #2 fell into the fire only two months after I got it, and then they stopped making them after that. I remembered the whoosh of flames as the polycarbonate fur ignited, and the smell of Gina's nightdress filled the room. My Nínís were one of the few things in the real world to interest me; I retreated even deeper after they were gone. And Rabbit came to take their place.

After a few days, the bacteria had all but died and, reluctantly, I focused myself back on the present, its petty concerns and stupid issues. Rabbit withdrew, and I knew that it was time to get back on the road. I had been locked in my room for days, and when I finally managed to stagger down to the lobby, the receptionist greeted me with a triumphal welcome. She was convinced I had died on her – left her with yet another *gringo* mess on her hands. If I hadn't turned up that day, she was going to have to come looking for me, and that was the last thing she wanted: yet another overdosed waster wiped out on too pure cocaine. She was steeling herself for the inevitable fuss: the police, the press, someone from the embassy, the forms, the fumigation, the grieving parents flying in from Gringoland and their shock at the squalor. All extra hassle she could do without. I was the best thing to happen to her that day. It was the fourth day, and as she explained to me in exuberant detail, she normally waited a full five days before checking a room so that the gastric juices had time to secrete and do their thing. Once digestion was well advanced, the police would feel less inclined to hang around investigating. She often wondered what was so terrible about the West to make its young come here and kill themselves.

Before I left Colombia I wanted to check out San Agustin. That was where the shaman in the *Observer* had said the statues of pure love were to be found. I took a bus south to the nearest village and from there got myself a horse and rode out into the foothills along the Magdelena River. Hitching up at an acacia tree at the gates of an archaeological park, I continued on foot, although I wasn't sure I wanted to be there at all. Archaeology disquieted me, reminding me of the years I had wasted in university. I felt I should be focused on the present, not looking back; but as the shaman was the main reason I had come and I was meant to be looking for love, I felt I ought to check it out.

I trudged on through the park of mimosa and mowed lawns, trying not to resent the other backpackers who all looked so fit and burnished, and so damn happy – hugging and joking and clinging out of each other like the drones they were. They made me feel more alone and inadequate than I already was. The statues were scattered haphazardly around the grounds, placed there by God knows who, God knows when. There was a fat frog in a bank of ferns above a river, a monstrous fat-bellied bird with a stubby snake grasped in its beak and claws, and various other totem-like figures. They were all carved out of volcanic rock by a culture that had long vanished before Columbus arrived. There was something really odd about their eyes – either stretching across their faces in sly squints or bulging outwards like volcanic eruptions. By far the most beautiful thing there was a riverbed with serpents and salamanders carved into it, which, when the water swirled through, seemed to come alive and slither slightly as light filtered down through a grove of bamboo. Whoever had carved these must have understood the connection between all things, the idea of everything being one. I settled down by the river to eat some nuts and soon fell asleep.

My head was throbbing from the sun when I woke again and set off stumbling up a hill trying to reset my bearings. The views over rolling hills and scrubland grounded me back in the present, and I was just arguing with Rabbit about whether it was better to experience these things on your own or with others when I became aware of something overhead. Looking up, I saw towering in the sky a monstrous, semi-human beast with fangs like a cat and molars like a bear. It was the sheer incongruity of it that got me. I just wasn't ready. It was so huge and stark, with the garish remains of thousand-year-old pigment still smeared on it. How I hadn't seen it when I first came up I don't know. Perhaps it was the heat, or the last vestige of the fever, but it felt like it was somehow more than just a lump of stone. Archaeology is by definition supposed to be inanimate – the remains of something that once was alive – yet this stone felt different. It was like a battery, its eyes the most charged part. Disproportionately huge and round, they were like winches trying to reel me in. It wasn't at all a nice feeling. As I came closer, I noticed that clinging to its shoulders was a wild animal. A jaguar. But it wasn't attacking the figure; from its expression I realised it was its *Rabbit*. But unlike my Rabbit, the jaguar seemed to make its owner happy; a delirious smile stretched across his face. That was what I wanted. My eyes scanned up along the seven metres of totemic body, first human and then feline, and I imagined I saw in the jaguar's alluringly luminous face what could have been a sun streak but seemed more like an opening, a labial overlay that expanded into a circle as I watched.

I turned away and went off exploring the rest of the park, but I was still feeling weak from the illness and had to rest a few times. I was sitting under a tree drinking something fizzy for the energy fix when I heard someone call my name.

"Mocha! . . . It's not yourself, is it? Well, by Christ, surely it is! How the bejaysus are you?"

Looking around I saw someone I only half recognised approaching me with nauseating eagerness. Scouring my brain, I tried to match the face until it finally clicked that it was the Irish bloke from the plane. His skin was burnt coral pink and whole strips of it were peeling off.

"How are you?" he bellowed. "How are you, at all? Are you okay? The name is Paddy, remember? Paddy Gish. Isn't there a fair bit of heat in that sun, huh? Isn't there just? And isn't it some crazy class of a country altogether?"

He laughed uproariously, then gushed on about the coincidence of our meeting and how synchronicity is the machinations of the gods and should never be overlooked. I grinned wanly. Machinating gods had less to do with it than the confluent effect of the Pan-American highway, which runs the entire length of South America, roughly along the meeting point of the Andean highlands and tropical lowlands, and tends to channel everyone in on top of each other. With everyone en route to the same towns and sights, you were constantly meeting those you had just left behind.

Things hadn't gone well for Paddy. He had bought what he thought was cocaine in Bogotá, but which turned out to be *pasta básica*, a crude form of jungle crack made from the stuff that leaches out of solvent-soaked coca leaves. In fairness to the dealer, he had warned Paddy to smoke rather than sniff it, and it was this that presumably saved his life. But even smoking the mix of cocaine, kerosene and sulphuric acid could easily have killed him. Paddy had taken it back to his hotel and rolled up a joint. It knocked him flat out, and when he woke next morning he was blind. Panicking, he didn't dare seek help in case the doctors reported him. Everyone knew of some friend of a friend languishing in a South American jail as revenge for the thousands of Latin Americans in northern jails on drug charges. The whole thing was basically a game of international draughts.

Paddy had spent three days locked up in his room, gradually going crazy, with every fear in his soul rising to haunt him. There was no phone in the room, and he didn't dare step outside in case of what might happen. Finally, on the third day, his sight began to improve and he summoned the courage to go out and buy some food. I met him on the fourth day, and his world was still a haze of indeterminate shapes; nevertheless he assured me that he was certain God would ensure his full recovery. It had scared the "bejaysus" out of him, he said, and he still hadn't been to see a doctor. He told me he was getting the hell out of Colombia, he was returning to Ireland and giving his life to Jesus. It was part of the deal he had made with "the Man above".

Paddy told me that all his negative preconceptions about Colombia had been proved right. It was a vicious, dirty, godforsaken place and should be flushed down the sewer. This struck me as odd as I had been thinking the exact opposite: that I had been so wrong to believe the country would be dangerous. In my short time here it already seemed one of the most welcoming places I had been. I felt embarrassed now for my behaviour in the bus station in Bogotá, where I had arrived in storm-trooper style with my shopping bags clasped to my stomach, looking around me like a sniper on reconnaissance. I felt even stupider for having believed the people who told me I'd be robbed within days. It was because of them I still only had the two flimsy shopping bags as luggage. They were in shreds by now, yet I couldn't bring myself to spend my meagre budget replacing them. I understood why people were worried when I went to Africa – there were lions and rhinos and hyenas there after all – but South America just has people, people trying to get on as best they can like everywhere else. I said this to Paddy, and he said I was talking through my arse.

He pulled out a 9mm handgun from his money pouch, saying, "If you have any sense, you'll pick up one of these little chickens."

"Chickens?" I said.

"Oh, surely to God, yes – just watch it blast a few eggs out its arse at any bastard that dares come at me. I got it in the market. At $25, you'd be a fool not to. Huh? Am I right or am I right? The bloke would have thrown in a grenade for free if I had wanted."

When I told Paddy I was heading south to Ecuador, he quickly forgot his conversion to Jesus and wanted to tag along, but I managed to convince him I needed to be alone. It was a lucky escape; someone told me later that he had been pistol-whipped by transvestites in Cali a fortnight later and then arrested in Bogotá airport while getting on the plane home with a snake in his lunch-box.

It was late in the evening when I finally got back to my horse and found the saddle missing. I didn't have the energy to do anything about it, but a local farmer came along and offered to sort out a bag of oats and some water for me, while I went around asking neighbours if they knew anything. Fortunately everyone knew everything, and I was directed straight away to where I'd find it.

Don Luis Mandango was an old man in his seventies, with wonderfully curly hair and gold teeth. He was a *mestizo* with the ideal mix of Spanish and native blood, which lent him a strong Roman nose and the heavy, bold jaw of an Indian. His lustrous grey hair and mahogany skin were pure indigenous. Most Colombians are a cocktail of Indian and Spanish, with a drop of African and Portuguese mixed in, but few were as perfect a blend as Don Luis. Full-blooded Europeans and Indians looked like crude caricatures in comparison. Don Luis was sitting on a bench outside his mud-hut with corn-cobs scattered all about. Inside in the kitchen I could just make out a rifle rack and a nest of horse tackle hanging on the wall. He invited me to share a cup of mint tea with him. But I ignored the offer and asked straight out whether he had taken my saddle.

"*Sí, sí, claro, amigo*," he drawled.

"Well, can I have it?" I asked.

"*Sí, sí!*" he assured me. "*Tranquillo, amigo*. We will drink some tea and talk a little, no? Just talking, *sí?*"

I didn't have much choice.

He asked me did I know about UFOs.

"What?" I replied.

"You know," he said. "UFOs."

This was all I needed. It had been a long day, a long few weeks.

"Not much," I said.

"Ah, everyone knows something," he said. His accent was so strong it was hard to tell whether he was speaking English or Spanish. "*Cigarillos* in the sky, you know? Saucers with glass domes."

"Well, of course I know, it's just I've never really thought about them."

"That's what all the *gringos* say. You need to think more. Around here, we think about them very much," he said. "Everyone – all the time. The armies and universities up and down the Andes, they make research departments here. They say it's minerals in our soil; maybe the volcanic activity, too. These things attract them, you see? Yes, yes, now you are seeing. They are attracting the funny folk."

He was chuckling warmly to himself and clearly deranged, but I had no option but to listen.

"Me, myself, I am thinking it is because it is easy for them to hide in the valleys," he went on.

"Look," I said, "I just need my saddle. It's been a long day."

"I had one of my men bring it here," he said. "Is that such a crime? It's just a little game. No harm, yes? Just fun and games."

I ignored the comment.

"How much to get it back?" I asked, tugging off my money belt.

He gaped at me open-mouthed. "We are *amigos, compadre!*" he said in horror. "I would not take a single *peso* from you. I just want to talk. You're Irish, yes?"

I nodded grimly.

"You Irish, you are knowing things," Don Luis said. "I see you around, so I asked my friend to bring you here. Where's the harm? It's okay to talk a little, yes?"

Normally I loved meeting people. It's always the impassioned, the obsessive, the dispossessed who prove most interesting. It's what travel is all about. But I just wasn't in the mood. It's always the same: you can be hanging out on the street drinking coffee waiting for a bus for hours and no one will come near you, but as soon as it's most inconvenient . . .

"Do you know of the Q'ero people?" Don Luis asked.

"What?" I snapped.

"The Q'ero," he said. "They are from Peru. We call them the last of the Incas, no? Many years ago, they fled high into the sierra to escape the conquistadores and have lived there ever since. Maybe, for five hundred years. Until 1955. In 1955 they came down from the mountain during the Fiesta de la Vuelta del Pleiades. I was there. Actually I was just a young muchacho on my way to follow Che Guevara. It just happened I was in the right place at the right time, you see? The Q'ero had never spoken before; suddenly they had something to say.

"They talked about a new time. The end of chaos, they said. The end of our stupid ways. Soon we would begin to realise we were god, they said. It was good news, no? Like your New Testament."

He raised his eyebrows, seeking a response from me. I just stared blindly. He shrugged and went on, "But that is not what interests me today. No, no, no. The most interesting thing the Q'ero told us that night was about 'a tear in the fabric of time'. That's what they said, '*un rasgón en la tela del tiempo*'. They said it would bring *oportunidades*. It would let us see for the first time what we were becoming, not just who we had been.

"*Comprende, amigo?*"

I shook my head.

"No, neither do I," he laughed. "Not for sure. But I think the tear they speak of is here, yes?"

"What?" I asked.

"It is here – you think?" he repeated.

"How should I know?"

Don Luis chortled. "That is what they all say," he said. "Maybe you want to stay longer, my friend, yes? You will not be needing the saddle."

This was ridiculous.

"Just answer," he said. "I am an old man, I don't know for sure. Maybe you feel something, maybe you didn't."

If anything was clichéd, this was. I mean . . .

"Okay, perhaps," I said. "But I've been sick – my mind's been playing tricks."

"You on drugs?" he asked brusquely.

"No!"

"Well then! You came here – I mean, to South America – looking for something, yes? Everyone does. Watch out – you find it. I think you felt the tear today – the UFOs."

"Sorry?" I said.

"Almost every month the air force goes up after something here, but there is no such thing as unidentified flying objects. There is something, but they don't fly and they are not objects. I think they are peep holes into other worlds; that's what the Q'ero were trying to tell us. Rips in time and space. So don't worry, it was just you from the past."

"What was?" I asked.

"What you saw."

"I didn't see anything," I exclaimed.

"Yes, you saw the tear; you saw through time. It is like this ranch: we're here and this is what we see, but we are not aware of Doña Lola washing *aguacate* in the kitchen, or my grandson asleep in his room. We look up in the sky, but there is nothing there. It is all happening in rooms alongside us. This is what the Q'ero were saying. I think the statues, maybe they are periscopes."

At that point Doña Lola called from the kitchen, and Don Luis immediately stood up and patted my back a few times absentmindedly before going inside. A few minutes later a boy came out with my saddle, and I was left to make my way home in the dark.

Chapter 4

Q UITO MADE ME miserable. It was full of happy, fun-loving *gringos*, all of whom seemed to know each other and have had great adventures on the road. I had followed the exact same route as them and only met Paddy Gish. While they spent their afternoons gossiping over coffee and their nights drinking and dancing, I traipsed along cobbled lanes and side streets, exploring the old city. I had nothing to compare to their tales of wrestling crocodiles in the Amazon or romancing the daughter of some cocaine magnate. Me *not* having sex with a naked girl or having my saddle stolen by a senile old man weren't in the same league. I should never have come here; should have gone to North America instead.

I took a bus south to Baños and spent a few days there hanging out with the Salasaca Indians in the outdoor thermal baths. I found their sweet, musty aroma of beans, herbs and smoke reassuring. I liked the way it never washed off. Sitting sweating in a limestone pit of blood-warm water watching mothers and daughters comb their tresses with the Andes soaring up behind was almost sacramental. Of course, I didn't fit in any better there than in Quito, but there was less onus on me to do so, as the Salasaca only spoke Quichua and very little Spanish. We just sat together smiling.

There's only so much time you can spend in the bath, and in Baños' *gringo* joints I was still the outsider because I wasn't up for climbing every mountain or smoking every drug or exaggerating every adventure. In the local zoo, I sought out the condor crammed into its rusted cage and sat with it – its misery reassuring me in an unhealthy, codependent way. The cage was six metres square while the bird's wingspan was three metres, which meant there was just enough room for it to fly one beat of its wings before crashing into the bars. I found it misanthropically appropriate that the animals were all as sad and shifty as myself. Like loveless couples bound together by force of habit, they had long since grown to hate each other but knew there was no one else. I was reminded of Rabbit's idea that hating someone only made you hate yourself more. The bear pit was the worst: a four metre trough in which a pair of schizophrenic bears circled continually through their faeces. I marvelled at the evolutionary leap that had suddenly made people in Europe and the States feel compassion for animals in captivity in the last few decades. There was a Salasaca Indian couple staring at the condor, and I wondered what they made of it.

Memories of the Screamers were haunting me; maybe I should have done more. Mixed up in all their anger and bitterness, I sensed real passion and idealism. I should have reached out more, I suppose. I admired them for choosing such an extreme way of life. Some of them were so mixed up and angry they wouldn't have been able to function in the real world. They would be locked up or at least on medication by now if they had stayed within the system. I admired them for finding another way. It was the children I felt concerned for. They hadn't chosen that life, but no child ever does choose, I suppose. And anyway, what could I have done? Social Services in Ireland had already tried and failed.

I was becoming ridiculously morose, which only added to my sense of isolation. I might as well be depressed at home as here. I certainly wasn't going to find love in this frame of mind. Something had to give; and when Rabbit grabbed me by the shoulders and took me hiking up into the hills, I willingly followed. It was the first time I had felt a rush of enthusiasm about anything since I had come here.

After an hour's hard hiking, when I was almost winded with exertion, he turned on me, saying, *What the hell are you up to? If you want to go home, go! But, you're in South America, man! You're young, for God's sake!*

He softened when he saw he had my attention.

Look, this is your life. It's up to you. Do you want a work of art or a tragedy? You choose; you decide. You were brave enough to come this far, now don't let me down. Live a little!

As usual his words resonated. He was a master of platitudes, but they had an uncanny knack of sounding sincere. I was thinking about what he had said when suddenly the thought came pounding into my head, like ammonia fumes assaulting the synapses, that the Amazon jungle, the most alive place on the entire planet, was just a few miles east of here. If Rabbit wanted me to chase life, where better than there? Amidst the macaws, toucans, tapirs, jaguars, snakes, piranhas, freshwater dolphins and who knew how many plant species.

I walked down from the mountain and straight to Café Hood to celebrate myself over a decadent lunch of Sumatra coffee and chocolate-biscuit cake. Early next morning I rented an old mountain bike with fifteen gears – only three of which worked – and took off tearing down the Andes on dirt roads toward the canopy of rainforest that stretched out forever towards Brazil. The sense of buds burgeoning and sap swirling and the heady smell of leaves composting filled me with hope, and I let my mind free to soar to that imaginary point somewhere in the centre of my forehead which, if I allowed it to, would open like a smoke ring and expand until it dissolved so that everything became included in its alternate world. It was like a backdoor into Neverland, an escape hatch that had been there since childhood but was becoming ever more elusive now. My brain would always try to dismiss it as just a transitory chemical rush, but only because it knew it was more than that. That's what made it so uncomfortable: it was a direct challenge to the cerebral cortex. Over the years, the rational side of me had developed a series of counter-manoeuvres to distract me, like making me hungry or flooding my blood with hormones or even, as a last ditch measure, pleading that it was only looking out for me, that it was worried for my sanity.

This time the brain had a new trick: it tried focusing my attention on the damage Texaco had been doing in the area – pumping gallons of waste oil into the rivers, corrupting the remaining forest tribes – but it didn't work. Once I had entered my alternate world, everything seemed to glow. I saw convoluted reasons why everything was appropriate. I was the three monkeys, and evil just couldn't register. Life was a mystery, part of the ever-adapting and infinite cocoon that nurtured us. As my mind drifted further away, pulling focus back and back, from the microbes in the water that had caused my fever to the sun that kept the earth in orbit and back down all the way to the sweat on my handlebars and the mosquitoes drinking it, I could see it was all too huge and variable to be affected by anything one stupid multinational might do. It was a presumption to even think it might be.

I tore on through the jungle with its flagrantly brandished leaves spinning past me and blue clouds of parrots above, while below me the grainy Rio Pastaza charged along. Gazing across its Coca-Cola-coloured water into the impenetrable wall of foliage beyond, I imagined the life that must right now be thrilling through it: jaguars silently dropping on their prey, anacondas slithering through the undergrowth, streams boiling with a mass of piranhas gorging on dying flesh. I thought to myself, *This is it – this is what it's all about.* All around me were great and terrible things, but what was most valuable was that I was experiencing them. I had to somehow embrace it all, accept it.

I was about 20km out of Baños, and the road was levelling off as the mountains dropped down into the Amazon basin. It was beginning to dawn on me that I would have to cycle the whole way back up again, but it didn't worry me.

Rabbit, I thought, *this is why you wanted me to come, isn't it? This is what it's all about?*

I heard the dog before I saw it.

Above the clattering of my mudguard and the grinding of the rapids, the barking echoed against the tall wall of wood on either side. It was unlike any barking I had known: frantic and frightened – the sound of anguish turned to anger. Something was wrong. Then I saw it: a black dog, big as a panther, tearing towards me out of the forest. Instinct made me ram into lowest gear and peddle as furiously as my calves would allow. Whether this may have incited it even more, I'll never know. But now its bloodshot eyes locked on to me, and it bore unremittingly down more frenziedly than ever. I pushed myself to the limit, certain that I could outpace it. It looked sick and exhausted, but something was goading it irrationally on. I begged my thighs to keep working, and screamed back, *"Buail abhaile!"* – a near magic Irish phrase that will turn any dog back to its owner. It had never once failed me. But this time the dog kept coming; bounding relentlessly on, driven as if by delirium. I had hoped if I outran its territory it would give up.

My knees grew ever weaker, and my feet began to slip off the pedals as I lost co-ordination. Suddenly I felt the hot saliva on my ankle, and its jaw tore through my skin. I lost my balance, and the bike keeled into the dirt. Had the lorry not come at just that moment, I hate to think what would have happened. It almost ran us down. I dived towards the ditch, and the dog backed into the trees in fright. I don't think the truck even saw me. It charged onwards, leaving me sprawled in the dirt with blood spurting from my leg. I was sure the dog would return at any minute, and after pulling myself to my feet, I hopped along as best I could. When I was sure he had gone, I clambered down to the river and stuck my foot into the roaring water until the blood stopped flowing. It was only then that I remembered the piranhas and pulled the leg out again as quick as I could. I pissed on the wound to disinfect it, rubbing a bit of earth in to help it congeal. It wasn't too painful, but I knew if I got on the bike again the wound would open and it wouldn't close so easily a second time. I limped back up to the track and waited until a jeep came along and gave me a lift back to Baños.

By the following day the cut had already healed. I hauled myself up to the thermal baths to soak my muscles, which burned from exertion. Some of the Salasaca Indians recognised me from before and at lunchtime offered to share their beans with me. In hand signals, I told them about my adventure the previous day, and one of the women got her son to ask me, "*Pienses que el perro tiene rabia?*"

The thought had never even dawned on me.

"There is much rabies in the forest," he continued. "You must be careful. Mama has a poultice she can make, but I think instead you should go to clinic."

Was there really rabies here? Was I vaccinated? I got straight out of the water and went back to Café Hood, where the usual motley gathering of stubbly Israelis, druggie London girls and unmarried mothers from Germany were killing time sipping *aromaticas* and picking on banana bread. I asked if any of them knew anything about rabies and got the usual scare stories about a friend of a friend, none of which were likely true. This was before the internet, when all one had for information was the guide book, which only said that rabies was dangerous: avoid getting bitten.

The owner of the café, a puppeteer from San Francisco, overheard us and asked, "Who's been bitten?"

I told him what had happened and where, and his face went pale. Ecuador had one of the highest rates of rabies in the world. An eradication programme had been running, but the marginal zone buffering the forest had yet to be tackled. Rabies was rife.

I went straight to the clinic and asked the doctor for a rabies test, but he told me that by the time the results were back I might already be dead. It all depended how quickly it reached my brain; it needed anything from a few days to a few months to incubate and then to travel up my spinal column. By that stage, it was already too late; my neurons would slowly turn to jelly, killing me. I was lucky I had been bitten on the ankle, he said. The virus had a long way to travel before it could activate. He promised me I would be fine for five days; after that no one could tell. The vital thing was not to get excited or stressed, he said. That only triggered the spread of it faster. He told me the government were now giving the vaccine out for free and I should get it immediately. It involved fourteen shots in the stomach of a compound made from the brain tissue of infected sheep. It was just as painful as rabies, but at least you lived. He had none in supply, but he said I could get some in the missionary hospital in Puyo, an oil-mining town in the jungle.

I had heard too many stories already about the rabies vaccine: people had been known to take their own lives rather than endure it. The first few shots were okay, but as the abdominal spasms and muscle aches became more excruciating with each shot, the patient lost the will to live. The shots tore through the nervous system like barbed bullets. I feared I couldn't hack it.

"There must be an alternative?" I said.

"Not if the dog really had rabies."

How would I know? The dog had seemed pretty crazed to me. I definitely saw its slavering mouth and bleary eyes. *Something* was wrong with it.

"If you can find the dog and check he's vaccinated, you're fine. But make sure you actually see the certificate; don't just take someone's word. If there's no cert, keep an eye on him for a few days, and if he remains calm and isn't frothing, you should be fine; although to make absolutely sure, you need to cut his brain open and bring it here to me. I can test it straightaway. Whatever you do, do it fast. You have only five days. And believe me, you don't want to die this way. I've seen it too often: the swelling pupils, the hallucinations, the fury. Just before paralysis, your mind starts to fear water and you refuse to drink, and that's the worst part of all, slowly dying of thirst over a few days until you fall into a coma.

"If it was me," he said, "I'm telling you I wouldn't risk looking for the dog. I'd get myself to hospital and start treatment."

There was no bus to Puyo until the following morning. I went and got drunk with the guys in Café Hood. Suddenly I was the centre of attention. I had a better story than any of them: I might well be living out the last days of my life. They could dine out on this in backpacker hostels and banana pancake joints for weeks. The spotlight of the *gringo* trail had fallen on me, and my status suddenly soared. They bought me beers and Pisco Sour chasers, and argued amongst each other about whether they would rather die than face the fourteen-pronged torture and the risk of brain damage that went with it. It was the owner of Café Hood who told us about the brain damage. It seemed that even if I got the vaccine in time, I risked being made a vegetable by it, as it contained traces of rabies which at times reacted against one's immune system.

The Israelis thought this was really cool. "It's like Russian roulette," Aviz, a former tank commander, drawled.

But the girls were concerned and sincere. They got me to promise I'd do everything I could to avoid the shots. I told them I'd try, but that wasn't enough. Over a round of Pisco Sours, they made me swear I'd hunt down the dog and even persuaded Aviz to give me his bowie knife to cut its brains out. The young German mother asked Beth, one of the London girls, to look after her daughter so that she could stay with me through the night. Beth was meant to be taking the night bus to Peru, but she cancelled her ticket for my sake. I was now the *Über-gringo*.

The road to Puyo was the same road I had cycled two days earlier. It was a long, windy, endless strip of dirt track, broken only by a few bridges and a dozen or so wooden shacks. The open-sided jalopy of a bus wound its way along it at a speed even slower than my bike. I knew the chances of remembering exactly where the dog had been were slim, but I had to try. Everything had happened so fast – my soaring spirit, the barking, the bite – the last thing I was aware of were the surroundings. All I could remember was the endless curtain of forest that had risen up on either side, broken in parts where the river meandered towards the road. Maybe there would be a shack near by that I would recall or even traces of blood in the dirt. Maybe the shack would be owned by some lonely gold-digger or an evangelist and his whore, and they'd bring me out back to show me their Alsatian who had run away, driven demented by lice, but who was now back home and fully healthy. They would show me their bright pink vaccination certificate and everything would be okay. I would be free to continue my self-absorbed existence, searching for whatever it was I was after.

It was a long shot, I knew, but I had to try.

The road stretched out mile after indistinguishable mile. I remembered one or two points: the crater that had almost knocked me off my bike; the metal bridge that swung precariously; the tiny farmhouse with a roof made of Coke cans where the children had waved joyously; and the semi-camouflaged barn guarded by men with assault rifles. I tried to recreate my journey around them, but it just wasn't enough. There were too many gaps. I had been off with Rabbit for most of the time. It was like trying to chart a dream: at some point the monster had attacked, but where and when I wasn't sure. And anyway, it was difficult to see anything at all with the passengers sitting around me, with their ponchos, bean sacks and chicken baskets blocking out the windows. I didn't want to jump off at the wrong place and be stranded, or even jump off at the right place, in case the dog was actually there and came after me again. It was an exasperating ride. After two hours we reached Puyo, and I had to face the fact that I had failed. Somewhere back there was a dog – either dead or alive – but I had no idea where. Maybe if I found the man who had given me a lift back to Baños he'd know – but where was he?

I was beginning to accept the fact that I would have to get the vaccine. The hospital was near the bus station. I went straight there and, after giving my details at reception, sat down resignedly. I was so frightened. I could see the fourteen shots pointing at me. For about twenty minutes I waited, the fear mounting exponentially with every minute. Suddenly something came over me, and I decided there was no way I could go through with it, not without one last attempt to find the dog. I ran straight out of the hospital, down the steps and into a jeep, gave the driver almost all the money I had and told him to drive me back along the same road I had come. I would find him.

We set off, me goading my mind to remember anything it could. Franco, the driver, was excellent. He stopped every jeep we passed and asked had they seen a black dog, but no one had. After an hour of driving back and forth, I had narrowed the attack site down to a two-mile stretch which had only one shack of any description on it. If the dog belonged to anyone, they must live here. I jumped out and banged on the door, but there was no reply. And we were just about to drive off again when the door opened a fraction and a woman nursing a baby peeked out. I raced up to her.

"*Usted tiene un perro?*" I cried. "Do you have a dog?

She said nothing. I thought perhaps she didn't speak Spanish, so I asked Franco to try asking in Quichua and in Shuar, but she hand-signalled that she was deaf. I grabbed my diary from my bag and wrote the question out, but she signalled that she had no Spanish. I asked Franco to write it in whatever local languages he knew, but he couldn't write, so I got him to speak the words to me and I tried to write them out phonetically. I must have garbled it up, because she could make no sense of it. Somehow she signalled to us that her husband would be home soon and he might be able to help us. We sat on the porch and waited for an hour until he finally came along holding a machete with a stack of fodder piled on his back.

His name was Orlando and he spoke good Spanish. At first he was very welcoming, saying what an honour it was to have a foreign guest in his humble home and ordering his wife to open a bottle of *gaseosa* for us. When I told him about the dog he got cagey.

"This story is a very, very bad one," he said. "A sad one for you, my friend. But why is it that you tell me? Why do you come here, to my home, and to the home of my wife and my child and tell me this sad story? Why is this, sir?"

With as much conciliation as I could muster, I said I needed to find the dog, to check it was okay. I was worried about it, I said. And I asked him again, did he happen to own a dog?

He got very agitated. The sweat was pouring off of him, and his wife had to bring him a tea towel to wipe himself.

"What are you like, *Gringo*? You come to my house and you accuse me of what? Of having a dog? Of attacking you? Of trying to kill you? Get out of my house, boy! I have no dog. I am a poor man. I am very sorry for you, my friend; but I cannot help."

"Please sir! The truth, tell me the truth," I cried. "If you have a dog and it has been sick and has run away, please, just tell me. I need to know! Nothing will happen to you, I promise."

"No have dog," Orlando reiterated. "Now, on my mother's life, you go!"

He looked shaken, really shaken. But whether it was just because a lanky *gringo* was interrogating him on his own doorstep or he actually had something to hide I couldn't tell. I was possibly the first *gringo* he had ever spoken to, the first he had ever seen even. He hardly deserved this imposition. There was nothing more I could do here. It was getting dark, and I realised I would have to give up and accept my fate. I apologised to Orlando and his wife for the intrusion and asked Franco to drive me back to Puyo.

Franco was all buzzed up on the way back.

"We will bring the police back with us and arrest him," he said. "He is a liar. He is not telling the truth."

While I had been talking, Franco had snuck around the back and found a crude corrugated kennel amidst a load of other junk and debris. The kennel was empty. Orlando obviously had a dog at one time, but whether it was mine or not I wasn't sure. Usually when a dog gets rabies it runs away; but if that was the case, Orlando wasn't telling. Involving the police would just drag matters out, and time was the one thing I didn't have. I thanked Franco for his concern, but told him to forget about it and to bring me straight to the hospital before it closed.

When I finally got to see a doctor, she told me she couldn't administer the vaccine until I had reported my case to the local health board, and it wouldn't be open until the morning. Franco insisted I stay in his house, which was just near by in the village of Shell, a depressing trading post built by the oil company of the same name and now an American missionary centre and a command post for the Ecuadorian army in their long-running dispute with Peru.

Franco's wife cooked us a great dinner of fried plantain with coriander salsa, and next day he drove me back to Puyo to the offices of the health board. I told him he could just leave me there, but he insisted on waiting outside. Things went smoothly at first; they took down my details and handed me out the vaccine straight away. I was back in the car again before I noticed it was the anti-vaccine for an animal, not a human. It was probably my bad Spanish that was to blame. I went back and they carefully wrote the words *vacuna de la rabia para gente* on a piece of paper and sent me upstairs to a fat man at an empty desk who spent at least five minutes perusing the piece of paper which had nothing else written on it except that. Finally he asked me when I was bitten and where. It was now three days ago. I had two days left before the first symptoms might develop: anything from fever, nausea, to a general malaise or a persistent cough. By the time they appeared, it was already too late. In all of medical history, only one person has ever survived their onset.

The fat health official seemed to reflect on my case for a long time, twirling his moustache and blinking nervously. Finally he said he would put in an order immediately, and the vaccine should arrive within two days. He'd then arrange for the first five shots to be given over the next five days. In fact, he said, he would book my bed now just to make sure it was kept free.

"You mean you don't have the vaccine here?" I screamed.

"You are very fortunate, Señor, that you were bitten on the ankle. Lady Fortune has smiled on you, you might say. You could not have been more fortunate. Most people are bitten on the arm and we are talking a few days to find a vaccine. With you there is no problem. The vaccine will come in two days, and you will still have a few hours before your time is up. Believe me, I am professional. I know this. Don't worry."

I asked him how sure he was the vaccine would arrive in time, and he said, "It's certain – more or less."

The words more or less – *más o menos* – were the last things you ever wanted to hear in South America.

"That's no good!" I yelled. "I need it now!"

"Not possible, my friend. You wait – no problem."

"I'll die," I cried histrionically.

"No, no. You'll be fine, young man. *Vaya con Dios.*"

An indigenous Indian sat opposite me – a faraway look in his eyes as if he could never understand our world and didn't want to. I understood.

I left the office in floods of tears. I didn't want to die. I was too young. There was so much I wanted to see. I didn't care how sore the shots would be any more; I wanted them now. I tore straight back to the hospital and told them the health board didn't have any vaccine in stock and that I would die without it.

"You must do something," I begged. "Surely you have a supply?"

They assured me they hadn't. Outside the hospital, I collapsed on the steps, whimpering.

So this is why you brought me here, Rabbit, is it? Is this what embracing life is all about? You asshole! I should have stayed with the Screamers. I could be lying in Gina's arms now, losing myself in her multi-orgasmic body. Well, screw you!

If Rabbit's great game of life involved vicious slavering beasts infecting you with death, I was glad to be rid of it. Yet, in truth I had never been less ready for death. The idea of *true* existence being beyond the veil suddenly seemed farcical. I had told Franco to leave me alone, to get out of my sight, and I collapsed in a heap on the hospital steps. And eventually he had left me, reluctantly. I was still sitting there,

fuming with white-hot rage, when a gleaming Toyota pickup pulled
into the forecourt, "HCJB Christian Radio" emblazoned on the hood.
A soft-faced, matronly woman in a dazzling blazer jumped out and
almost tripped over me as she ran toward the front door.

"Wooaa-ah, hey there! Sorry, fella," she called in a Louisiana purr.

I ignored her. On her breast pocket were the words "HCJB –
SPREADING THE WORD".

"American?" she tried again, but I refused to reply.

"Why the long face, sweetheart? What's the big problemo?"

Her name was Guinevere. I think she decided I was her act of mercy
for the day. She was electric with compassion.

"American?" she asked again.

I mumbled, "Irish."

"Come on, fella, it can't be all that bad? Smile those famous Irish
eyes for goodness' sakes! Where's your pot of gold today?" she said in
a teeth-grindingly awful Darby O'Gill impression.

In spite of myself I couldn't hate her, and looking up into her face,
I thought of my mother, and the tears came flooding back. Maybe the
Screamers were right and I was still tied to her apron strings. All I
wanted was to be at home, safe from everything. Guinevere, to hide my
embarrassment, started telling me how she had just got back from
"witnessing" with some far-off tribe, the Huaorani. They were famous
back in the fifties, she said, for killing some missionaries. Things must
have gone really well for her there because she was all stoked up, and
when my crying finally died down, she crouched down beside me with
an open face and said, "Come on, tell an old Yank what's bothering you.
I'm one-eighth Irish after all; can you tell?"

I found myself nodding in the affirmative, which sickened me even
further.

She added in that same awful brogue, "Sure, it can only help to
talk."

Somehow she made me start blathering, and before I knew it I had
told her the whole thing from Gina trying to kill her baby to this.

She let out a long whistle at the end, saying, "Oh boy!" Then she stood up and turned my face to hers, saying, "First off, you don't want to be getting those nasty shots, okay? You listen to me now and you listen good. What you want is the new Vero cell culture. They have it up in Voz Andes in Quito, and you want to get yourself there pronto, honey. It's just one shot and you don't feel a thing. It is expensive, mind – $400 – but it works a treat, and you feel no pain. I've had it, and I can get bitten by every rabid dog from here to kingdom come and it won't do me a blind bit of harm. I just wish I could have thrown myself between you and that beast."

She laughed loudly. She was on a real high, I think purely from the exhilaration of "witnessing" – but in the post-Prozac era you never can tell. She hunched close into me and in an exaggerated stage whisper said, "Between you and me, when I'm on mission I go out of my way to get bitten by dogs, bats, coons – anything rabid! Nothing impresses the natives more than an immortal preacher. It can be mighty sore, believe me, but if it saves souls . . .

"Of course, I should really tell them it's the vaccine that's doing it; but the way I see it, the Lord, He needs all the help He can get around these parts. Anyways, after all, who else makes the vaccine but Him on high?

"What am I doing nattering on, and you dying at my feet! We can't have you hanging around here mopin'. We gotta get you up to Quito. Howabouts I drive you to the airfield in Shell, and we'll see if we can't find us an army plane headin' north?"

What were the chances of her just appearing like that? I recognised I was in the presence of a miracle. In case it was somehow Rabbit's doing, I sent him rays of thanks before throwing what remained of my shopping bags into the pickup and climbing into the cab. Guinevere talked the whole way to the airfield about how she only got to see the Huaorani a few times a year and each time it sent her heart soaring. It turns out one of the missionaries killed by the Huaorani was a close friend of her father's. She was only ten when he died, and she had idolised his memory ever since. She had come out here twenty years ago when her husband had left her, to avenge her father's friend. At first, her heart was set only on retribution, but over time the pastors and members of the local ministry had turned her rage into a zeal to spread the Word. Now her life's wish was to bring sinners to the body of Christ. Each time she saw the once "savage" Huaorani kneeling before the tabernacle reading Scripture, a sublime sense of ecstasy overcame her. It was like the blush of first love, she said; and she would be in bloom with it for weeks.

Seeing how God had transformed these "cocoa-coloured, coarse-haired killers" humbled her anew each time, she said. One of them in particular stirred her soul: Chenwie. He was the last surviving warrior of the group who had killed her father's friend and the other missionaries. Now, almost half a century later, Chenwie was the community pastor. Guinevere felt only compassion and love for him, and over time, she had begun to realise the courage it took for him to attack the frightful albino Mongoloids who had come with Bibles held aloft. As Chenwie saw it, he was protecting his tribe, his way of life, and nothing could be more honourable than that. As far as he knew, the Mongoloids had come to eat him. And he was right in a way, but I didn't say that to Guinevere.

Earlier the same morning, when Guinevere was leaving the camp, Chenwie had had his tribe kneel by the camp-fire and sing hymns for a safe flight home for her. It was so moving, she said. He had looked deep into her eyes and promised he'd pray for her. What grander prayer could there be, Guinevere asked, than that of a former heathen brought to the light of Christ? Each time she met Chenwie, her belief in the power of the Gospel was reaffirmed and she felt reborn.

I mumbled an awkward "Alleluia", for want of anything better.

"Halleluu-yi-jah indeed, my pet," she said and stroked my cheek.

We drove into the airfield which, although just a simple runway with a few shacks around it, was buzzing with army trucks, missionaries and CIA men. The border dispute with Peru was hotting up, and everyone was getting ready. Guinevere hopped out of the cab and asked me would I kneel with her in prayer, and like a fool I agreed. She got me to crouch down by the tailgate of the pickup, watched by a line of orphans led by a nun and some Ray-Banned pilots striking apathetic poses. She told me to repeat after her the words her father's friend had sung on the fateful day of his massacre.

> We rest on Thee, our Shield and Defender
> Thine is the battle, Thine shall be the praise
> When passing through the pearly gates of Splendour
> Victors, we rest with Thee through endless days.

There was a bunch of fresh-faced recruits being led under the whirring blades of a plane into a cargo hold crammed with vegetables and crates of live guinea pigs, whose whiskered snouts twitched against the vibration of the engines. Guinevere got up off her knees once the prayer was said and gave me a big gutsy hug before scampering off to find me a plane. Within minutes she was back with news of a four-man Cessna sitting on the tarmac ready to leave for Quito within the hour. She got them to guarantee me a seat and offered to wait around until it took off, but I assured her I'd be fine. She had saved my life; what more could she do?

Only when she had gone did I realise that the flight would cost $200. I certainly didn't have anything like that much. My budget was $35 a week, and I had only $16 left. There was $500 in my bank account, but I couldn't get to it here, and anyway I would need it for the vaccine. So I left the airport and hitchhiked back to Puyo. From there, I was lucky: I got a bus leaving straight away for Baños, and from there a *collectivo* over the mountain to Ambato, where I was able to catch the night bus heading north towards Quito.

Arriving in the capital at dawn in the central bus station, I walked the four miles across the city to Voz Andes hospital. I was beginning to feel really sick, but I couldn't tell if it was tiredness or something worse. Even thinking about it made me stressed, and I knew that just increased the risks. I was now on my fourth day; the clock was ticking.

Voz Andes was high-tech and impressive: a plush private hospital built by evangelists for themselves and petrochemical workers and anyone else who could afford it. I felt embarrassed in my sweaty T-shirt and frayed shorts. A Peruvian consultant sat me down in a luxurious office and massaged his chin contentedly while I explained the situation. He told me he had never heard of a one-shot vaccine, but he did know of a five-shot dose which was also pretty new and had no side-effects. He had none in stock at present, but it could be flown out from the US in twenty-four hours. He said that since the old vaccine was free, not many people chose the new one. It would cost $300, which I would have to pay upfront. This all sounded fine, but it had already been four days; by 5 p.m. tomorrow, my time was up. If my neural circulation and haemoglobin levels were especially efficient, the virus could have reached the brain by then and it would all be too late.

The consultant tried to reassure me that it was unlikely to spread that fast. He knew of cases where it lay dormant for months; but he couldn't say for sure what would happen. All I could think of were the hallucinations and hydrophobia. I didn't want to die.

"Relax, my friend," the consultant intoned.

I was beginning to hyperventilate.

"You could try asking your embassy: sometimes they keep a supply in stock for themselves. It's possible they may take pity on you and give you the first dose while the rest is being flown out."

Without even waiting to thank him, I raced out of the office and into a taxi while looking up the embassy in the guide book. Ireland only had a consulate, but it would have to do. It was an apartment in the rich quarter, and a pompous man with an Oxbridge accent answered the intercom, but he refused to let me in.

"We don't handle illness here. I suggest you go to a hospital. Try Voz Andes," he said before hanging up on me. "They're very good."

It was the taxi man who suggested I try the British Embassy.

"You, English, Irish, you all the same," he said. "You just say you're different. England will help you. They owe you big time – like Spain owes Ecuador."

The first secretary in the British Embassy could not have been more charming. She gave me a cup of tea and listened as I ranted on, but said there was no way she could let me have the embassy's own dose of vaccine. I begged her, and so as not to cause a scene, she said she'd make a few phone calls. She came back a minute later with the address of a private clinic out near the airport which had a batch in supply that they were willing to sell me for considerably more than it would have cost in Voz Andes. They couldn't see me that day, but they made an appointment for first thing in the morning.

I didn't sleep much that night. I stayed up with Rabbit on the roof of the *Residencial Marsella* looking out at the equator just a few kilometres north and the Amazon stretching east, thinking that if I did really have to die somewhere, no place could be more auspicious. Of course, I did my fair share of whimpering, too; my diary contains twenty fraught pages of mawkish emotionalism which I still haven't had the stomach to read fully. I wish I could say I faced death nobly, like I had before in Africa, but things were different now. I was beginning to feel more and more clearly that I really would find what I wanted if I just kept after it long enough. This time, I wasn't going to be beaten. No way would I give up.

The following morning I was camped outside the clinic hours before they opened. The secretary arrived at eight and told me that I'd need to pay in American dollars before they'd even see me. This required a wild, two-hour goose chase back and forth between various banks, but by noon I was sprawled over a starched sheet, mooning at a sweet-scented, saintly nurse who opened a double-sealed, stainless steel refrigerator and from its aureole glow took out a single dose of immunoglobulin. As I stared at the pristine white floor, this great Nightingale pumped me full of concentrated rabies antibodies, and with that one shot of her syringe (and another four vials to take with me to be injected each week), it was all over. I was saved.

I walked out of the clinic into the seething throng of smoking buses, waspish taxis and emaciated peanut sellers, feeling reborn. Never had the world looked so supersaturated with colour, so sumptuous, so ripe with possibility. I could feel life pulsate through me. I held in my hands every and any potential. I was a palette and this was my easel. What would I paint today?

Chapter 5

THERE WAS NO doubt about what I wanted first . . . watermelon. I wanted a watermelon. I wanted to break open and bury my face in the blushing flesh of a syrupy, seedy watermelon. I walked through the Parque El Ejido to the fruit market where the Monterey pines looked more melodramatic than ever, their bark as richly textured as sods of turf. I gorged myself on the smell of their lush lime needles. Even the dog turds smelt nourishing and important. I was 3,000 metres up in the Andes, and I could feel every metre. I was alive, on top of the world. Above me was nothing except the diamond snow peak of Cotapaxi soaring towards the sun.

In the market I picked out the lushest, largest watermelon and told the seller how *linda y preciosa* her daughter was, and may she marry the most handsome *caballero* in all Ecuador. She beamed blessings back at me as I walked away to the shade of a magnolia tree with my great green ovary and my heart overflowing with warmth. Unsheathing Aviz's bowie knife, I sliced through the creamy yellow spot where the melon had lain on the earth sunning itself and through into its spongy slurry. Its life dripped down my sweaty T-shirt, and I felt bathed in its goodness. I made no effort to spit out the seeds. These ova of potential were too sacred; their potency echoed my own. I shivered with the momentousness of the idea that this flesh that fed my future dreams was the product of the sun, the moon, the earth and water. A Quichua girl in multicoloured alpaca shawl came by selling bracelets, and I offered her a slice. We sat together in silence eating slice after sweet slice. Then she took my knife and began carving smiling faces into the discarded skins. It was sacramental.

Later I decided I should celebrate. I washed my hair and dug out my only good shirt. I intended to let rip like a roman candle, but when I got to the clubs off Juan León Mera, I realised I wasn't prepared to allow my newly saved body anywhere near cigarette smoke. And even the thought of filling it with alcohol repulsed me. Rabbit sneered. He said he preferred the dying me to the born-again, but he didn't understand.

I set off along Amazonas where the Otavaleños were selling carpets and ponchos, and as they called their greetings to me, I saluted each one in turn like a star at a premier. Outside the Museo Shuar, I happened upon a young European girl crying. She was sitting on the street with her head in her hands. I thought back to myself on the steps of the Puyo clinic just two days before and bent down to ask what was the matter. She took me aback a little, by not saying "oh nothing," or "I'm fine," or even, "I'm just a bit sad."

In a prosaic Danish singsong, she began, "When I slept with Manuelo in Santiago the condom tore, and now my period is late and I think I'm pregnant, and my friend Tina doesn't care, and I don't know what to do, and so I tried to harm myself, but . . ."

She stretched out her arms to show fresh bandages on her wrists. I stared. I had no idea what to say. She was so young, so innocent. She couldn't have been more than eighteen – her skin the waxy alabaster of a twelve-year-old, the texture of pre-fired clay. She should have been tucked up at home and never let out alone. I sat with her without saying a word until she collapsed back and fell asleep against my chest. She had been drinking *aguardiente*, and her breath reeked of bubblegum and the kerosene fumes of bad alcohol. I tried waking her, but it was no use, and in the end I brought her back to my room and put her to bed. I settled myself on the floor beside her, but I couldn't sleep. I spent the night perched on a stool, mesmerised by the almost imperceptible swelling and falling of her marble cheeks, thinking about where I should go from here. The rest of my life lay at my feet, and I had no idea where to begin. All I knew for certain was that I had to leave Quito later that day as it was a Wednesday, and Wednesdays were tear-gas day – the day students invariably held protests and were sprayed with o–chlorobenzylidene malononitrile by the police.

The girl and I shared breakfast, and then I headed towards the bus station, where, at the gates, the usual scrum of hawkers were desperately trying to sell off the remaining seats on departing buses, screeching like gannets over a shoal.

"Ambato! Ambato! Ambato!"

"Esmer-aldas-Esmer-aldas-Esmer-aldas!"

Adding to the cacophony were the ricochets of "*El Comercio*" and "*Diario*" from the newspaper boys. A coked-up backpacker was screaming that he refused to pay bribes, while one or two patient strangers were trying to explain to him that it was just the regular charge for using a locker. I noticed the headlines were full of the usual swagger about *footballistas* and *contrabandistas* – the same old stories. Nothing had changed in the real world.

A young girl in a tattered pink gown came to me and whispered, "Vilcabamba?" in the sweetest, softest tone, and I nodded, more to give her the commission than anything. She grasped my fingers in her tiny hand and led me through the crowd to a ticket booth, where I bought a ticket primarily so that she could have the pleasure of pushing me towards Gate 37 and pocketing her few *pesos*.

Before I knew it, I was on a chrome and Formica bus headed for Vilcabamba. As good a place as any, I thought. I had been hearing about it since I'd arrived. A remote valley in the foothills that had been cut off until a road was built twenty years ago, it was known as the Valley of Longevity because its inhabitants claimed to live into their hundreds. Octogenarians whose dads were still alive were said to be common. I liked the fairy-tale aspect of it, and flicking through my guide book I found someone had pencilled in some recommendations: I was to stay in Hostel Caravanserai; scrawled across the page were the words, "*Its chocolate brownies kick ass*". It was as good a tip-off as any. I often got people heading the opposite way to annotate my guide.

Eight hours later, on the main square of the tiny village of Vilcabamba, I clambered out of the bus and asked a backpacker at a café to point me towards the hostel.

"I saw a woman riding on silver wheels," he said, "and I called her disabled." He looked hard at me for a moment, before continuing, "Of course, we are the greatest enigma of all, aren't we? Why can we never *see* that? Why must we always be the enemy?"

"Caravanserai?" I repeated. "It's a hostel."

"Look, look!" he implored. "It's all light. Just different frequencies, you see? What's your name, my friend? Your name?"

"Mocha," I sighed resignedly.

"Of course you are! You're looking for a hostel, aren't you? Hostel Caravanserai?"

"Exactly," I said.

"Yeah, yeah, yeah," he agreed. His accent had the unmistakably jilted tempo of an Israeli's, and like all Israelis he used his jaw like a ventriloquist's. "It's about one click back up the road, but take the river route; it's prettier."

Hostel Caravanserai was impressive: a winding track through acacia trees and giant aloes led up to a low adobe farmhouse which peered out from under a heavy terracotta roof. Acres of fruit trees stretched up the mountain behind it, and on either side were cottages among the trees, some made of bamboo, others of logs and huge river-washed stones. Streams wound their way around them, and in a grove of papaya trees was a tiny azure swimming pool cut into the mountain.

An Australian girl sat me down on the veranda and checked me in. The price was $7 a night including breakfast and dinner, she chimed. It was way beyond my budget, but I didn't care. I was alive. And anyway, if I spent nothing else all day, I could just about cover it. I left my bag on a bed in the bamboo dorm and went to wash the road dirt off me. In the showers, I literally bumped straight into Beth, the girl from London who had been in Café Hood the day after I was bitten. She shrieked with delight to see me alive – my Lazarean recovery, as she called it.

"Bollix, we all had you dead long ago, mate!" she cried. "How in hell are you?"

Beth went to hug me, but stopped, "You still infected, eh?"

I assured her I wasn't, but she was dripping from the shower and I avoided the hug. She said that we had to celebrate my survival. I should come to Loja with her, she said, she knew of a great guinea pig restaurant.

"I can't believe you're not dead. Everyone is talking about you. They say your brain liquefied and spilt out your ears!"

Beth stopped to think for a second, then said, "I have a surprise for you – just give me five minutes."

Half an hour later she was on the verandah in a sarong and T-shirt.

"Okay, this is going to be so great!" she said breathlessly. "We're going into town – you ready?"

She was literally leaping with excitement as she led me to her horse.

"What are we going to do?" I asked.

"It's a surprise, Lazarus," she said throwing a blanket across the horse and fixing the halter straps. "I'm afraid the saddle is tiny. You'll have to sit bareback behind me."

We rode back into town and she made a beeline for the café on the square where she hitched up right beside the Israeli from earlier, calling out to him,

"Mordechai! Hey, Mordechai! You'll never believe it! This is the dead man I was telling you about." Then she turned to me, "Lazarus, this is Mordechai."

"Hi Laz," he said. He didn't recognise me.

"It's okay if he tags along?" Beth asked.

"Sure," he said lackadaisically.

Mordechai threw a few *pesos* on the table, then hopped on his own horse, and we rode out of town and up into the Rio Yambala Valley through freshly cleared cloud forest. He pointed to an old Indian hunting cabin way off in the distance on the far side of the valley, saying that that was where we were headed. At first I thought they were joking, but no one laughed, and the horses set off up a narrow track just wide enough for one. The track was slippery and wound its way precariously along the side of the valley, making it necessary for the horses to tread carefully. Eventually it dipped down to the river, which was deep and strong and surprisingly difficult to ford. We emerged dripping and shivering on the far side, but the exertion of pulling the horses up the steep slope had us dry by the time we reached the cabin two hours later.

Sitting on the porch waiting for us was a lanky, dour-looking man with a leather sombrero and an equally emaciated woman who had the boldest snake eyes I'd ever seen. They ignored us, and Mordechai made no effort to greet them. He just walked straight by, giving the briefest nod before entering the cabin.

"What's going on?" I asked Beth.

"Indeed," Mordechai intoned in reply.

The place smelt of rodents and wet horse blankets. Beth led me straight into the kitchen, which was no more than a few old planks stretched across wooden crates, and she pointed to a saucepan of thick, green soup on the stove.

"That is!" said Beth, laughing. "That's what's going on."

"What is it?" I asked.

"You don't know?!"

"Vichyssoise?" I ventured.

At the birthday party of a school friend, we had been offered this instead of sausage rolls or marshmallows, and I still remember my sense of disgust. One boy said it looked like phlegm, and the mother had started to cry.

"It's San Pedro! Cactus of San Pedro," Beth said at last.

I had no idea what she was on about. I looked quizzically, and she stared back at me in disbelief.

"San Pedro cactus!" she repeated in exasperation. "Mordechai found it yesterday in the mountains. He's been boiling it all night. You must know about it? There's only a few places on earth it grows. Shamans use it to meet God. It's sooo beautiful, Laz."

The more I travelled the more I realised how little my schooling had prepared me for the real world.

"Mordechai took some this morning," Beth explained.

"Whoooeee, it's beautiful. The real deal," he assured us. "It's like . . . out there. Like you've frickin' died and gone to heaven."

Beth frowned, reminding him that I almost *had* died and gone to heaven.

"No offence, mate," he added amicably.

"I've *so* always wanted to try it," Beth exclaimed. "'You've just got to have some, Laz. To celebrate you're alive. You know?"

Mordechai got out two glasses and filled them. It was snot–coloured and slimy, like pond scum or primordial soup. He handed one to me and the other to Beth. My brain tried to evaluate the pros and cons, but everything was happening so fast. It seemed churlish to hold back. I was miles from anywhere and didn't really know my way home, and anyway Beth was right, I was alive after all. I managed to ask what was in it as Mordechai cut up a lemon and handed us each a slice.

"Mescaline, my man," he said waving his knife at me. "Like peyote."

As I knocked back the drink with no idea what it would do to me, I thought of Alice choosing between the one that made you larger and one that made you smaller. *If she was brave enough, then so must I*, I thought. It tasted like rancid borscht, and my stomach did its best to reject it, but I could hear Mordechai's words, "Keep it in. Try and keep it in. That's the boy. Tiny breaths. Take tiny breaths."

Strands of mossy sludge stretched between my mouth and the glass, and yet more dribbled down my cheek. I breathed slowly through my nose until the urge to vomit passed. I could see Beth's face contorting as she downed hers. Then Mordechai took another shot, just for good measure.

I sucked on the lemon to kill the taste and felt a profound sense of anticlimax. *Now what?* I thought.

"How long does it take?" I asked.

"Oh, you'll know," said Mordechai.

The three of us sat down on the cabin floor, looking at each other awkwardly. My eyes ranged over to the porch where the man in the hat and the woman were still seated. I had no idea what they were doing there. I caught the man's eye, and he gave a brief, surly nod. I nodded back.

"Hi," he muttered in a melodic Welsh drawl.

He looked out at the mountain before turning back, saying, "Wanna go on a trip to the edge of the world sometime, son?"

I think I already was, but I didn't say that. He seemed a little drunk. He had a bottle of sugarcane spirits in his hand, and I got the sense he wasn't comfortable with what we were doing. He had been shifty ever since we'd arrived and had ignored us until I addressed him directly.

He offered his snake–eye friend a slug from the bottle and then stared back out into the mountains.

Finally, he turned to me saying, "You know, you don't need that shit. I can bring you places that will really blow your mind without using drugs – just the way-out beauty of it. Gimme $40 and I'll take you on a trip you'll never forget – food, horses, sleeping bags, everything included. We'll go right up into them mountains, if you want. The name's Rory. This is my wife, Luna."

He stood up, shambled over and shook my hand and began to talk volubly and ramblingly into my face about everything. He and Luna had come from a village near Snowdonia in Wales ten years earlier, he said, convinced the world was going to end and that this was the only place they might survive. They had bought a thousand acres of pristine cloud forest high up in the Andes which Rory was determined to preserve. It was his church, where he hoped to convert mankind, one by one, to an understanding of the sacredness of nature. He now spent his days hanging around the square in Vilcabamba, drinking beer and needling backpackers to take a trip into the forest with him, to see and feel its fragility, its beauty. Although he only managed to bring a few hundred up a year, he believed backpackers, and particularly the ones ambitious enough to come with him, would become the most influential and powerful people in society when they were older. The fact that they could travel around the world to new and dangerous places on a pittance proved they were innovative, motivated and had breadth of vision, he said. How could they not thrive?

At least, this was what he was staking his life on. By influencing these people when they were young, he would ensure that they in turn would set the world to rights later on. It was a long-term plan, and already he realised he was running out of time. Every year farmers were encroaching nearer and nearer his forest, planting sugarcane for which the government paid subsidies. The farmers would slash and burn a section of forest to sow seed in, but often the fires would get out of hand.

That was the reason Rory was down here now at the cottage. He had seen smoke on the edges of his forest earlier in the day and had come down to warn the authorities; to let them know they should send a spray plane up. But he and Luna had only got this far when one of his mules died of exhaustion. The other was too lame to go on, and he had sent his children down to Vilcabamba on foot to raise the alarm while he waited to give the remaining mule a chance to rest.

Talk of her children caught Luna's attention and she glanced over. She had made no movement the whole time her husband was talking, as though she were hypnotised, entranced by the varnish on her nails. She looked completely bored. With her black designer jodhpurs, crimson blouse and large brass eagle brooch, she was an unlikely figure to find sitting in a shack in the Andes. Her mane of petroleum hair was groomed to perfection, and her eyeliner and nail polish matched her blouse. Compared to her beat-up, outback husband, she looked like a Victorian doll, or a cross between a doll and the opera-singing hookers one saw in the saloons in old Westerns. It was she who taught me some weeks later about the whole concept of defining people by their *energy*. And it is true to say that her energy was definitely her defining attribute. It was slithery and alluring and seemed to fit perfectly her job as a masseuse. Luna gave me my first-ever massage some time later.

Directly afterwards she commented, "I haven't felt such energy in my life before. You are a god! I'm so electrified I could take you down and rape you right now."

At the time, I regarded it as an unusual liberty for a masseuse, and it was only later I learnt that it was her usual practice. Even on this, my first encounter with Luna, I was intrigued. She was just so different from the backpackers I had been around and seemed so at odds with her husband, who oozed honour and honesty.

After a long pause, Luna flicked her glowing mane and asked, "How much did you take?"

"Sorry?" I said.

"How much Pedro?" She had a slight lisp and a trace of Spanish through her Welsh accent.

"A glass," I said. "Is that all right? Will I be okay?"

"You're going to have the time of your sweet young life," she hissed. "There is no more I can say – it would be like describing pink to a blind person. You'll know all you need to soon enough. Don't be scared, whatever happens. Remember there are only two things you can control: intention and thought. Believe you can, and you can."

In her slithery, Spanish-Welsh accent, this sounded profound, and maybe it was.

"You won't hallucinate," she added. "At least, not that much. It's not like LSD. Your brain will talk to your senses – your ears and eyes and taste buds – in a new way, and when you consider that everything you know comes from your senses, it's kind of freaky. Without them you'd only be your thoughts, right?"

Just like Rabbit.

"Think of it like you're an astronaut," she purred. "It's been years since humans first set foot in outer space, and we still can't navigate inner space! Enjoy."

I already am, I thought. My muscles were beginning to tingle, and I could feel my body being washed in warm waves, like I was coming alive for the first time – connecting to everything, expanding outwards and delving inwards. It felt good. There was a column of ants meandering between an old jam jar and a hole beneath the porch, and I watched them transfixed until Beth came and sat beside me.

"Mordechai is going to put on some sounds," she said. "Any requests?"

I shook my head.

"The Rolling Stones?" she said.

I shrugged.

"Okay, Laz," she said and stroked my hair. I could feel each strand react.

When I heard the sweet soprano boys' choir rise up to meet the soaring violins, I knew I had already left this world. I was far away by the time Keith Richards' clashing guitar came thrashing through to meet Jagger's voice.

I saw her today at a reception
Glass of wine in her . . .

It was as though the music were alive and I had entered it. I could hear Richards' nails strum the steel strings and the young boys suck in air. It was all liquid and light. I closed my eyes and lay back on the porch. Cinemas appeared inside my eyelids. Haloes and lattices appeared; they were cobwebbing through chequerboards. Every note of music and every colour contained worlds within worlds which were more alive than anything I had known. Catacombs. It saddened me to recall how little of *anything* I had really heard up until then. My reality had been a mono, black and white television, and I didn't even know it.

Mordechai came and asked us did we want to go for a walk, and I got to my feet. The dusty track we had walked up earlier had become a swirling, Van Goghian tunnel of trees and bushes that shrank and expanded, seemingly on a whim. Catacombs: I was sure I sensed tunnels spreading out through the ground beneath my feet like a fairy fort. I wasn't frightened. This was no alien force, quite the opposite: I had eaten a part of my surroundings which somehow allowed me enter it more deeply than I had ever entered anywhere before. On some levels it made more sense than anything I had known up until then. *This* was reality – never mind the pale and meagre façade I had known before – as full of potentials and probabilities as a game of chess, as evolution. From here I could see *all* the options, not just the one my brain chose to focus on. It reminded me of the worlds I used to visit from my tree stump in the schoolyard. Somehow the cactus had widened the parameters to reveal the marginal worlds which were infinitely more vibrant and chaotic. Nothing was static, and nor need it be, I realised. Everything could react and interrelate with me.

When we got down to the river, Beth sprawled on the bank to soak up the sun while Mordechai went off climbing a eucalyptus tree. I kicked off my sandals and plunged my feet into the water. My legs were spirals screwing into liquid vortices, and I could feel the H_2O molecules come and kiss the scab of the bite wound, and I cried inside, cried out of sheer joy at being alive. I wondered what preoccupied scientist in a laboratory in India or America or wherever had isolated immunoglobulin and given it to the world? I needed to find him or her and thank them. I should dedicate my life to them. How many animals had been killed testing the vaccine? Could I make it worth their while?

I could feel my body dissolve into the water; my legs were already gone, flowing towards the Amazon. I yearned to allow all of myself merge with it, to just let go and escape the suffocating matrix of my body. I was drifting far away, and it was Rabbit who eventually caught up with me. I was deep in the weft and weave of my T-shirt – literally trekking through its fibres, following individual strands on their heroic journey from hem to collar. All that remained of me was my T-shirt; my body had long since been swept downstream. Rabbit somehow found me and pulled my eyes up to the sun; it shone with alien incandescence.

Mocha, he called out.

I wasn't in the mood.

Mocha? he repeated more urgently

Yeah, I sighed eventually.

Do you have any idea who you are?

Mocha. I'm Mocha, I said impatiently.

No, who you really are?

I'm Mocha!

Yes, but who else? Come on! You know. I know you don't normally know, but now you should. Think!

Really Rabbit, I'm Mocha. That's who I am.

He shook his head, saying, *That's only partially true. Only the last bit is, really.*

Huh?

I AM. That's true. You are! So am I. Don't you see?

I AM? I repeated dubiously. *You're saying, I'm nothing else?*

He shook his head again. *You're EVERYTHING else, you fool! Can't you see?*

I could see him pause, trying to find the right words. It was hard enough to follow him normally, but I was barely holding on now, with every word exploding into pictograms and linear sequences. My focus was melting around the edges.

Believe me, you have no idea who and what you really are, he said. *You are light. Can't you feel it? Can't you feel it burning through? That's you. It's me. It just is.*

Of course, I felt it. I could feel anything now, everything.

That's who you are, Rabbit said. *It's everyone. You ARE.*

I was valiantly trying to keep up with him.

You hate hearing that, don't you? he went on. *It means you're responsible. You can't blame me or anyone else. If you don't want it, you can choose again.*

Look, Rabbit, I'm having a good day, I said. *Can't we just leave this for another day?*

No, he said. *No, I'll never catch you like this again. Just give me a chance here. I only want you to know who you really are – a billion times bigger and brighter than you think. A million times more than me.*

Yeah, right, I said. *So that's why you're always on my case?*

Just listen to what I'm saying; that's all I'm asking, Rabbit said. *You were willing to cram yourself into that lanky body; now allow yourself to remember what it's like being free. It's easy for me. I can vanish when things get tough – just switch off, move elsewhere. You're here all day, every day.*

Yeah, I've noticed, I said.

And you know why that is, he said. But I didn't.

I was free of the fibres of my T-shirt jungle now, and my attention was fully on Rabbit. I could just about see him. He was floating. He looked like Níní only bigger, and his fur had all grown back.

Today you're seeing my perspective, he said. *The unlimitedness, the intensity. I've never once seen what it looks like for you. 3-D is the hardest there is.*

Tell me about it! I said.

But you came here on purpose. To live. To learn. To experience.

Feeling was beginning to return to my feet. They were wet and cold.

The whole thing is a game, Rabbit said.

Cedar and Lana, Rory and Luna's children, came crashing through the water on a pony. With Cedar in his leather chaps and Lana in a smock, they looked like Wild West pioneers. Luna had told me that they were the reason she stayed on in South America. She would have gone home long ago except for them. They had been living for so long in the mountains they were practically feral. She wondered if they could ever adjust to life back in Wales, or if they would have to stay here their whole lives. Cedar was fourteen and Lana eleven, and although they attended the local school and spoke perfect English and Spanish, they didn't have many friends. Their mother didn't like them hanging around with *campesino* children.

81

Cedar leapt off the pony, approaching me and asking where his parents were. He looked anxious, and I could sense the panic in his heart. There was much sadness in him, as though his cells had been infused with all of his father's despair. Mordechai climbed down from the tree and put his arms around the boy, asking him what was wrong. He just pointed up the valley where vast plumes of smoke were rising above the trees. The fire was still maybe five miles away, but it was spreading fast.

"There was no need for us to go to Vilcabamba," Cedar said in his dusky Latin–Welsh drawl. "They could clearly see the fires from there. But they aren't sending any planes. They say a storm's coming and it'll put it out."

We looked dubiously up at the bright blue sky.

When we got back to the cabin, Rory was even more morose than before. He had been watching the smoke spread across the skyline, and it was breaking his heart. The bottle of spirits was long gone, and it hadn't killed the pain. Hearing that there was no help coming made him flinch as if he had been whipped. He had devoted not only his life to the forest, but his wife's and children's, too. The forest was his final hope in what he believed was a poisoned world.

There was nothing to do now but wait and hope for rain. I lay down on the verandah and stared at the sky until Rory told the children to fetch the mule down from the mountain where it was grazing, and I asked could I go with them just to get away from the cabin and Rory's mounting despair. It was getting dark, and it would be dangerous to leave the animal up there through the night. Pumas often came down this far, and while there were just as many vampire bats around the cabin as up higher, at least if they attacked here we would hear the mule's cry and could come help. Although a bat bite wasn't fatal (unless it was carrying rabies), if enough anticoagulant got into the wound, the blood could flow all night.

Cedar grabbed a lasso and we set off through the forest calling and whistling, but the mule didn't want to be found. We trekked in circles for maybe an hour until finally the animal coughed, revealing itself scratching up against a podocarpus tree. Cedar tied a halter round its neck with ease, but there was no way it was going to follow us back down the mountain. It had found a juicy patch of alfalfa and was feasting itself. The poor thing looked gaunt and exhausted. The late *El Niño* rains had reduced grazing to a minimum, and all the animals were suffering.

Coaxing the animal back towards the shack took for ever. It was an exhausting ordeal, but being with the children made up for it. It was exactly what my over-exposed soul needed, to be among people who weren't completely pinned down yet, who could still dream. Cedar, the elder of the two, was already losing his innocence; he had taken on as much of the weight of the world as his fourteen-year-old mind could and was infused with the same inspiring, stoic sense of righteousness as his father – like an old John Wayne hero. His sister Lana was that rarest of things, a child of light-incandescent and seemingly infinitely wise beyond her years. I could feel the compassion off her like from a wise old dog. Being in their presence washed away some of the desperation stirred up by the fire. It helped ease the choking, congested feeling I was having as my spirit wound its way back into its cage.

As we took turns beating and dragging the mule back, I could feel Lana's optimism gradually wane as we saw and heard the fires spreading closer. Rationalising Texaco's damage was one thing, but this was something else. It seemed to be a more personal vengeance. I turned on Rabbit.

If this is a game, it's a sick one, I said.

You always make it so hard, he agreed.

Me! I said.

All of you. I didn't light the fire, after all. Can't you just trust that it's appropriate somehow?

No! I cried. *That's mind-Prozac. Novocaine. Bullshit.*

I stopped myself: raging at an imaginary figure wasn't a good idea. I had to stay balanced, to remember that it was just the bitterness in the cactus lashing out with a final slash of its barbs and making the world seem a tragic, desperate place. I never knew whether to trust Rabbit or not. At times he was so cutting, and at others he could be so compassionate. I was beginning to suspect there was more than one Rabbit, but how could I tell them apart?

When we finally got back to the house, Rory had ground up some corn and was frying tortillas for dinner. The others were dozing. I threw on an old poncho I found and sat down on the porch to watch the flames eat their way through the forest. The walls of the shack swayed slightly like a veil in the breeze, but otherwise the magic had all but drained away. I made one last effort to grasp at it.

I'm not sure I want to go back, I told Rabbit.

I suddenly understood those people who end up in institutions, who could never bring themselves to return.

Yeah, Rabbit agreed. *You're not as obsessed with it all any more, are you? You've lost the hunger. That's why you don't connect with people. But give it one last chance. I'll keep an eye out for you, I promise. I'll send a wind to dry your tears.*

I felt a gust against my face. It was so gentle, no more than the lightest breeze. Rory and the mule raised their noses instinctively, sniffing frantically for more. It had been so gentle – perhaps we imagined it. We all held our breath, remaining poised like weathervanes until at last it came: a slight but unmistakable wind blowing in from the coast with a touch of chill that it could only have picked up over the Chimborazo volcano. Rory's face cracked into an almighty smile.

"Watch out," he said. "I reckon you guys are in for the storm of your miserable lives. Sit back and enjoy!"

Sure enough, along the western horizon, a phalanx of cloud cavalry came riding in, dark, swollen and rain-drenched. Within an hour it was on top of us, hanging heavy and threatening above our heads.

"Let rip, you bastards, let rip," Rory screamed, but the clouds were oblivious and rolled right over us and onwards down into the Amazon. Lana burst into tears, and nothing her mother said could reassure her.

The fires were so near now we could hear the crackle of burning trunks – ancient teak and mahogany reverting to carbon and water, a pall of black smoke suffocating the canopy.

It was another hour before the rearguard appeared. It came in riding lower and even heavier than the first, and Rory broke into a cry of pure joy. There was no way these monsters could make it over the mountain without breaking, and sure enough, moments later, we heard the first crash of thunder, and the rain began to pour. It poured and poured, and with it came flashes of lightning that lit up the sky from the equator to Peru. Mordechai dug out a bottle of beer and gave it to Rory to celebrate. He tore off its head as though it were one of his hens and shoved its neck to his mouth.

"Thank the Almighty fucking Christ for that!" he roared.

The rain was torrential and it continued through the night, quenching the fires and washing away the last vestiges of our magical journey. We were back on earth, exhausted, a little demoralised, but alive.

Chapter 6

IT WAS ONLY when I got back to Caravanserai and unpacked my bag that I remembered the vaccines. The clinic had injected the first dose of antibodies, but I still had four more to take over the next month, and in the meantime they had to be kept refrigerated. The doctor only gave them to me on condition I bring them straight to a fridge and keep them there.

Hoping that they hadn't spoiled already, I went straight to the kitchen and asked Marialena, the housekeeper, would she mind them for me? It confused her at first, and she tried using them on the dogs and then promised to send them back to Quito for me. Eventually I got the Australian girl at reception to explain that I wanted them kept in the fridge. But I realised that as I couldn't keep bringing them from fridge to fridge with me for the next five weeks, I would have to settle down somewhere. I asked the Australian if there was any chance of a job in the area. By sweet coincidence, she told me she was leaving in a week and that I should ask the owner of Caravanserai, Nadine, for her job.

Nadine was from Seattle and lived with her husband Demofilo and their children in a large ranch house on the edge of the estate. She was as alluring as Luna and far more elegant, dressing in flowing folds of mauve and olive and wearing her hair in complicated plaits. When I arrived at her door, looming down on her in my huge sandals and pasty face looking for a job, she didn't react well. Hers was a hip, laidback joint for cool, laidback people. I was awkward and unkempt, not really what she had in mind. But I was so desperate for somewhere to stay that I told her I'd work for free; I'd even pay a little for my bed and board. She agreed to think about it. She told me to help the Australian girl in her last week and see how I got on.

At first I was awful – self-conscious and disjointed – but as I got to know the place and built up information about the locality, a transformation occurred. I found for the second time in my life – the first was on the farm – that I was actually of use, and it felt good. Guests arrived in off the road, tired and dusty, and I would find them a bed and nice food and tell them where everything was – the best hikes, banana bread, place to rent good horses – and I loved doing it. I bloomed. I was enjoying myself so much I didn't even take the bribes offered by the local shops and services, so that I could be genuinely objective in my advice – although I used to get a free massage for every four clients I sent to Luna. But I would have recommended her anyway, because she was the best and I always got good reports back – especially from men. Suddenly people appealed to me. They were all manifestations of the life I had been given a gift of by the vaccine, so how could I not love them?

Within a week or two I was running things so smoothly Nadine had little to do. She paid me $30 a week, and for that I organised the staff in the kitchen, and the gardens and the fields and sorted out the guests' problems. Basically, Caravanserai was more or less mine, and it felt great. I found myself thanking the poor dog for bringing me here.

To really fit in, I knew I would have to earn the trust of Nadine's husband, Demofilo, the scion of a political dynasty on the coast who I was told was now a pale imitation of the blustering Lothario he had once been, when he had arrived in the area twenty years before and swept Nadine, a wandering flower child, off her feet. His aristocratic poise was now tempered by a deep melancholy, and from time to time he would rub his eyes, letting out a weary, heart-wrenching sigh.

The only way of getting close to him was through colonic irrigation. He was an absolute devotee and could actually smell the intestines of people who didn't wash inside. He found it hard to be near them for long. "Would you allow a mangy dog lick your face?" he used to say. His family underwent weekly clean-outs, and it was Nadine who hinted that I should consider it, too. When I finally relented, Demofilo gave me a great hug and yanked out reproductions of Hieronymus Bosch paintings of people defecating gold to show me the rewards that lay ahead. From that day on, Fridays were wash-out day: one of the staff would come to my room with a hosepipe, a funnel, a tube of KY jelly and a plastic bucket. Demofilo only stood watch the first time, and, I suppose, I could have just pretended after that, but somehow I felt honour bound, particularly as the maids had prepared the five litres of cold coffee and I didn't want to see it go to waste. The worst thing was that I actually grew to like the blissed-out, fleecy feeling it gave. It felt like how I imagined the womb must be. But I drew the line when Demofilo said he would teach me how to push my lower intestine out my anus, insisting that it was the only way I could be sure it was fully clean. That was a step too far, and I didn't weaken even when he explained the incredible feeling it gave as it rubbed up against the perineum on its way back in again.

Of course, over time, the novelty of the job wore off. Telling people where the best milkshakes were for the hundredth time loses its magic, and you begin to see the idiot *gringos* for the knowledge-sucking parasites they are. I remembered why I preferred my own company and decided that once I'd taken the next four injections I'd head off again; in the meantime, I became more discerning and only helped the guests that I thought were interesting.

We were all sitting around on the verandah having dinner one evening when a girl sitting a few seats down from me said, "Wow, what's up with the horses!"

I ignored her. We had no horses. There was always some fool jabbering on about something; if I wasn't in the mood I could just tune out. This girl went on, however, "Hey . . . Moo-khaa – isn't it?" she asked.

"Yeah," I said.

"Wow, what's up with that?"

"With what?" I asked.

"You rose up like a team of horses there," she said.

"I did what?"

"Woo! Giddee up, boy! You reared up on those hind legs something awesome. What's up with the donkey? You and Wendy, yeah? You wanna get it *on*!"

"I have no idea what you are on about," I replied and went back to my dinner.

I had just overheard someone say moments before that Wendy, a Singaporean guest, was planning to spend New Year's Eve up in the cloud forest with Rory and Luna. It had bothered me because I liked Wendy and didn't want to be left alone with the rest of the guests for New Year's. But I hadn't said anything about it. Now somehow this girl was suggesting I had reared up like some charioteer. I tried to forget about it and enjoy my dinner, but it rattled me. How could she have known? I never even opened my mouth. Yet her horse metaphor was so apt, it was exactly what I had done. I had reared up inside, but then reined in my feelings almost immediately. How could she have known? And who was she anyhow? I made my excuses and went to the kitchen to eat with the staff.

So many guests passed through the hostel that they became a blur. I racked my brain to remember who this girl was. After checking the ledger, I found out that she had arrived the previous day with an Ecuadorian boy. I remember casting a quick glance at her, but lost all interest when I saw him: a typical Latino stud, the coke-smuggler type from Guayaquil. They regularly brought their *gringa* conquests here because their families frowned on foreign girls. At Caravanserai the only Ecuadorians were the staff. It was a *gringo* republic, and the locals disliked it for this. The idea of dorms and shared showers didn't appeal to them, and the food was too Anglo, with granola for breakfast instead of *huevos rancheros*.

The Ecuadorian boy who had come with this mind-reading girl hadn't said a word at check-in. She had done all the talking, asking me where to rent horses and then later in the day where to get lanolin as her "ass was saddle sore". I had been curt on both occasions, particularily the second – it had definitely been more information than I needed. Looking around now, I noticed the boyfriend wasn't at dinner, and after checking the guest book, I found he had checked out that morning. I noticed, too, that she would be paying by credit card, which was rare among backpackers at the time. She was obviously a *real* tourist or possibly a Peace Corp volunteer. I was intrigued.

I went back to the table, shooting secret glances at her while pretending to listen to whoever else was talking. Let's say her name was Eve. Backpacking girls from America and the Mediterranean are often beautiful, but there was something else about her. She simmered with doubts – not in any morose way, but like an anxious cat. She was raucous and just seemed so alive. I was drinking her in. Her skin was dusky and sallow, her hair *campesino* dark. She was in a league of her own, about as far from all the rest as the Andromeda galaxy – a whole different species; in fact, she was like a tennis ace, like a burnished, Californian tennis ace, except that you could never imagine a tennis ace backpacking.

Wendy had said she was having a party, and I thought I'd ask this girl to come along.

"Sure," she said, in that non-committal, self-assured way Americans have. "Sure, I'll stop by."

The party was in Wendy's room. She had baked hash brownies, and everyone was sitting around on her bed talking rubbish. An Israeli boy in dungarees was murdering the usual mawkish anthems on a guitar.

Soooooo.
So, you think you can te-eeh-ell ,
Heaven from Heee-ell.

He was one of those classic Zionist poster boys, sculpted in kibbutz fields and tanned on Tel Aviv beaches. All the girls were enchanted, mesmerised by his henna locks that swung gently as he sang. That was the problem with backpackers: too many of them were perfect specimens that made you feel even more inadequate. I noticed that the patchwork quilt on Wendy's bed was identical to Fiona's, and it set me thinking back to Gina. Was I really prepared to let that baby die? It still made me shudder. Maybe I hadn't fully understood the situation at the time. I was half asleep after all, and anyway, what could I have done? They had set themselves beyond the law – that was one of the reasons they had moved to Colombia. They were reverting gradually to a form of tribalism, and some tribes discard unwanted babies as a matter of course. But that was no consolation – I had known that her parents were sending help; all I had to do was keep him safe until then.

Eve suddenly arrived at the door, and we all shoved up on the bed to make room for her. God, she was beautiful. Her eyes burned with a glint like they were under photographic lights. I've since seen the same characteristics in women in Lebanon, and in some parts of Mexico too, but nothing quite like her. The sort of person you imagine pounding adobe floors in art movies filmed in Arizona or New Mexico.

When the Israeli finally shut up, a Scottish girl working with street children in Quito started telling dull jokes, and I tuned out until I heard Eve speaking.

"I used to think dancing was just organised wobbling," she said. "I always felt self-conscious, but that all changed with the Doors. Suddenly I realised it's everything. It's the basis for life, you know? That's what Jim Morrison was on about, setting free the demons, opening up. It's shamanic."

An accountant from Düsseldorf, who had spotted the hash brownies in the kitchen and eaten one without knowing what they were, interrupted her with a loud rat-tat-tat. His arms were locked into machine-gun barrels in front of him, and he was firing at a moth fluttering about the room. It was the first thing he had said all evening. Wendy had invited him along only because she felt she ought to keep an eye on him. He rat-tat-tatted a whole minute before falling quiet again and never said another word all night.

Eve just nodded her head and said, "Yeeaah."

Her voice was deep and peaty, with the sound of a long Camel habit she had just kicked. She oozed an aura of wonder, of expanse.

The following day I woke up late, my mind in tatters. All I could think of was her. Nothing else mattered. Something inside my head had tweaked in the night, and I couldn't explain it, except that she now filled my entire brain. I had been dreaming about her. All I knew for sure was that she and I were separate links on a chain that had somehow fused, and I was now being pulled uncontrollably towards her.

Deciding that the hotel could run itself for a while, I went straight to her room, but she wasn't there. The kitchen staff told me she hadn't appeared for breakfast, and no one else had seen her around. I searched the farm, panicking that perhaps she had been an apparition, a final fantasy from the cactus sparked off by the brownies. The very idea that it might have all been in my mind frightened me to the core. You can't just meet someone like that and then have them vanish, can you? Of course you can. How often in my dreams had I met the perfect partner, a soul mate, only to wake in the morning alone? Yesterday could have been just a hyper-realistic dream. The thought pushed me towards despair; and yet the alternative, that she had actually been here and was now gone, was even worse. I checked the register and found her name still on it. She hadn't yet settled her bill. Circling out from the hostel, I searched the surrounding farms and sugarcane fields and kept on going through the higher up cocoa-bean fields and papaya groves until eventually, around noon, I spotted her lying beneath a banana tree in the coffee plantation above the hostel.

She didn't see me coming, and instead of approaching her directly, I crouched down in the grass and watched. I was in awe, so in awe I couldn't bring myself any closer. She was glorious, everything about her, even just the way her fringe fell, the way the strands of hair danced. The way her collarbone rose when she breathed made me . . . I dunno

. . . melt, I suppose. I had never seen anyone in this way before. It was like my eyes had new filters attached, or more likely, old filters removed. Like my heart had been recalibrated.

I stared greedily on, watching, imagining, until Rabbit appeared and called me a creep. He said I was a coward, a spineless voyeur, and that if I was any sort of man I would at least approach her. But I had no idea what to say. How could I tell her that something inside me told me I had known her for ever, and that even if we never met again, I still would. We were one. How do you explain that?

Coward! Rabbit jeered. *After all our talk, and you can't even say hello to a girl. It's a GAME for God's sake!*

It was only when Eve pulled down her jeans a bit to put more lanolin on her bum that I felt so sneaky I had to reveal myself.

I stood up and walked forward.

The day was magnificent with a bright blue sky and a high hot wind that sent the clouds racing across the sky.

"Hey, tiger," she said. She wasn't at all ruffled. "How's the head?"

It's my nerves, my breathing, my heart that's at me, I thought.

"Okay, it's okay. How about you?" I said. That's when I spotted it: the scuffed black Kodak canister.

"What's in there?"

But I already knew. I had seen them too often before. It was a dose of Don Miguel's watered-down, homebrew San Pedro. You could buy it in town for a few *pesos* if you knew whom to ask.

"It's quite a ride," I warned as she opened it. "It might be particularly bumpy after the brownies yesterday. You think you're up to it?"

"We'll soon see," she said, bringing the canister to her lips and swallowing a mouthful. "Are you coming?"

Oh, Christ! I thought. She had just checked out, and I knew that there was only one way I could follow her. If I didn't I might never see her again. Who knows how long she was staying in Caravanserai for. My mind and stomach were shouting, *Don't*. Once was enough. It is ridiculously intense and exhausting, not something you go through twice. I fought with myself back and forth, trying to find out what Rabbit thought, but he was nowhere to be found.

She handed me the canister, "Here."

I had no choice. I had no time. I had to.

I took as small a sip as I could, only a fraction of what I had taken before, and set off back down the same path. This time following someone else. It was lucky that I forgot to warn her not to vomit and she coughed up most of it. It meant neither of us had taken all that much, and we soon found that Saint Peter wasn't going to steer us too far away – opening the gates just wide enough to peek into other worlds while staying safely in this one.

Eve lay back in the grass and I settled down beside her, saying nothing for what seemed like for ever. I reached up to brush a cricket off her shoulder and asked her what she did back home.

"Ha, ha," she said.

There was a convention among travellers not to talk too much about their lives. It restricted you. Travelling was about living in the *Now*.

"No, seriously," I said, "I'm interested."

There was a long pause, and she just smirked.

"Well?" I said.

"Oh! Right," she said jokingly, and with odd emphasis, as though she were speaking to a child, "I'm a butterfly collector."

"Butterflies," I said. "Wow, that's brilliant. Where? In Arizona?"

She paused a while looking at me, and then with an eerie grin, said, "Exactly. In the desert. All kinds of desert insects."

"That must be fascinating," I said, but her smile was so wide I added, "What?"

And she, trying to seem serious, said, "Oh you know, just the insects. They get you thinking. Like metaphors, you know?"

I didn't know.

"Is it for research you collect them?" I asked.

She looked at me with an expression that was both comic and

paranoiac. "No. No, actually, not for research. I put them together with other insects and sell them."

That idea seemed to please her, and she broke out in a loud, scornful laugh.

"But that's enough about me," she said archly. "What about you?"

"Me?" I said, stalling for time. I was actually a bit worried about her behaviour. She was being oddly self-conscious or affected. Everything was out of synch, like there was a time lag. We weren't connecting. There was something wrong.

I was caught up in these thoughts and didn't answer her question, and so she went on, "Do you collect butterflies too?"

"Oh . . . no, I don't," I said with increasing concern. What sort of question was that? "I work on a vegetable farm."

I told her a bit about myself, but it was all very stilted, like we were out of time, as though the drugs were playing tricks on us. But they couldn't have kicked in yet. She obviously wasn't who I thought she was.

We fell quiet for a long time, both of us worrying about the ride we had condemned ourselves to. I took a gulp from my water bottle and offered it to her.

She looked skew-ways at me with her face set and serious, and said, "You do know, don't you?"

What? I thought. I looked at her quizzically.

"Like really, you know?" she repeated.

Oh Christ, this was freaky. I was getting worried.

"What?" I managed to say. "I know what?"

"Who I am?" she said.

"What? What do you mean?" I asked.

She could see how worried I looked.

"You don't! Oh my God, I'm so sorry!" she cried. "I thought you knew. I thought you knew! I'm *so* sorry. I didn't mean to play games. I thought you were joking. I'm not a butterfly catcher."

"Oh," I said.

"I'm an actor."

"Oh," I said again. "Sorry, I didn't know. I wouldn't really – I've never been to America."

"No," she said, "in Hollywood."

And she named a few movies. I was mortified.

"Of course," I said. "Sorry, I should have known."

Actually I had never heard of her. She wasn't quite A-list, but still had a house in Beverly Hills and Johnny D and Keanu and Winona as friends. River had only died a little while before, and it had set tremors through them all. The dark reality of their lives had suddenly become clear, and they were all taking stock. The *National Enquirer* had been on their backs ever since, bringing to light the excesses that had come to define their lives. It was a bad time, and being forced to confront it in public wasn't easy. Eve had just wrapped on a big shoot in Vancouver and had fled here to recover. It was her first holiday in years, she said. She was hoping it would be a step in rebuilding her life.

Once I admitted I had only seen one of her movies and hadn't really noticed her, we put the whole career thing aside. Dublin is small and so littered with big names drinking in the same pubs and hanging out in the same places as everyone else that they appeared familiar. Everyone knew a cousin or a friend or an employee of one of them, and it would have been impossible to deify them. I think Eve was a bit suspicious at first, but after an hour or so of sitting together not saying very much, she seemed to accept that I really didn't care about that side of her life, and I could feel her letting go of the game of hide and seek she was used to playing around the parapets of her private life. She began to trust me, and over the course of the day, I sensed that the chain that had fused inside me might have found an anchor hold in her, too.

I don't know quite how it happened. There was no epiphanic moment, but somehow we just gelled, like it was meant to be. I asked her what she disliked most in the world, although I already knew she would say something about men, some type of men – priests, officials, bankers. I just knew.

"Men in dark polyester suits," she said, and I smiled. "Because they either want to trap you or sell you something or, worst of all, hug you. I hate perfume pollution, too."

I could have put money on it that she was going to say children when I asked what she liked most.

"And not because they are cute," she clarified, "but because they are free and can still piss on the carpet without having to say 'please' beforehand or 'sorry' after. They know who they are."

Later a wasp came dive-bombing at us – a huge Amazon wasp. I tried killing it, and she said, "Why? He has as much right to be here as us. Let him live out his annoying, buzzy little life."

And the wasp flew off straightaway. I could have married her right there and then.

I loved how when I asked her about growing up, she started telling me instead about her granny's recipe for a tonic of heather and herbs and honey and one other secret ingredient that made it magical, but which had been lost when Vikings came and killed nearly everyone in her village to get the secret ingredient. Eventually only Eve's great-great-grandfather and his son were left alive, and as they were being tortured, her great-great-grandfather cried out, "Kill my son and I'll give you the recipe," because he was afraid the son might talk if he was the only one left.

That was all she said about growing up, as if that explained everything. And when I told her the Vikings were a thousand years earlier, she just giggled. It didn't matter. And when I queried about how her family line could have continued if everyone in the village was wiped out, she just shrugged her shoulders and said, "In vitro?"

Why this would captivate me, I don't know. I'm just trying to explain what happened. Even looking at her, listening to her, sent a tune ringing through my mind. There was no moment of transcendence – nothing like that. Just being there was enough. Breathing.

I felt like a fish in a pond, conscious of a world beyond the plane of the surface, a magical world of warmth and humour and support, and all

I had to do was leap into it. I was intrigued by it, and petrified, too. But somewhere at the back of my mind was the awareness that not only was it possible to do it, but my entire species had done it before me. Made that leap out of the cold and into the light. All I had to do was trust.

Whatever the reason, by that evening, using some unfathomable channel I didn't even know existed, we were able to express ourselves in the barest of words. Intuitively. Using a language so eloquent that the words of a thousand alphabets couldn't translate it. Like how cells share information, like how an orchid knows it's time to bloom, or an apple knows it's time to fall.

"Take your name, for example," Eve said at one point. "There's no way it could ever get near to describing you – the expanding and contracting you, shimmering and shifting and swerving like a wave, a cloud, like turbulence.

"But even that rock," she said pointing at a pebble. "It's changing, too: as the sun and shadows play over it, it changes shape, heating up and cooling down; becoming one with that snail for a while and then falling back alone. The molecules in it are dancing, constantly dancing.

"Reach out and touch it," she said. "Go on!"

She took my fingers and stretched them towards the stone.

"What do you feel?"

"Stone," I said.

"Yea, but what?"

"Well, it's grainy and bumpy. And it's hot."

"Exactly!" she said delightedly. "Some of its heat comes to you, and it only really has texture when you feel it. How do you sum all that up in 'rock'?"

Although it's pointless to try and say what we talked about – all the silly details that were so fascinating to us and would bore anyone else stupid – she made my head spin. One of her grandfathers was half Choctaw and had encouraged her to follow her impulses.

"That's why I'm here," she said. "I had the impulse to do the movie in Vancouver and then afterwards another one to come here."

"Wanting to kill the wasp was an impulse for me," I said.

"No, it wasn't. That was fear," she said.

"What about River Phoenix," I said. "Look where his impulses led him."

She didn't agree.

"You trust the impulses of your cells, don't you?" she asked. "And of your body – it got you this far, didn't it? From foetus to toddler to today. It didn't try killing you or anything. It didn't try raping or pillaging, did it? If you don't trust yourself, you close all that down, all those urges and inclinations. You become unbalanced; that's what did for River.

"You can see why religions want to cut us off from them, to control us. That's why Freud was so big. He was saying more or less the same thing: impulses are bad; we all want to fuck or kill our parents. Freud was such a warped son of a bitch. Imagine if a dog or a bird distrusted itself, was constantly second-guessing itself. How messed up would that be?

"What's your greatest impulse every day?" she asked. "Do you have one thing you have to have each day? Like take a walk or phone a friend or whatever?"

"Coffee," I said.

"I've given up," she said.

"If I don't have a coffee every day, I fall apart," I said.

"Tell you what, you can have my machine. It's a Victoria Arduino, original vintage with the brass cylinder and pressure like a piston engine. It has one of those huge golden eagles on top."

"Sounds great," I said, "like those statues on car bonnets."

"Except it's far deadlier," she said. "If I don't clean the tappets regularly, it comes flying off the cylinder at me like Kato in *Pink Panther*. Someone told me it's the biggest killer in Italy – death by espresso machine – but at least the ambulance gets there quick, hoping for some of the coffee."

I had always thought human beings were separate, isolated entities;

now I found out that sometimes, only sometimes, two people can become one. I could almost have jumped into her skin and become her. Is that stupid? How else do you explain coalescence? Rabbit tried to muscle in, but I didn't need his mean, meagre mind now. Either he was going to claim credit, or advise caution. Either way, I didn't want to know. This eclipsed everything. So what if there was an element of the prima donna about her? I could easily overlook a few mood swings. At one point she yelled at Carla, the laundry woman, for daring to smoke too near her. And as she had recently quit, I understood her sensitivity, but still it was extreme – virtually a tantrum – and it went on far too long. It wasn't hard to imagine her in her Winnebago on set lashing out at some minion. But, ultimately, none of it was her fault. She had been commoditised for too long, and part of her had begun to believe the hype.

Over dinner on that first day, we played backgammon and rolled consecutive doubles twelve times in a row. Twelve times! We knew this was special. She wrote me a letter that night and left it outside my dormitory.

Hey there Tiger,

That was a good day. Actually, it was great. Every now and then it hits me and hits me so hard how alone I am. Maybe it's part of the job – everywhere in the galaxy stars are spread far apart with dark matter in between. For once I'd love to be a cluster or a nebulae, that would be great. Even an imploding universe, maybe – for the adrenalin rush!

Sometimes at night I get so scared. My manager showed me a death threat just before I left. What's up with that? I feel I have to tell someone before I crack. You're here now, but what about later? I want you on my phone – on speed-dial, okay?

River was so fuckin' beautiful, Mocha. I wish you'd known him. I do! The day before the ceremony a few of us headed down to the sea and took our clothes off and just danced – danced like no one else existed, danced like it was what we were born to do . . . releasing the despair and anger and back-stabbing necrophilia of the newspaper reports. An hour of pure

*brilliance in an evil week. I want more of that. Today was like that – a
day of love in a messed-up year.*

*I don't know what to do, Mocha, and it frightens me. I haven't done
drugs since the funeral, so it can't be that. Anyway, I had these feelings
long before. I need to know if I'm here to make crummy movies or what?
Is this what I was born to do? And if so why do I feel like I'm not doing it
right? And what about the donkey sanctuary, for real this time?! I wish I
knew so that I could at least know. You know what I mean?*

*It's what I came here for. To find a soul gas station. I knew it existed
somewhere and my impulse told me here. I didn't know you'd be the pump
attendant! I didn't know that . . .*

*Looking forward to granola and yoghurt in the morning, and being
with you,*

See ya on the flip side,

Eve

The next few days were a dream. We planned our future: I was
moving to LA or else she was coming to Ireland and setting up a
donkey sanctuary in County Kerry where I would grow vegetables and
paint. We promised we wouldn't make love for at least a month. The
currency of sex had been debased so low in her life that we were going
to start afresh. What we had was too precious. This would be different.
We agreed that all too often people used relationships to get someone
to love them so they wouldn't have to love themselves; or else, to prove
to themselves that despite how much they hated themselves, someone
else was capable of loving them. They ended up hiding so much that
things rarely lasted; the relationship would stagger on, but the love
wouldn't. We didn't want that. We wanted it to be a long-term
adventure exploring what made our eyes flicker, smile spread, voice
come alive, laughter ring out – a journey into the unseen essence.

It was on the third day the call from her attorney came. Nadine came
up from the ranch to tell us someone had been phoning all night,

insisting he speak to Eve. She had told him she'd pass on the message in the morning, and now here she was, the executioner delivering her sentence. Eve's face fell. If LA was stretching out its claw to her, it could only be bad news. I unfurled my arms from around her neck and we walked back to Nadine's place arm-in-arm to phone the attorney.

It was such a silly little thing. Such a stupid inconsequential thing to shipwreck us on. Eve had allowed some new friends housesit while she was away. They were actors she met on a New Age course, and she felt she should support them. It was a "no brainer", she said: her beautiful house with its pool and gardens would be lying idle for weeks. She might as well give someone else the pleasure of it, allow someone other than herself be pampered by Jorge, her macrobiotic chef. It was about being generous. Sharing. Living right. All those sweet ideas LA pretends to champion. Eve was suddenly being shown that they might in fact be just candy-cane decorations.

Her new friends couldn't believe their luck at first, and they behaved impeccably – watering the gardens, ensuring the gates were kept closed, keeping the pool clean – but after a few days, they began to get a taste for it and became greedy.

Now, here we were in Vilcabamba with Eve's attorney screaming down the phone at her about fraud and larceny. Her new friends had stolen her credit card details and were trying to access her bank account. When her agent had gone over to the house, he found the locks changed. Her PA caught them trying to pawn stuff.

Eve freaked. It was all too much – too dark a reminder of the shit she had fled from. It was as if someone was trying to send her a message, to let her know that it wouldn't be that simple. She had dared imagine a new beginning, and this was what she got. In the course of that phone call, she saw the stark truth: if you sell yourself to Hollywood, you don't get out that easily. Paranoia set in. As long as she had her looks, they'd never let her go. Hollywood would find some way of pulling her back. It was mostly the residue of the cactus stirring up trouble, and I tried explaining that to her, but she wouldn't listen. She believed she was a slave – in a less opaque way than in the old studio days, but still a slave. All the turmoil and tragedy since River's death had set a lot of her friends on the same track as hers – hoping to slip away and start again – but it wasn't going to be that easy. The industry was beginning to pull them in close again in any and every way it could. If not through drugs or money, it would be something else. The puppet strings were practically translucent, but Eve swore they were there. She was as much in control of her destiny as Pinocchio, or the love interest in a two–bit movie.

This was a lot to grasp in the space of an hour in Nadine's front hall. The whole conspiracy idea seemed far-fetched, but Eve believed it. It was as though one of the satellites hanging above earth had fallen from orbit and was coming careering towards her. Nothing I said could reassure her. It was too late for that. Her eyes had turned into glaciers. She didn't tell me to fuck off or anything but instead raised a shell around herself, an impregnable sarcophagus that more or less removed me from her reality. I didn't exist any more. She looked across to Nadine and took out a roll of dollars, handing them over to cover the costs of the calls she would be making, and then spent the rest of the day ringing her lackeys in LA, shouting and issuing commands. There was nothing I could do but back away, leave her alone and hope she came around.

When I did approach her again a few hours later, she was a fraction more affectionate, but every tendon in her body, every synapse in her mind was still stretched to breaking point. I couldn't possibly understand, she said. This was bigger, this was so much bigger than I could ever imagine. I was a potato farmer, she said. Nothing more. I was Forrest Gump. There was no point in even discussing it.

That night I went out walking, and suddenly the words of the tune that had been playing in the back of my mind ever since I had first met Eve came back to me. It was Bob Dylan, the soundtrack to my childhood:

Sweet Melinda
The peasants call her the goddess of gloom
She speaks good English
And she invites you up into her room

> *And you're so kind*
> *And careful not to go to her too soon*
> *And she takes your voice*
> *And leaves you howling at the moon*

It had been revolving around my mind since that first night at dinner, but the words hadn't come until right now. I never imagined it was a warning, that it might be Rabbit sending up flares, waving red flags. Now it was too late. I was howling at the moon.

Walking back towards Caravanserai, a farmer beckoned me over towards the flurry of moths dancing above his head. I sat down on his verandah, and he told me to pour us both a drink while he unscrewed his single light bulb and brought it to the socket outside. We sat in silence there, looking up at the sacred Mandango Mountain for maybe an hour before finally he stood up and said, "You know, sometimes at night when we are awake, we are actually dreaming. Other times we think we are living, but we are asleep."

He bade me goodnight, and I finished off the rum and headed home.

Eve was waiting in the dorm. She hugged me.

"Sorry, Tiger," she said. "It's not your fault. This – you and me – should never have been. You come from somewhere else, another world, you know?"

She dropped something into my hand. It was a pebble, a tiny sea-washed pebble with a turtle on it, made by some tribe on the coast in Canada, she said. It helped you find your way. Then, looking into my eyes, she urged me to smile, to make it all okay, and I tried. I really did.

"Will you do me a favour?" she said.

"Anything."

"Forget I ever was."

I reached out to touch her, but she said "Don't", in a voice so cold my hand dropped limp. I just stared at her numbly, like a patient, like a patient after electrocompulsive therapy. And when eventually I found some words, her eyes glazed over, and I could see I had lost her.

"You *are* . . ." that's all I wanted to say to her. "You *are*."

"Look, can you get me a taxi?" she said quietly, trying to infuse the words with warmth. "I need to be at the airport."

And that was it. A *collectivo* drove out from Loja and took her away from me.

Chapter 7

WHAT DO YOU do after that? Where do you go? You can't just forget. Even if you try your whole soul best to be positive, you realise it's futile. I was left with the carcass of my former life, and I could have tried to put a brave face on it, to pretend it was all okay, that I actually liked carcasses, but instead I fell apart. Love had burnt itself into my nerve endings, and they were numb to anything less.

I walked straight out of Caravanserai without even saying goodbye to Nadine and Demofilo, heading south into the desert of northern Peru. I needed to be alone. I spent a few days walking through the sands and on up into the mountains, realising I was too weak to end it all, but wanting to do nothing else. I just kept walking, fuelled by pity and self-indulgence. Of course, I tried ringing her in LA, but she just hung up. I had letters couriered to her at great expense, but they came back to the poste restante address I had printed on them in bold, black, super-clear marker. She had moved out of her place on Mulholland Drive and had told her agent and lawyer not to say where she was. I was just another stalker now. Added to the list.

I wandered aimlessly, walking until I was exhausted, then hopping on a bus, not caring where it brought me. From one town to another, one bronze general on his horse to another. I avoided the backpacker hangouts: my story was beginning to spread through that claustrophobic, gossip-mongering subculture like a virus. It seemed everyone on the Pan-America highway knew about me. They all wanted to tell me their favourite movie she was in, or some gossip they knew. And even if they hadn't heard, I found myself telling them. I couldn't help it: what else was there to talk about? I learnt a lot that I hadn't known. The dodgy B-movies. The *Playboy* shoot she did early on. The alleged affairs with one of the *Breakfast Club* crew and a Baldwin. The rumoured extent of her wealth.

After a week, the bus I was on broke its axle in the mountains and nearly careered off a cliff. I was stranded in a town called Huaraz, which was plagued by locusts that kept smashing into me, driving me nearly demented. Eventually they moved on and torrential rains came, washing out the road, and I was stranded there for a week. All day long sheets of horizontal water lashed down from heaven, turning the town to muck and its inhabitants to shivering, freezing wrecks.

I hated myself. I was damaged goods, and there was no way of forgetting. From now on life was downhill. A long-drawn-out disappointment. I really dived, and I suppose the vestiges of San Pedro in my system didn't help. It may have been why she reacted so badly to the news also; but if that was the case, did it also explain why she had been so warm to me up until then? She only liked me because she was stoned. How had I not seen it? For her, it was just another binge. I really *was* Forrest Gump.

Rabbit tried to butt in in my defence – to reassure me – but I told him where to go, that sick, sycophantic do-gooder. I realised now that he had never been on my side; his whole plan had been to try and get me committed for hearing voices. It was all a game to him. I was just a player. He spouted on about it being appropriate in the grander scheme and how I had learned valuable lessons and not to see myself as a victim, but I told him, that smug, pontificating fool, that until he had lived an actual human life to keep his mouth shut and, in fairness, he did leave me alone after that.

Just when the rains were dying down and there was a chance of getting out of Huaraz again, I did what I had most feared I would do ever since

I arrived in Peru. The country has a lunatic shower system in which the water is heated through a bare 120v coil bolted to the showerhead and attached to cables that spark and fizz when water hits them. As a safety precaution, there is a large metal crank beside the shower which must be pulled to turn the current on, so that the place is only live when you are in the water: completely counterintuitive, but anyway. To put it simply: if by mistake you make contact with anything metal while you are showering, you fry. All I did was pick up the soap which was balanced on the water pipe, and I ended up flipping around in the shower tray like a fish out of water.

I was found eventually by the owner and had to be carried out under a blanket and brought to the clinic where they dried me off, put me in a bed and kept an eye on me for a few hours. It was at the clinic I met Renaldo. He was a nurse with great English and a pudding bowl haircut in the style of the Amazon Indians. That evening when I was let out of the hospital, he lent me some clothes and brought me for a drink with his friends, most of whom were environmentalists and wannabe witchdoctors. They smoked a huge amount of grass, which I resolutely refused: drugs had tricked me once into a false, empty world, I wasn't going to let it happen again.

Over the course of a night's drinking, they told me about a job they had been given by an English environmental agency to help write up an impact assessment report on the Amazon. Renaldo said they had been appointed as Sting's local representatives, but I think they were more like volunteers who had been asked to keep an eye on things in the rainforest and to report back on any meetings they had with native Indians or oil workers. I doubt Sting had anything to do with it. The agency had sent them out a computer and some money for stationery to help set things up, but they were finding the work more difficult than they had imagined. While being well-intentioned and passionate about the environment, they were basically dropout students and dopers. Renaldo was the only one with a regular job, and with the amount he smoked and drank, I was amazed he managed to keep it. I suppose a little town like Huaraz was grateful to get anyone. So although they had big plans to stir things up and talked a lot about organising investigative trips into the forest, none of it ever came to anything, and as far as I could tell, most of their time was spent arguing over what should be done and who should do it.

When they heard I could type, they latched on to me immediately. The agency back in London had been demanding a preliminary report for months, but nothing had yet been written, and most of them hardly knew how to turn on the computer, let alone type. They promised that if I hung around a while and helped write it up, they'd bring me into the forest with them. I said I'd think about it; anything to get my mind off Eve, and anyway I was still keen to explore the forest. I felt cheated that the dog had stopped me last time.

When I got back to my hotel that night, the owner was still up and was delighted to see me alive. He had been worried about me. He, too, thought he had another dead *gringo* on his hands. I was making a habit of this. He felt so guilty about the shower that when I asked him for a discount if I stayed on for a few weeks, he gladly gave it. And so, I thought, *Why not?* Huaraz was as good a place as any to hide out, and if I could help Renaldo and his friends, so much the better. If I wasn't going to be running a bloody donkey sanctuary, I might as well be here, and anyway, the rainforest was a pet concern of Eve's. If she ever heard about this, she'd be impressed. Also the name of the town, Huaraz, reminded me of another line from that same Dylan song,

> *When you're lost in the rain in Juarez*
> *And it's Easter time too*
> *And your gravity fails*
> *And negativity don't pull you through . . .*

And that reminded me of the fact that Eve had met Dylan in Harvey Keitel's kitchen at a party and had asked his advice about a movie she was doing and I liked the synchronicity of that bitter-sweet reminder – as if I could ever forget.

Before I could give the guys any help with the report, they had to decide what to put in it, and that was almost impossible. Over the course of a few days, we went to a local bar each evening where they batted ideas back and forth. I had rarely come across such divergent views among any supposedly like-minded group before. They disagreed on everything except their love of the forest. Everything came back to that. No matter where we began – people, literature, water, commerce, culture – it was always somehow connected. Someone would mention McDonald's or oil or cars or paper or Brazil, and we'd be back.

Renaldo would say, "We must write about the diseases the oil workers bring – how they are killing our people. How the oil bosses hate us. All they want us for is as prostitutes to fuck their dirty, fat workers."

Although both Renaldo's parents were *mestizo*, he claimed his grandmother was pure indigenous, and he identified heavily with the tribal people. His haircut was just the most apparent manifestation of this. He used to tell patients in the hospital, "*Mi corazón es pura indígena*" (My heart is pure indigenous).

This never went down well. The idea that their nurse saw himself as part-savage didn't reassure anyone.

I suggested to Renaldo and his friends that maybe they should offer solutions in their report as well as listing the problems. Should the Indians be taught Spanish, for example? Should they be taught to read and write? But this just caused more arguments.

"It's a Trojan horse," Renaldo said. "When the loggers and oil men hear they're educated, they offer money to come work for them and defend the company against other Indians and attack groups like ours. And who can blame them for taking the money? When they learn our language, they find out how we live and they want the same."

"We shouldn't teach them anything," Gabriel, a quiet-spoken black man from the coast, said. "They are perfect. We should write that it's up to us to learn *their* language. As long as we can't speak it, they won't respect us. They'll regard us as idiots."

"It's too late for that," someone else countered. "They must learn to cope, but language isn't enough. They need to know how to compete in our vicious world."

It was around about this point that Esteban would always pitch in. He was the most pragmatic of the lot. Sharp-minded and ruthless, he was the sort of person the CIA would have profiled as a candidate for cult leader. He was only twenty and had already been kicked out of the Shining Path, a formidable Maoist organisation responsible for the deaths of tens of thousands of Peruvians. Esteban's arguments always revolved around the same ruthless Darwinian precepts: he believed that the forest should be protected, but couldn't see any reason to protect the Indians. It wasn't up to us to play god, he said. We were the winners in a competition against hundreds of thousands of other species of humanoid: it would be against nature for us to reach down now and help one of them. "Does an oak bend to allow light get to the nettles?" was a favourite aphorism of his.

With regard to saving the forest itself, he saw no use in half-hearted campaigns.

"It's too late for that," he said. "Tell London we need guns. We need to do what the big boys do back to them, only harder. Poison them; frighten them; make their lives a misery. Helping a genetic dead-end tribe won't make a blind bit of difference. Most of them are either backward or scum."

Esteban knew all about the Huaorani, the tribe Guinevere – the missionary who saved me in Baños – worked with, the ones that had killed her father's friend.

"Murdering bastards," he called them. "That's what they are – they admit it themselves. More than half of them were killed by their own family or neighbours. Instead of crying over her father's friend, your missionary pal should spare a thought for the thousands of their own people the Huaorani killed before we came and saved what was left of them. Most of the children ended up as orphans when their parents were murdered. Only a tiny fraction of the tribe ever died of natural causes.

"*National Geographic* can get all gooey about their simple life roaming naked, hunting pigs with spears," he went on, "but they never show how the same spears are used on old people when they become a burden, or how unwanted babies are strangled with vines or burnt or even buried alive."

I liked Esteban. I liked his mind. He was the most original thinker of the group, and I loved how he had built himself a thriving little business in such a far-flung place selling forest recordings on CD. Five years earlier, he had got his hands on some recording equipment and started taping natural sounds of the jungle for New Age CDs. Right from the beginning, his recordings had attracted good reviews in magazines and some laudatory feature articles, although cynics sniped that his Shining Path friends had exerted undue influence to get these. The meditation CD business is a competitive one, Esteban told me. There is always someone somewhere getting a purer, more authentic sound – ramming the microphone further up the mosquito's ass, as he called it. But, having used his innovative mind to keep ahead of the rest, he was now a respected "aural anthropologist", and his work on rain patter, in particular, had got him attention in the United States. His sonic signature, the turtle cough, had been nominated for a Silver Lion.

He showed me letters from devoted fans who claimed to have been changed for ever – cured of depression, of insomnia, even of childhood epilepsy – by his sounds.

"A sonic alchemist who captures the very pulse of the earth and amplifies it," one of his *Acoustemology* magazines gushed. "A pioneer of ethnomusicology."

But there were also critics of his "more-real-than-real sound". His seminal frog spawn popping was compared to a squadron of revving bulldozers; if nature was a building site, it said, it would sound like this.

Esteban picked out one of his favourite CDs for me, and I tried listening to it a few times, but I didn't get it. It sounded like a casserole of owls, whales and marmosets being simmered to death. I was struck by one particular aural motif right at the beginning which made the hairs stand on end. I asked Esteban about it.

"It's the air reverberating to the thunder that hasn't yet appeared," he said.

I was impressed – it was so evocative, so pregnant with anticipation – and when I asked how he recorded it, he said I'd rather not know. It was all part of his technique of using unorthodox and frankly dubious methods to trap the sound. He told me that he was the only man to have got the mating gurgle of the pink river dolphin, and that was through even more questionable means.

His interests extended into the world of ambient music, and in particular techno-shamanism, which he said involved creating new tonal vibrations and percussive wavebands through electronics and trying to replicate the harmonic toning of Siberian shamans. He was considering using this as a weapon against the loggers and oil men. He believed it had the power to induce alternative states of consciousness in the minds of rave dancers around the world and influence them to come out and defend the forest. His great hope was to hypnotise them into attacking the multinationals and in this way defeat the oil men.

Of course, Esteban was a computer whiz kid and could easily have typed up the report if the others had allowed him, but they didn't trust him not to go off on a rant about his personal theories, which would get them all fired. The project was too important for that: they were hoping it would be their ticket to work visas in Britain. That's why it was so important to get the report written and make sure it was compelling. But after listening to them debating the situation night after night, I realised they were never going to agree. I started reading through the literature myself – the over-worthy environmental accusations and oleaginous oil company denials – trying to mash it into some kind of digestible matter that the organisation in London could feed to its donors. It had to prick their consciences without being sensational; to provoke them, but also provide a salve that their contributions were making a difference. I spent a week cutting and pasting, but no matter what I wrote, one of the others would disagree and refuse to sign off. We were getting nowhere, and Renaldo finally suggested that we make a trip into the forest together and base our report on what we found. I jumped at the idea. It made a lot more sense to go now, before we wrote the report, rather than after. That way we'd actually know what we were writing about. A jungle adventure would also take my mind off things, and getting out of Huaraz for a while would be a relief. It was a fine town, but the unremitting rain grew wearisome.

The choice was either to fly to the jungle city of Iquitos in Peru or drive back to Puyo in Ecuador, where the dog had bitten me. Iquitos was much closer, but the big rubber boom in the nineteenth century had wiped out much of its virgin forest. Renaldo insisted that to find real old growth and untamed tribes we needed to be in Ecuador. So, over the course of a few days, arrangements were made for the trip. We stripped down and serviced Esteban's old GM van, packed up whatever was needed and invented a story for the clinic about Renaldo having to attend a surveillance operation for the Peace Corp, which got him a week's leave and enough money to pay for diesel for the trip.

It was a month to the day since I had arrived in Peru when we all piled into Esteban's van for the long drive back up to Ecuador. It took almost sixteen hours to get to the Peruvian border, and we camped there for the night before continuing on north through Ecuador at daybreak. During the journey, Esteban took the opportunity to tell me what he knew about the Huaorani and the killing of Guinevere's father's friend.

He said that at the time of the killing, fifty years ago, the Huaorani were living in terror of each other. There were so many feuds and vendettas between them that they were gradually killing each other off. At any moment, they risked being speared by someone close to them – a cousin, a brother, a neighbour, a friend – but they never knew who. It was basically all the shamans' fault. Vendettas and reprisals that went back and forth for years almost always stemmed from misdeeds a shaman claimed to have seen in the spirit world which he would tell only one side about. He would reveal a crime he had witnessed a friend or neighbour commit, not on earth but in the spirit world, which the person then felt duty-bound to avenge. The sense of paranoia and terror running through the community was so strong that some of the Huaorani wanted to flee to save their lives, but there was nowhere to go. Outside of their tribe, they wouldn't have survived long on their own.

Guinevere's father's friend and the other missionaries had heard about the Huaorani's situation. They reckoned that in their desperation they might be easier to convert than other tribes, but the problem was how to get to them. Twelve Shell workers had already been killed after stumbling upon them accidentally. Over a matter of years, the missionaries gave the problem a lot of thought and finally came up with what they hoped was a foolproof trap. They learnt how to fly aeroplanes and then spent months mastering the art of flying in tight circles over a fixed location so that if a cord and bucket were lowered from the plane, centripetal forces would keep it straight. Their plan was to send presents down to the Huaorani in a bucket, at various intervals spread out over a period of months. In this way, they wouldn't have to risk an actual landing until they were sure they had tamed them, luring them in slowly like animals.

By October 1955, their plan was in place, and the first thing they sent down in the bucket was a cooking pot decorated with bright ribbons. The Huaorani took it suspiciously. Week after week when the missionaries returned with more gifts, the Huaorani took them, until eventually the tribe sent a present of their own back up to this big generous bird in the sky. The trap was set.

A month later, the missionaries landed on a sandbank about four miles from the camp and waited until some Huaorani had the courage to approach. It took a few days, but eventually three Huaorani came along and, by making drawings in the sand, one of them asked if he could go up in the plane. As soon as he had risen above the canopy, he burst into tears at the sheer beauty of the carpet of trees flowing beneath him. It was a successful first contact, and the missionaries were delighted. They pitched their tents and began to build a simple chapel. But when the Indians went back to their camp the following day, some undisclosed intrigue led them to tell their tribe that the people of the bird had threatened them and killed a cousin of theirs. It was at that point Chenwie (the man who had prayed for Guinevere's safe journey back from the camp) and a few others went back and speared the missionaries to death. I asked Esteban if he knew whether the missionaries had been singing as they were being speared, but he didn't.

The trip north to Puyo took two days, and other than talking to Esteban, I spent most of my time reading his old Spiderman comics. He had a rare collection of seventies *Marvel* comics, most in their original wrappers, and for some reason he thought I would appreciate them. He was right; the ideas they contained were so powerful that I read until my eyes veined and spun like webs.

From the moment I read about the weak and bespectacled loner Peter Parker, who discovers within himself a divine essence which he chooses to use for the good of humanity, I was hooked. I loved the fact that he wasn't in any way Christ-like, like Superman – the last son of a distant, dying world – nor a super-rich but super-powerless S&M freak like Batman. Peter Parker was a mutant, who chose to use his weakness to fulfil a mission. That thrilled me. It was so redemptive. The fact that his blessing was also his curse moved me. I understood. He was not the saviour of the world, rather *a* saviour *in* the world who at times felt insecure and awkward, but in spite of everything achieved great things. None of us are gods, but we all have god inside us: that's what I took from it. It was a revelation. It was stuff I always felt but never understood before, and why it took Spiderman to make it clear, I don't know.

What touched me most was his isolation, his sadness in knowing that he could never fully identify with anyone. He had convinced himself that he shouldn't reveal his true self, and yet keeping it hidden was choking him up. I loved the moments he was forced to reveal himself, and having overcome his fear and reluctance, found he was treated with compassion by the citizens of New York. What a metaphor! And although my own miserable experience of love prevented me from rooting for him to have the courage to seek out Mary Jane's love or believing that she would accept him for all he was, I did in spite of myself feel the few remaining remnants of romance stir in me. The fact that, at least, Peter would no longer be alone was some sort of consolation.

I learnt from Spiderman that life was not about reaching a goal, but about taking each day as it came. It had that element Rabbit talked about of just *being*, not looking back or forward but enjoying the path. I wished I had explained that to Eve, that she didn't need to look back, she could start again any time. Life was a process of just being, of gradual evolution. It was ironic that she had told me to forget she ever was, when in fact that was precisely what I wanted *her* to do. I wanted her to forget who she had been. It obviously wasn't making her happy. I wanted her to choose again, but I had never actually said as much. Maybe if I had listened to Rabbit, he would have given me the words, given her the strength. It was too late now. Eve was gone, and I had turned my back on Rabbit. Reading the comics made me feel guilty about this: Rabbit was not so dissimilar to the gift or mentor that the superheroes had to help them through their dark times, and Spiderman had never banished his gift.

When we finally got to Puyo, I tracked down Franco, the taxi man who had helped me look for the dog a few months earlier. He told me he had been asking around about Orlando, and sure enough we were right: he did at one time have a large black dog, and as far as people knew, it had gone missing roughly around the time I was bitten. Franco said that although he couldn't prove it, he was certain Orlando's dog had given me rabies. He said that if I reported it to the police, they could arrest him for not having a vaccination, at least.

"It would serve him right," Franco said.

"Maybe he wasn't able to afford it," I suggested, but Franco pointed out it was free.

"Orlando was lazy, and his laziness almost killed you," Franco said. "Now he must suffer."

But I didn't do anything about it. I wanted to forget the whole thing, to move on. In truth I could never know whether the dog had been Orlando's or even if it had had rabies at all. And I won't be sure whether the bite was ultimately a good or a bad thing until my last day on earth.

I told Franco that we were hoping to make a trip into the forest to meet some Indians, and he said he could arrange it all for us. While the boys went off to wash away their road thirst in a bar, I set out to see if I could track Guinevere down.

"Baby, you're alive and you've come back to me. Praise the Lord!" she exclaimed when I pulled open her screen door and stuck my head in. I was afraid she was going to get down on her knees again there and then.

"I've been thinking and praying about you day in day out, my pet," she said. "He has spared your sacred soul. Praise be! Praise be on high! Just the sight of you standing there, tall and proud, has made my old heart soar."

I choked back the urge to Halleluiah again. I had left a message for her at the mission to say that I was okay, but it obviously never got to her. She sat me down and wanted to find out all about my life since. She felt she had a stake in me now, I suppose. I didn't imagine she'd want to hear about the San Pedro, and I certainly didn't want to talk about Eve, so I made up some generic adventures and switched the subject. Esteban's take on the Huaorani had set me thinking, and I was keen to find out what she thought of the missionaries and what they had done to the Huaorani. I felt bad that I hadn't had the courage to confront her last time. It had certainly been on my mind, and particularly over the last few weeks as Renaldo and Esteban filled me in on all the church had been doing to the Huaorani and the Shuar and the other tribes over the last forty years. Although Guinevere had been an angel to me back at the mission hospital and I loved her for it, I was still uneasy with everything she stood for. Notwithstanding the fact that tribal culture was latently dysfunctional long before the missionaries arrived, the damage that they had done since, like teaching them about sin and that their bodies were shameful, was still difficult to come to terms with. Now when I finally challenged her, she was adamant that it wasn't they who had destroyed the Indians; it was the oil miners, and the gold miners before them, who had done the real damage. Her dad's friend had only arrived after the Huaorani were being invaded by Shell and Texaco, she said.

"It wasn't the oil companies who took them out of the jungle and got them to settle near the church and the hospital in Puyo," I pointed out.

She told me how the miners would have committed genocide if they hadn't moved them.

"Anyway," she admitted, "that mission isn't really working for us any more. Medically it's a great success, but to be honest we have had few long-term conversions. The first generation of Huaorani took to *His Word* zealously to escape the cycle of violence, but the younger ones no longer care. It breaks my heart.

"Believe me, my pet," she said later, "it was the randy Spanish colonialists who are to blame. They're the ones who defiled the place, and although they gave it its independence a century and a half ago, they are still sucking the marrow out of her – riding the old strumpet until every ounce of life is beaten out. 'Scuse my French.

"We only came along to mop up the mess, to bandage their shattered souls. After the colonists had polluted the Indians' minds with fear, infected their lungs with viruses and broken their backs in the rubber plantations, they lost faith in their culture: their weapons, their medicine, their shamans had all been powerless, impotent against us. But, it was the loss of faith in their shamans that devastated them most. Their whole lives were based around them – but what good were they now with their silly potions and rattle sticks? Most of them were hoodlums anyway, addicted to power and status. They led lonely, outsider, celibate lives, and many of them were insane from too much *Iyuasca*. We've seen it in our own church too, I'm afraid."

Although Guinevere didn't say it, the collapse in belief in the shamans had left the tribes vulnerable to the missionaries who arrived in the fifties and sixties to scoop up their souls. They were a queenless hive, desperate for guidance. Esteban told me there had been one group of Huaorani who hadn't converted when the others did. They had fled deeper into the jungle, and over time had managed to end the violence within their group, but they had had no contact with the outside world ever since, and so still believed that the rest of us were as violent as they had been. Still today they live in terror of outsiders, killing anybody who comes near, even family and friends they knew in the old days. Every few years a logger or a miner stumbles upon them and dies. There are only about forty of them left, and the gene pool is degrading rapidly.

I didn't know what to think any more. I believed Guinevere when she told me the oil and gold miners would have wiped out the Indians if the missionaries hadn't come. They had done the same elsewhere, and I felt she wouldn't lie to me. There was no simple answer. I hoped meeting some Indians would clarify things.

Franco had all the arrangements made for us that evening, and early the next day we set off, passing first through the outer scrub forest where the spiky up-tempo syncopations of roadside salsa bars and the gnashing and grating of chainsaws drowned out any real jungle sounds, and only very gradually finding silence as we advanced deeper into the darkness of virgin trees. The signs of civilisation followed us for a worryingly long distance: big-wheeled oil and logging trucks hurtling along mud tracks littered with discarded oil canisters in the undergrowth. I thought of what Guinevere had said about sucking the marrow out.

Entering this massive incubator of life, I was struck again by how the grandeur of tropical forest lies in its subtlety. There were few cascades of bright flowers, just infinite shades of green in every form and texture, and a constant hum of biology, almost as if evolution were working in overdrive. It was a clammy, sweating fractal of which I was just a constituent element. I could almost smell the randy colonialists defiling its purity.

I had hoped that the tribe we would be meeting were the Huaorani, but Renaldo couldn't get the funds together for the flight in to them, and instead Franco had found us some Shuar near by who had agreed to see us.

Around noon, the road came to an abrupt end at a large, tannin-stained river. The land on the far side was owned by the Shuar. It was registered to them in the land commission in Quito, but as this had rarely protected them in the past, they had taken the precaution of chopping down the bridge built by Texaco. It now lay in pieces on the black sandy beach. A pair of egrets stood victoriously over it, keeping a dispassionate watch. Franco unwrapped some still warm *empanadas* and we ate them as we waited for his Shuar contact, Cristobal, to meet us. It was beautiful there with *chachalacas* bickering above us in a cloudless sky and a family of turtles mooching along the bank. After about an hour, two dugout canoes came paddling around the bend towards us.

"*Maravilloso!*" Franco called as he ran down to meet them.

Cristobal was tiny and as dark as chocolate. He had a flat Tibetan sort of face and a severe pudding-bowl haircut matted with dried red paste. There were two young men with him, one, I think, his son. Their arms were lined with zigzag tattoos, and the only clothing they wore was a string around their waist. All three of them had their foreskins tied to the string, for practicality I presumed. The boys had white plastic discs in their ears, but Cristobal's were removed, leaving his lobes dangling loose around his neck. Often in South America, I felt like an albino giant, but never more so than now.

We all climbed into the boats, and they brought us along a snaking, leaf-veiled tributary to a clearing which had palm leaf huts and a rusting crucifix. The place looked abandoned, but as we unpacked the canoe and laid out our gifts in the manner Cristobal advised, a number of dark brown bodies emerged silently from the undergrowth. They examined us and the penknives and salt pouches we had brought, and then invited us over to a log bench where we sat while Cristobal introduced us to the leaders. The rest melted back into the forest, and a young girl with only a tiny apron tied to her waist-string as clothing handed us cups of *chichi*, while the leader got Cristobal to translate a short welcoming speech.

The men were just about to go out hunting, and the place livened up as they got ready, checking their blowguns and spears and packing up little bundles of darts. Cristobal said there were too many of us to go with them, but he offered to bring us out separately with his two helpers later. It seemed that he had drawn the short straw to nanny us, and I wondered was this a punishment. I had a million questions to ask, and I wanted to get straight down to business, but Renaldo and the others were keen to try hunting first. It was a new experience for them, but for my part, having hunted with pygmies in Zaire, I was already all too familiar with it. Ripping your skin to shreds along trails designed for far smaller people is not something you do eagerly a second time, but at the same time it's not something to pass up.

While Cristobal and the boys gathered their spears and nets, I wrapped myself in my thickest jumper and jeans, and we set off in the opposite direction to the real hunters. Cristobal and the boys sped ahead into the undergrowth in an irregular hopping, trotting movement like pheasants through gorse, and we did our best to keep up. It was the same fast-slow run that the pygmies had, but since the Shuar weren't so small, their trails were fortunately wider.

I found the forest disorientating at first, an anarchy of green, neither dark nor light, like being at the bottom of a well. Hundreds of metres above me flashes of light shone through the dark canopy shooting random shafts downwards. Otherwise there was just a general sense of suffused light, with some places completely dark. Running over branches and vines was hard. It took concentration to see each new obstacle and to get a sense of the proportions of it. With no distance or even middle-distance to gauge against, everything was suddenly upon you, like in a dream, looming disconcertingly over you or spiralling around or tangling beneath. It was like walking through your mother's closet as a child, with smells, textures and shapes assaulting you.

The pace was relentless, and soon I was breathing hard. Esteban and Renaldo were panting like beasts. Now and again, Cristobal would stop long enough to show us something – the fruit of the *achiote* plant used for war paint, walking palms which sent roots out of their trunk, pulling the tree somewhere else – before he darted off again. As we weren't chasing anything, I couldn't see why we were going so fast, except maybe to test us, to hurt us just a bit. As a way of slowing Cristobal down, I asked him what we were hunting, but he just pointed at his nose and reached into a rotting tree to pull out some ants which he told us were delicious, and he was right. They were kind of lemon-flavoured.

He was explaining how to find grubs in old wood when suddenly his body tensed. I felt at first that we had done something to offend him, but then realised he had seen an animal move in the canopy. Glancing across at his two helpers, he gave them a signal. They took a few paces into the trees, then stopped stone-still, watching and listening. One of the boys moved on tiptoes around a fallen tree while pulling out a dart from his quiver and checking it for curare, a natural tranquilliser found in a local vine. He handed it to Cristobal who positioned it carefully at the tip of his blowgun. It was such a beautifully choreographed sequence, and seeing it in slow motion made it all the more graceful. The dart was the midrib of a palm-leaf shaved to a point.

We all stood in stasis for a time looking around as a trail of electric-blue butterflies floated past. Then at some imperceptible signal, Cristobal raised the heavy blowgun to his mouth and blew so hard his body contorted. The crashing sound from above revealed that a monkey had been hit and was dashing through the canopy in panic. This was the critical moment: lose sight of it now and they would never find it. The single dart might not have embedded itself fully, and anyway the effect of curare is not immediate.

Cristobal and the boys crashed so quickly through the trees that we made no attempt to follow. It was vital that they get more darts into the animal to finish him off. We could hear them calling to each other, shaking vines to force the monkey to move, and finally after a few more darts we heard the thud as it fell asleep and landed on the forest floor. The air was heavy with the weight of centuries, of years without seasons, of life without the rebirth of spring.

When we got back to the camp, Cristobal handed the monkey to the women while Esteban offered his cigarettes around and they all had a smoke. I could see Renaldo was awestruck by the experience. Never had he been more proud of his indigenous blood or had he felt closer to that side of himself. He was looking at Cristobal as though he were some mythic hero straight out of a comic book. For Renaldo, a life in the forest, hunting for food and communing with nature, was beyond imagining; it was transcendental. The heroism and mythology of it was beyond anything he would ever know. To him, forest tribes were divine, god-like beings existing in communion with the pulse of the planet. They were his yogis, his source of sanctity. I knew he was hoping Cristobal had noticed his tribal haircut. As far as Renaldo was concerned, the two of them were practically blood brothers now, or at least master and disciple. He put his arm around Cristobal's shoulder and asked what was the one thing in the world he wanted most. But Cristobal didn't understand the question, and so he asked again, "If the gods or Great Spirit could give you and your people just one thing, what would it be?"

"An outboard," Cristobal replied. "A really good one, a Honda, like the oil men have. We could travel all through the forest and hunt every tapir down. We would be safe from jaguars."

"Okay, but what else?" Renaldo said, clearly hoping for something more spiritual, more profound. "What could the world do to help you most?"

"Give guns," he said. "If we had guns, hunting would be easy, and the oil men would listen to us."

Renaldo, masking his disillusion, tried again. "What about something more personal. Something you yearn for?"

He was hoping for some esoteric gem, a profound quote to emblazon the front of the report – something so sagacious yet simple that it would leave the donors back home breathless.

"A new penis," Cristobal replied, with a straight face. "Mine doesn't stand up any more."

He waggled his waist-string, sending reverberations down his shaft.

One of the leaders heard us and came over. He must have had some Spanish because he understood what we were saying, but he got someone else to translate what he had to say.

"There is no answer to your questions," he began. "We need to be able to help ourselves. For that we need education, but your schools bring more than just Spanish; they bring your values, your prejudices. All we ask you is to stop the genocide. You no longer are sending us blankets impregnated with smallpox, and so you think things are better. You help us most by leaving us alone. Keep away! We cannot adapt to you; our culture is too different. Ours is about owning nothing, living from one hunt to the next. Yours is the opposite."

Esteban looked completely bored. He was still convinced that trying to help the Indians was futile. All he really wanted to know about was the state of the forest, not of the Shuar. He wanted to know about the changes they were seeing and the problems they foresaw. The leader patiently spent an hour telling us what he knew about the changing ecosystem around him, with Renaldo taking notes. Later some girls came out with fish wrapped in manioc and bunches of ladyfinger bananas and we ate greedily.

Esteban had brought a mini DAT machine and wanted to do some recording. One of the elders told him that to hear chanting or drumming he would have to go to the shaman, who lived on his own a distance away. I offered to go with him, and the others collapsed in hammocks for a snooze.

The shaman, who was named Lucho, was old, but he had a sharp mind and great Spanish. He looked up when we entered his hut, pointing out a wolf spider on the ground and, without saying a word, showed us how it jumped at a stick if his scent was on it. It was hunting him. When Esteban pulled out the microphone, Lucho immediately became more alert. He knew exactly what it was, but when we asked about chanting, he said he had no interest. Instead he wanted to talk. There were things he needed to say.

"The Shuar are not finished," he began. "Their work is just beginning. We need to teach the white man that he lives in a fantasy, that the things he holds dearest are not real. He can't see the thunder approaching or the dawn because there are no dollars on them. When he sees a tree or a herb, he sees only . . ."

"Yeah, yeah, very good," Esteban interrupted. "That's all great. The levels are fine. Now can you just do some chanting for me. In your own time . . ."

"Everyone must ask are they happy with what they are doing in life," the shaman continued defiantly. "Will it bring peace and contentment? Will it . . ."

"No, no, you don't understand. I need chanting; no talk . . . singing, yes? Thanks a lot. In your own time . . ."

Lucho looked annoyed, but he did begin to chant a little. Then he stopped and Esteban took off his headphones, saying, "I like it! I like it! Excellent, Lucho. Okay, one more time, but speed it up a bit, yeah? And would you normally be doing some drumming with that?"

Lucho shook his head.

"Right, okay. Well, can you do a bit of drumming for me, anyway? It'll add to the vibe."

It's possible I'm exaggerating Esteban's insensitivity here, but only because it's how it seemed at the time. He fiddled with the positioning of the microphone and then said, "Okay, rolling . . ."

Lucho remained silent. Esteban signalled that the tape was running, but still Lucho didn't react. Finally he said, "I am a shaman, someone who journeys to other worlds to help change this world, someone who knows the secrets. My role is to teach people about themselves, not. . ."

"Okay," Esteban said, rushing to turn off his machine. "Why don't we do both? You can first tell us about yourself, and then we'll record some sounds, okay? It's just that I've come a long way, and your music means so much to me."

Lucho grudgingly accepted the compromise and he began again, "I am a shaman, a transformer who takes the power of an eagle and puts it in a butterfly. Anyone can become a shaman. All you need is to hear the call and the doors open. A shaman is a bridge between the human realm and the divine. The world needs us, it needs many more of us, more now than ever. But it is a hard path. It means dying to the old and being reborn. It means sacrifice, years of aloneness in the jungle, years of sexual deprivation and hunger and nights by the river with dangerous animals.

"You cannot learn from someone else, but from the spirits inside of you. They train you in your dreams and in your life. It is not easy, but each single step is bearable. You need to know about plants, to feel them, to understand how they think. You need to know the dreams and chantings of your people; to die to your old ways and be reborn. A power animal rips flesh from bone and reconstructs the shaman in your place. It happens in trance or in real life: you are killed, dismembered, eaten, regurgitated and put back together by the spirits. Your bones are replaced with quartz."

As he talked on and on in heavily accented Spanish, I had the oddest sense he was speaking directly to me. I felt his eyes burning through me, although he wasn't looking at me at all. The words came as if through an echo chamber, and I could understand each one, where normally it was a struggle to keep up with Spanish. I experienced the eerie certainty that this was something I had always needed to hear, something he alone had been waiting to tell me.

. . . it means dying to the old and being reborn . . . years of aloneness . . .

years of sexual deprivation . . . nights by the river with dangerous animals . . . a power animal rips flesh from bone . . . you are killed, dismembered, eaten.

He had just described my life. My interest in plants, my herb garden, the attack by the dog, my not having sex, the spirit-figure inside me, right down to my grandmother having taught me the language of my people and our dreams and chantings. Was I a shaman? Was that what this was all about? Was I in training, and was this my Spiderman moment: the moment I got bitten by the atomic spider?

Chapter 8

MORE THAN ANYTHING else, the shaman made me realise I had to stop running. I had come to South America for a reason, and I couldn't just forget it all because of Eve. The answers still lay out there somewhere, in the sweetness of *Rica*, in the soul of *Ame*, and it was up to me to find them. I decided to go back to Caravanserai to take up where I had left off. Renaldo and the boys agreed to drop me in Baños on their way back to Peru, and after spending the night there, I took the bus back down to Vilcabamba. When Renaldo heard that I wasn't going to type up the report he was angry, but I didn't let it get to me. I was beginning to think they would never actually get around to deciding what to put in it. Meeting the Shuar had only set them firmer in their contrary positions, and anyway there were more than enough people out saving the rainforest already. It didn't need me.

Nadine and Demofilo weren't all that welcoming when I got back. I had really worried them by running off. They didn't know what had happened, and all they could find out from their staff was that I had been hanging around a lot with the girl who got the phone call, and then suddenly I stormed out. They were upset that I hadn't taken the time to explain it to them, and Nadine wasn't pleased to find herself with the responsibility of running the hotel again. I tried to explain how messed up I had been; I hadn't been capable of explanations back then. I think they understood. For the first few days, Nadine, and to a lesser extent Demofilo, tried to keep up the pretence of disappointment, but I knew that secretly Nadine, at least, was relieved to see me back. Her mother had suffered a minor stroke back home in Seattle, and she needed to go see her. I could run the hostel while she was away. I had arrived just in time.

And so, in a matter of hours, my life returned to its previous pattern of welcoming backpackers in off the road and looking after them. Once Nadine had left for Seattle, I was put in charge of the farm as well as running the hostel, which basically meant checking that the coffee groves were kept in order and the sugar-cane was harvested at the right time. Other than that, I was expected to oversee the staff payment once a week, which required setting up a desk on the verandah where the workers, with machetes swinging from their waists, would file up to be paid and to air any grievances they had. This was also the time for them to plead for any favours they needed, and I soon realised I was completely ill-equipped to know what to say when a labourer earning a dollar a day asks you for money to fly to Miami for the funeral of his grandson. Another thing that college doesn't prepare you for. Fortunately Manuel, the foreman, would stand beside me whispering suitable replies in my ear.

Luna, the overly eager masseuse I had met up in Mordechai's cabin, was particularly happy to see me back: she needed more massage bookings as she was running out of money and hadn't been getting clients referred to her while I was away. Things weren't going well for her and Rory. He had broken his arm and had acute pneumonia from spending three night out in the open looking for a tourist who had got lost in the mountains, and in some perverse way Luna blamed the whole thing on me. It seemed that after I had left, Nadine had taken down all the posters advertising her massages in revenge for a fight the two women had had many years before (possibly over Luna giving Demofilo one of her "special" massages). With massage money not coming in, and Rory not having much luck organising tours into the forest, things had got very tight for the family. When the children had gone without dinner for a few days and Rory had taken to drink to hide his shame, Luna kicked him out of the house and told him not to come back until he had food or money. He had hung around the cafes on the main plaza for days, offering every backpacker he met a cut-price trip into the mountains until finally he met two Swedes and an Irish bloke who agreed to sign up. Rory was wary of the Irish guy from the beginning. He had a tendency to ramble incoherently and was lumbering and inept, but on sight of his crisp, clean dollars, Rory brushed all concern aside and went off to load up the ponies.

Things went well on their first day. Although the Irishman was a bit of an idiot, he had a great stock of stories and kept them all entertained. It was on the second day, when they were high up on a ridge in the cloud forest, that a heavy mist fell, obliterating everything. The Irish lad, who had walked ahead some distance, instead of retracing his steps kept on going until he took a wrong turn and got lost. Even then the fool didn't turn back. He went on, hoping to link up with the main trail further on. It was the most treacherous part of the ridge, with sheer drops down to dry creeks and riverbeds. Rory told the Swedes to sit and wait while he tried to fetch the Irishman back, but he had no luck finding him. Once the rain began to fall, the trail turned to sludge, dislodging rocks which slid down past them towards the river; at any moment, a landslide could have brought down half the mountain. Rory and the Swedes were forced to bivouac beneath a rock for the night. The following morning, he led the Swedes back to town before returning the whole way up the mountain to hunt for the boy. He spent two days roaming the trails, climbing up and down cliffs calling out to him until finally, on the evening of the second day, a call came back. The Irishman was about 80 metres below on a ledge, and although Rory tried his very best, he couldn't get down to him.

The only thing the Irishman said was, "Oh, I was wondering where you were," as though he had just left him a minute before. Rory was exhausted to the point of collapse, he hadn't slept in two nights, and although he didn't know it yet, he had broken his arm in two places in a fall. But all he could think of was saving the guy's life. He was his responsibility. The lad meanwhile was lying comfortably on the ledge beneath him, calling up to Rory every now and then, "Would you happen to have a cigarette on you, at all?"

Rory shouted at him to make his way down to the river, but the boy said he couldn't. "I'm stuck. I'm well and truly stuck," he said. "Haven't I told you that? I tried everything these long days."

Rory had no option but to run back to town and call the army rescue from Cuenca and then run the whole way back up again, with his broken arm stabbing with pain, so that the boy would have someone to spend the night with until the helicopter arrived in the morning and winched them to safety.

At dawn the following morning, the Irishman was dropped down into the main plaza of Vilcabamba by helicopter and welcomed like a hero by the Red Cross and the Irish consulate. The same official who had been so dismissive to me about the rabies vaccine now stood proudly to have his photo taken with the returning hero. The staff in Caravanserai even baked him a cake with an iced shamrock on top.

He said to Nadine, "Ah now, and there was I thinkin' I'd never be seein' the likes of that again. Sure, you're a star – that's precisely what you are. May God be good to you."

He had them all charmed, all eating out of his palm. They thought he was a fool all right, but a charming one, a simple Irish one. No one gave poor Rory a second thought; they blamed him for losing the boy in the first place. When the doctors checked Rory out, they discovered his broken arm and took him straight to hospital, where he was diagnosed with double pneumonia. Now, with the hospital bills weighing down on them, he and Luna were poorer than ever, and Luna regarded it as my responsibility to find her more clients.

It was only when Rory showed me the video of the boy's heroic arrival in town and I saw that same pasty, sunburnt face that I realised who the Irishman was. It was none other than Paddy Gish, Paddy from the plane. They had refused to allow him leave Colombia until he paid the fine for smuggling the snake, and since he hadn't been able to afford it, he was still here. Maybe I should have let him travel with me after all, I could have kept him out of harm, and who knows, he might have kept me away from Eve and that bloody dog. Maybe all my bad luck would have gone to him.

I slotted easily back into life in Caravanserai. It was nice to be helping people again, telling them about the place, and there was no problem finding clients for Luna. She still insisted on giving me a free massage every week, which she was becoming ever keener to elevate to something more – to take my mind off Eve, as she said. I was still trying to make sense of the shaman's ideas which were tumbling around my head, not to mention Rabbit's various pronouncements and the repercussions of the whole Eve fiasco. I still didn't know if I could get over her. I needed somewhere to work it all out, and Caravanserai was as good a place as any.

I had had a very strange experience in Baños when Renaldo and the guys had left me off, which I was still trying to come to terms with. It was an omen of some kind, but I had no idea what. It was late in the day when we reached Baños, and I decided to stay the night rather than go straight on to Vilcabamba, in case Caravanserai was full or Nadine wasn't prepared to take me back. I had gone to sleep early, exhausted from meeting the shaman, and at some point in the night had woken with a blinding light burning inside my mind. I opened my eyes, but the room was completely dark. Turning around in the bed, I looked towards the door which led straight out on to the front yard and saw a bluish white blur burning in around the jamb and through the curtains. It was the colour of a magnesium camera flash, but magnified a thousand-fold. I pulled myself out of bed and yanked open the curtains, but there was only darkness outside, and the light had disappeared from behind the door. On the back of my retina, I could still see its afterglow; it was fading slowly. I was sure I hadn't imagined it. Somehow I had seen the light inside my head first, but then when I woke up and turned to the door, I had definitely seen it with my eyes for a few seconds. It never dawned on me that it could be alien. It seemed more natural than that. I got back into bed, keeping an eye on the window, and sure enough just as I was about to fall asleep again, the light returned, blazing through the window and around the door frame. It was as if someone was shining a lighthouse beacon directly at the hotel. As far as I could tell, it was coming from beyond the hills. I got out of bed and rushed to the window. The trees and valley were silhouetted by an electric blue light burning in the sky. My nerves were tingling, and I bristled with alertness as though the air had too much oxygen. It lasted over a minute, then went dark again, before coming back seemingly even brighter and lasting longer. My mind tried to seek an explanation: could lightning blaze for that long? It was simply too blue, too electric to be fire. In the end, I thought an electrical transformer must have exploded. But I had heard no noise.

Next day there was no official talk of any accident or explosion. The papers didn't mention it at all, but everyone on the streets was talking about it. Almost all of them had woken at the same time and had seen it. Some were aware of high-pitched noises, too. Of course, I thought back to Don Luis in San Agustin. He would have said it was a tear in the fabric, but that didn't seem right. Whatever it was, I decided to take it as a sign, that it was time to pick myself up and get back on the trail. Things would work out this time.

I had been back at Caravanserai for a few weeks when Demofilo came home from Loja one evening with a ream of faint, grey print-out tucked under his arm and slapped it down in front of me. He knew how crushed I had been about Eve, and as a surprise had decided to trace her on the internet for me. It was the very early days of the World Wide Web, when it was still only a collection of interlinking shared files, and finding anything without a specific server address was a challenge. The Banco Del Andes was the only place in Loja with an internet connection, and as a special favour Demofilo had asked the manager to run her name through various gopher databases and automated catalogues to see what turned up. This mound of unformatted courier script, acupunctured with hyphens along the left margin, was it.

It was sweet of him, I know, but . . .

I knew immediately I shouldn't read it. It would do nothing but reopen the wounds. I had already refused Demofilo's offer to watch one of her videos. Every night on the verandah, we used to show a film, normally Disney's *Aladdin* or *The Emerald Forest*, which were the only two we had. Demofilo had offered to order one of Eve's from Quito for me, but I got him to promise not to. All it would do was prolong the pain. I had to start afresh. I really did. And yet now with the print-out lying there in front of me, how could I resist? Those squadrons of dot-matrix characters lined up like ants on the march might reveal everything. I might find out why. What had triggered her mind. I might catch a glimpse of her soul.

I did resist nonetheless. I resisted valiantly. Or at least tried to. I pushed the mound of tickertape back across the table at Demofilo and thanked him, but told him I wouldn't be reading it. I just couldn't. He was his usual magnanimous self, purring sympathetically about how he quite understood, how I was being most sensible but that maybe I should consider it more over an enema and that he would leave it with me anyhow, just in case.

I managed to hold out for almost a week.

The first few files were from the Movie Query Review Engine at the Carnegie Mellon mainframe, which had reviews of most modern films. They listed all eighteen she had made and gave details of the director and her co-stars. I knew about most of them already from her or from people I had met since, but I'd rather have been spared the barely euphemistic line: "Eve's bold, brave performance does not shirk from revealing all in this raw, gripping thriller." It just set my mind off.

The database of a San Francisco-based anarchy collective had the names and network transfer details of files containing nude photos of her, but fortunately the Loja bank had a text-only screen and the photos weren't included. Overall, it was all pretty anodyne up until then, consisting mainly of biographical details and harmless gossip, and I was actually rather glad to have read it. At least it proved she wasn't a figment. She did exist.

It was on the bulletin board of a microprocessor company based in Atlanta that I found the real grime. The nasty, low-down dirt. (The general tone of the internet has crawled so low since that it's hard to convey a sense of quite how odious it appeared at the time, quite how degenerate.) The thread began vaguely enough with techie-speak about the Rodent-Oriented Netwide Index on an Intel 8088 and then, halfway through, suddenly swerved towards a question about Eve. Someone posted about whether anyone on the board had seen her latest movie, and out of nowhere some socially retarded Neanderthal replied:

```
I don't care what the people in the meedia say.I
don't believe that anyone hass ased Ms Eve about
the current clinton scandal. I just wish that I
could see more of her body. I agree with her on
so many things. The movies and such that EVE has
appeared in can be found 8here.Looking for nude
pictures of Eve? Try WAIS server.

She's is so cool. Or at least near the top.Yeah,
I know — so what?Three cheers for EVE. I'd bet
that Eve looks great nude.I agree with her on so
many things.That's something the whoo world can
agree on.My cousin told me EVE enjoys brazilian
but I have no idea to verify that.

Look at the feet of EVE, I'm not into feet but
they are nice..You can't be a heterosexual man
unless you want to see nude pictures of eve and
do things, you know. Like to her. I have a telnet
link with pictures of her herr.
```

I can't describe how sick it made me feel, as though the ship I was on had suddenly listed twenty degrees and was taking in water and about to keel over. That freak, that techno–obsessed, emotionally retarded freak was drowning me, pulling me down into his fetid realm. I thought of him staring into the globular abyss of his putrid green screen, pleasuring himself. It was all too horrible, and yet I couldn't help but admit to myself that Eve did have nice feet.

All my good intentions gave way after that. If everyone else could have her, why couldn't I? I rang one of the studios in Hollywood and begged them for her address, but that got me nowhere and just sent my name higher up the stalker list. So instead I turned to Demofilo and asked him to get whatever videos he could from Quito. It took a week for the first one to arrive, and although I tried in the intervening days to promise myself I wouldn't watch it, it was no use. The rest of the guests were so excited to get a break from *Aladdin* and *The Emerald Forest* that there would have been mutiny if we hadn't shown it.

The beginning was fine. The first scene of a remote ranch somewhere in Maine was really pretty. It was autumn and a shiny Volvo pulled up outside – all beautifully framed and subtly lit. The introduction of the characters was well executed, and I was beginning to settle down and look forward to what was to come. Eve, of course, looked divine; her character was strong and well-rounded. She was a fantastic actress. I felt so proud. It was about ten minutes in that the whole thing suddenly jack-knifed towards the gutter. I suppose I had Eve on such a pedestal that seeing her as anything other than the Lady of Shallot or Joan of Arc would have hurt me. This was a straight-to-video thriller; I should have known what to expect. I should have anticipated the sex, steeled myself for it. I had spent enough drunken evenings during adolescence watching this sort of thing, shouting lecherous insults at the screen. But I'm not sure anything could have prepared me for what was to come.

I didn't know such degeneracy was even allowed outside of porn films. Stilettos and smeared lipstick: it was horrible. In comparison with the director, the internet freak was a paragon of virtue. I couldn't believe such scenes were classed as family entertainment. Each new camera angle left me more violated – like being kicked in the gut repeatedly. The other guests were peering out of the sides of their eyes, tickled pink at the reaction each scene provoked in me. I'm not sure how long I managed to endure it, but as soon as I thought my feet would carry me, I got up and chased out. I couldn't risk there being any more, or worse to come. I was strong – I had taken everything the Screamers could throw at me – but not that strong.

It was a Monday, the day after the day the Americans and Israelis took their malaria tablets. It was always a bad day. A bunch of them would invariably fall into severe depression brought on by the drugs, and it seemed their doctors never warned them about it. Because of the day that was in it, I wasn't too surprised when I was woken by one of the maids, just when I'd finally managed to fall asleep. She said there was a *gringo* crying up on the hill.

"I'll be right there," I said, pulling on my trousers.

Carmella, the maid, led me up past the first coffee plantation to the scrubland beyond, and there, cowering beneath a large boulder, was an Israeli boy crying like a seal calf. This wasn't just the usual malaria tablet blues, but something Nadine and Demofilo had been seeing more and more of during the previous year. The situation on the Lebanese border had deteriorated; Hamas were making frequent incursions into northern Israel, and the Israelis were retaliating hard. They had been told to fight back any way they could, which normally meant going after the refugees in the camps. For the young conscripts, it meant taking a step further away from their own conscience, which had repercussions that only surfaced when they were safely out of the Israeli army and thousands of miles away up in the Andes.

San Pedro has been used for ever by shamans to drive out evil spirits, to reconnect one to one's soul, and the Israelis hoped it would do the same for them: it would wipe away the stain of the three lost years of inane orders, punishments and shootings. Caravanserai had been planned as a centre for San Pedro therapy when it was first built. Nadine and Demofilo had helped find and cook the cactus for the string of confused, argumentative ex-soldiers who turned up each year. But this all ended when a local shaman heard about it and put a curse on them for misusing the sacred plant, for daring to call in its spirit outside of the proscribed ceremonies. Locals claimed the curse was behind every bad thing that happened in the hostel – Eve included. And although Caravanserai had nothing to do with San Pedro any more, the soldiers still came. Each year fifteen thousand conscripts were released from the army, and those that didn't end up in Kashmir turned up here as part of their annual circummigration of South America, the primary aim of which was to lick their wounds and heal their minds. They sought out and found San Pedro, hoping it would do the trick, as it had for so many of their countrymen before them. But sometimes it just didn't work. Sometimes it wasn't powerful enough to cope with all the memories, all those hours of lost youth, of atrocities, and they found themselves spiralling into a bad trip. Demofilo had trained the staff to deal with it, to give them sips of coffee and stay with them until they were okay, but sometimes it needed more than that.

When I called out to the boy on the hill, he stopped crying for a second and looked up. That he could hear me at all was a good sign. I offered him some bread which Carmella had brought and he took it. Maybe this wouldn't be so hard after all. He tried to say something, but he was still dry heaving and it was difficult to make out the words. I waited as he pulled a chunk of bread off, chewing it languorously, which seemed to calm him. After a moment he repeated what he had said.

"Uri," he said. "Uri!" and pointed up the hill.

I left Carmella with him and went up beyond the next rise to see what he was on about, but there was nothing there. I stopped and looked around and that was when I heard it: the same whimpering I'd heard before, like the wailing at a Jewish funeral. Following the sound, I came upon a hunched figure, scratched and bloody, hiding beneath an acacia tree. He was completely naked and had shit smeared in his hair.

"Are you okay?" I said. I was rushing forward, but I stopped dead as he began to scream. I squatted down low on my hunkers until he grew less frightened and fell quiet again. Even from this far back, the smell was awful. I never knew what to do next, how to reach out to someone who was drifting into darkness, how to get them to trust me. I just hoped that if I sat and waited long enough they would come around eventually. The other Israeli came up behind me with Carmella.

"How is Uri?" he asked and then called out something in Hebrew, but Uri just moaned in reply. He reminded me of a rabbit I had once run over – the same lost, panicked eyes. If he was this far gone, there was no knowing how long it would take to get him back. If ever. He wouldn't be the first to have arrived in Vilcabamba in perfect health and left like a zombie on Telegraph Avenue. Some paths were so dark that they only went one way – wormholes that never quite led back to earth. It fell to their embassies to pick these lost ones up and fly them home. In fact, one of the original Merry Pranksters (a sixties beatnik group that travelled through the States in a psychedelic bus turning people on to LSD and countercultural thought) was living just outside town; he was fine now, but it had been touch and go for a long time.

Uri lay sprawled out like a star staring into space, like da Vinci's Vitruvian Man, his trousers and underwear hanging in shreds in a thorn bush beside him. He was uncircumcised, which was odd, and he had a leaf tattooed just above his pelvis, which I was sure was against the Torah or Leviticus or something. I had read somewhere that since the Holocaust, tattoos were seen as disrespecting those branded in the camps.

Raban, the other Israeli boy, tried to approach him, but it just set off the wailing again and he retreated, squatting down beside me. He looked choked with concern for his friend.

"Will he be okay?" he asked.

I nodded assuredly, thinking that it was what was expected.

"We just wanted to make it all better," he said. "To make it go away and start afresh."

"Uh-uh," I mumbled.

"Uri has a girlfriend in the West Bank, see?" Raban went on. "It's been three years since he saw her. They told him it was safer to keep away while he was enlisted; for her own safety, you know?"

"Sure," I said. I was exhausted, but Raban was keen to talk.

"Sometimes neighbours pour battery acid and stuff over Arab girls who go with soldiers, so it's better they don't know. Uri wanted to go see her straight after he was demobbed, but the lieutenant said they would still be able to smell the army off him; better to wait till his hair grew and he looked human again. He was worried his head had become so fucked up by all the shit he had seen and done she wouldn't even recognise him. That's why we came here, to take Pedro, to make it all better, that's why. To remember how to live again, how to love nature and people, not just other fucking soldiers."

Raban took another chunk of bread from Carmella, chewing it slowly without ever taking an eye off Uri. His compassion was palpable, almost visible. If I half-closed my eyes, I could see tendrils of light coiling out from him towards Uri. It didn't phase him that his friend was naked and shit-covered, scratched and battered like roadkill. He didn't see any of that.

"Everything had been going so well," Raban said. "We come from the same region, see? Went to school together and all. Our mothers were so relieved when our platoon was sent to build a hangar out near the Dead Sea. We hadn't seen any fighting the whole time, but we had to have our fucking Uzis with us anyway – always, all day, all night, even when we were mixing concrete, even dancing at the disco. The girls danced around their handbags and we danced around our submachine guns. Only in the Promised Land!

"We both felt guilty about it, you know? How we had got off so easily. Waking up sweating, hearing God, like an accountant, looking over his steel-rim glasses, saying, 'Haven't you boys been lucky, eh? When others have paid such a high price guarding My Land? Let's see can We balance the books a little here, Messrs Lucky. Huh?'"

"It was the first weekend's leave that I hadn't come home with him. I had met a girl in Tel Aviv, see? But I told him not to tell my mom; to tell her instead I was doing shift work. He lives in a kibbutz just outside my village, one of the last traditional ones, self-sufficient. They still share all their clothes and stuff and play games instead of watching TV. It's about being peaceful, living and breathing Zion. And the one thing they hate most is guns. So Uri always had to hide his in my house.

"Because I wasn't with him this one time, he brought the gun home. It only dawned on me that it would be a problem after I had left him, and I tried ringing his family to tell him he could leave the gun at my sister's, but it was Shabbat so they couldn't answer the phone. Some rabbis say you can listen to your answer machine without desecrating Shabbat, but obviously not theirs. Anyway, they didn't get the message. Some of those kibbutzniks are real devout, you know? As I say, it's a real orthodox place. Uri ended up digging a hole and burying the gun in a field behind the kibbutz kitchen. It was the usual shit. We'd just got off a six-day rotation with two hours sleep a night. I don't know how he even got the energy to dig – I remember I fell straight asleep in my girlfriend's arms – and the ground there is baked hard like rock . . ."

Raban paused – his mind adrift, probably back home somewhere in the Negev. I got up to stretch my haunches, and it seemed to bring him back. He took up the story again, more slowly this time, more contemplatively.

"He mustn't have buried it well," Raban said, "because some goats, they dug it up in the night. And when he woke up in the morning, he saw the local kids playing with it outside the window. He ran out screaming, and they got such a fright that one of them accidentally let off the safety catch. It had a full magazine – firing-speed of ten rounds a second. I don't know how they got off so lightly. The boy must have dropped it after the first burst. And only one really hit home. It was so lucky. Only one injury. It was the son of a friend of ours. He's fine now, just that a bit of 9mm lodged in his back so he's in a little steel chair. We had been so lucky up until then."

Raban looked away to hide his eyes, and we both stared at Uri, who was so far away he could have been in a coma. Raban rushed over to feel his pulse, which set him contorting back to life, writhing and moaning on the earth, oblivious to the stones and thorns that were piercing his skin. He only quietened again once Raban had backed away. I noticed Raban was exhausted, on the verge of fainting, and I told Carmella to bring him back to the hostel and feed him. But he wasn't keen to go, to leave his wounded buddy in the field. It was this sense of comradeship that most drew me to Israelis. It was something I had never known myself, and was jealous of. The bond formed by what they had been through was at the core of their travelling in large groups, like a military campaign with every route and site planned out. They needed to stay together; no one else would understand. Back home in their barracks, they spent hours poring over maps and consulting handwritten manuals passed from generation to generation, listing everything from how to perform a tracheotomy to the price of toasted sandwiches and granola yoghurts between Venezuela and Chile.

Before Raban went back down the mountain, he made another effort to approach Uri, and this time the fit of writhing he provoked was less severe. Raban didn't back away from his friend but held on tighter, whispering reassurance into his ear until eventually Uri quietened. Raban cradled him like the Pieta, like a war movie, and when Carmella handed him a cloth he wiped Uri's brow and began to clean him like a cow with a newborn calf. I was bowled over by the scene: these strong Jewish soldiers with more experience of the world than I would ever know and a far greater capacity for love. It's what Israel was all about, I suppose: looking out for each other, cooperating for the common good. Despite all their squabbling, they were prepared to die for each other as much as for their country. Israel would never have worked without that – that willingness for sacrifice. That unconditional love. It was something I hardly understood. Would I have died for Eve? Not likely. My grandmother had been a freedom fighter and risked death numerous times for love of her country, but the hero gene had skipped me. During adolescence I had toyed with the concept of continuing her fight, but soon realised that such passion was so raw and impulsive it could too easily slip into fanaticism. It was what had turned idealistic patriots into an army that kneecapped Protestant boys for kissing Catholics. It's what made the Screamers who they were. Nevertheless, as I watched the boys clinging to each other, I knew I was seeing it in its purest form, and I was moved.

Over the course of the morning, Uri gradually wound his way back to sanity. He allowed me throw a blanket over his shoulders, and I watched as he struggled to stitch back together the pieces of his tattered mind. I wondered was this what the shaman had meant: how in your visions you get killed, dismembered, eaten, regurgitated and put back together by the spirits. Was that what was going on? Did making the shift from soldier to civilian require a similar process? It was at times like this, staring into the startled eyes of yet another lost Israeli, that I wished I could somehow tell them about Rabbit, to introduce them to the equivalent inside their own head. Although Rabbit could be a temperamental bastard, he did tend to want the best for me most of the time. Somehow he always knew what to do.

"I am blind . . . No . . . small, black bits scurrying," were the first semi-coherent words Uri spoke. "It's a cockroach? No! Thousands of them! See?"

I told him I couldn't and got him to tell me everything he was thinking and seeing, so I could tell him if it was real or not. I thought it might help guide him back.

"You can't possibly know," he said, absentmindedly picking the dried shit from his hair.

"Just tell me; tell me where you are," I said.

"There's nothing. Look, coming out of your veins and there, in lines across the earth. See?" he shouted.

I promised there was nothing there.

"Don't look! Don't even think about it," he cried. "It is terrible. A shadow, it's cold. So cold."

His teeth began to chatter. Sweat was still running down his forehead.

"What?" I asked. He was panting now. "Tell me! You must tell me."

As he pummelled my hand in a vice-grip, I reminded him about the cactus and what it did to your mind. I reassured him that he was almost home and that he mustn't give up. I gave him sips of coffee whenever he let me.

"Everything is so polluted, so plastic," he said. "I'm frightened. We need weaponry. Look, ball lightning there, in that tree."

"It's a leaf," I said. "It's only a tiny leaf. I promise."

It went on like that, him crawling through various neuroses and psychoses until eventually he found his way back.

After looking hard into my eyes, trying to place me, he said, "Oh, it's you."

"Yeah," I said. "Are you okay?"

"That was fuckin' bad. So bad."

"Are you sure you're okay now?" I asked.

"I dunno," he said, pulling his blanket tighter around him. "You're an anti-Semite, yeah?"

"I am?" I said, surprised, I thought he might be about to thank me or something.

"Yeah, I heard you play David Bowie in the bar."

"I like him," I said.

"Well, you like a Jew-hater."

"Bowie doesn't hate Jews."

"Wrong!" he said triumphantly. "He wore a PLO scarf. I saw him."

I said nothing. I didn't mention how ironic it was: these Israelis coming to South America to rebuild their lives, just like the Nazis had done before them. I kept quiet because I had a sense of how hard things were for them, of the weight they carried, the legacy they represented. Looking at them, you could almost imagine their ancestors scribing the scriptures, carving the Temple, prostrating themselves in sackcloth. Before we dared imagine that God might be within us, anyone who wanted power had to control the holy places, and with the Jews living near the holiest sites of the three major religions, things were never going to be easy. Mordechai had told me that when he was on San Pedro, he realised that what was needed was a new Exodus. If the first was out of Egypt and the second into the new Israel, then the third had to be, not to a new location, but into the heart, into the spirit. That sense of oneness Uri and Raban shared had to be extended beyond the tribe so that a new Temple was built, not on the foundations of the old one, but throughout the world.

Chapter 9

THE LONGER I spent in Vilcabamba, the more it lost its shine. What at first had seemed a paradisiacal valley in which the water was so pure, the climate so perfect and the soil so fertile that its inhabitants lived for ever, became like anywhere else: neither good nor bad. Even the famed notion of longevity that had first attracted me wasn't as clear-cut as I had believed. While the simple farming lifestyle ensured that heart and lung disease were rare, the claim of long life had more than likely begun with someone boasting they were well over a hundred and attracting so much outside attention that others were willing to go along with it to the point of even adding a few decades to their own age. Anthropologists, seeking to make a name for themselves, had come and written vague but positive studies about the phenomenon, and the rest of the world, keen to discover a remote Shangri-La, knew better than to ask too many questions. Since births weren't registered until the late nineteenth century, there was no way of knowing for sure, and whatever church records did exist had had their early pages mysteriously ripped out. Either way, it was a tranquil place, and it did seem to have more than its fair share of old people.

After a few years of celebrity in the seventies, with articles written about it in *National Geographic* and *Reader's Digest*, the longevity myth had backfired on the locals when a string of seekers, dreamers and assorted oddball refugees had come looking for paradise – all with their various ideas and idiosyncrasies, crusades and dogmas. Most just messed about for a time until disillusionment set in or money ran out and they went home again. However, a few from each wave – the most committed, the most desperate – had remained. They would buy a patch of land, a mule and some chickens and set up homesteads as in the Wild West. It became a frontier land of maverick misfits, eccentric apostates and seceders. Many had been through the same communes and crazes together and had built up the scar tissue of old fights and rivalries. Now, finding themselves running cafes, hostels and treks, and dependent on the same small pool of backpackers to provide their income, the old wounds became reinflamed, and there was a continual undercurrent of tension. Competition and jealousy were rife. I did my best to stay out of the infighting between Rory and Luna, and Demofilo and Nadine, which had become poisonous over the years. All these outsiders adored the place and had a real passion for the environment, but what was missing was the cooperation and community feeling that the *campesino* locals – forced to strive together over centuries – so evidently had.

From what I could gather, almost all of the foreigners had been involved with Johnny Lovewisdom at some stage. Johnny was the type of guru one only finds in paradises. He was known as the Greatest Saint of the Andes and claimed to have been John the Baptist in a previous incarnation. He believed that living on a diet of pure fruit had made him clairvoyant, clairaudient and able to levitate. He came to Vilcabamba following his dream of restoring paradise to earth through a new race of humans who would live for ever, having attained enlightenment by eating fruit.

All other food was contaminated with radioactive fallout, he claimed. The most dangerous of all were the reproductive parts of plants. Seeds, grains and nuts were poisons that stimulated sex-drive and incited one to issue one's own seed, which in turn made one go to seed.

Johnny Lovewisdom had set up a commune in Vilcabamba in the seventies, which he hoped would form the core of a new society of fruitarians who would never have penetrative sex or even ejaculate. The body could not ascend to spiritual purity, he claimed, if one fuelled the fires of sex. He had brought sixteen vestal virgins with him, who dressed in capes of crimson. These were to be the seed stock of the new race, and would become pregnant through spiritual intervention (immaculate conception) once the energetic intention of the community was resonating at a high enough frequency. Needless to say, the girls caused a stir in the village as locals watched on in bafflement and concern as they paraded regularly through the valley, and as devotees kept coming from all over the world, and as Johnny and his communards guided spiritual pioneers from acclaimed journals and academies through the back alleys of the village. It was Johnny's set-up here that inspired Viktoras Kulvinskas to write his influential work, *Survival into the 21st Century*.

As with all such movements, it lasted only a few years. The men found it too hard not to ejaculate, and the women couldn't handle Johnny's six-month, seventeen-day fast. Everything fell apart amid sordid scenes in the village plaza of committed fruitarians breaking their fast after four years and gorging like pigs in a trough on meat and cigarettes. The vestal virgins were defiled while the locals watched on, shaking their heads in bafflement. It had all happened twenty years before I arrived, but for the locals it was like yesterday – their Kennedy assassination, which will stay with them for decades. After the break-up, most of the communards returned to their homes in California or wherever, and the handful that remained were some of those now running the hostels, horse tours and other backpacker ventures.

Johnny took the cream (a fruit metaphor is more appropriate – the figs, the cantaloupes) of his remaining devotees deep into the forest, where he set up a smaller commune. Things went well there for many years. While his disciples laboured growing fruit trees and gathering berries, he wrote a word-for-word translation from the Aramaic of one of the lost *Essene Gospels of Peace*, which had recently been discovered among the Dead Sea Scrolls, and over time he became highly regarded in Gnostic circles. But the locals could never quite get over the scenes they had witnessed. Suspicion and rumours grew about what he might be up to in the woods, and without proper information their minds imagined the very worst. There were all sorts of dark stories about him, and when a young boy went missing in the forest two years after the debacle, it was said that Johnny had taken him to use in some depraved ritual. The locals immediately formed a hunting party and went chasing after him. Johnny was forced to flee deeper into the forest towards the Amazon.

It was Rory who told me about it. He and Luna weren't in Vilcabamba at the time, but they had talked to people who were. They were sitting outside their house roasting coffee beans when he told me the story, surrounded by avocado, mandarin, papaya and pomegranate trees that he had been influenced to plant by Johnny's teachings. Below us was a whole field of more trees (passion fruit, sweet lime, maracuya, guyabanana, pineapple plants) that the communards had grown from seed. Rory was so inspired by their legacy that he rarely ate anything other than fruit, and he said that it was for the hops within beer that he drank so much of it. As we talked, he was sucking on the spawn-like innards of a passion fruit, slurping it around his mouth and spitting the odd seed into the coffee beans on the pan, to sweeten them he claimed. He told me the names of all forty-two types of fruit that grew on his holding and got me to write them in my diary.

"If only Johnny had talked more to the locals," Rory said, "and explained himself. If he hadn't thought he was on such a higher plane. They were just curious; they wanted to know what he was up to, that's all. If he had allowed them come visit, even once or twice – shared a cup of *café con leche* – things would have been different. If they had seen him tapping innocently away at his little typewriter, consulting his dusty old tomes and dictionaries, they would have known he was harmless – just a dreamy old fool. But as it was, when the young boy went missing everyone panicked. There was no time to think, to reason, to give the benefit of the doubt. The boy had to be saved; Johnny had to be caught."

Rory took the frying pan off the flame, chewing on a bean to check for flavour, before continuing.

"The locals are all *campesino* farmers now, but this is only a recent thing – a phenomenon of the last hundred years or so. Before that they were hunter-gatherers. Although they had been developing the settled man's fear of the forest, still inside them pulsed their old tribal blood, and now it rose again as they fanned out into the trees, excited and afraid what might lie ahead."

The hairs on Luna's dusky skin bristled as she listened to her husband describe the hunt: the fear and foreboding as ancestral memories were re-awakened, the adrenalin pushing them beyond endurance. Rory's account was so vivid I wondered was he perhaps remembering his own hunt for Paddy a few weeks before.

"The mob found Johnny's followers first," Rory explained. "They didn't do them much harm, only frightened them a bit to find out what they knew. It gave Johnny a day's start, and he was safe that first day. The following morning the trackers set off early, but they were no match for the Greatest Saint of the Andes. Too much milk and eggs and rich farmer food had made them flabby, and Johnny knew the forest better than any of them. A life of fruit had left him lean as a panther. Some say he got away on the second and third days by levitating over the forest, and it might be true. I saw him do it myself once, but not that high and only for a few seconds. I doubt even he could have managed it, but who knows? I only got to know him as an old man. In his prime he might have been capable of anything.

"Whatever miracle it was that saved him those first few days, he was damn lucky. The locals would have ripped him like hounds on a hare if they'd got a hold of him. As it was, they were approaching dangerously close and were little more than a mile away when the news finally came through that the boy had been found. He had turned up alive and well at his granny's house. He had wandered up a dry riverbed on an adventure and only come home because he was hungry. The hunt was called off, but no one told Johnny. No one could find him; he had gone so deep into the forest he simply disappeared. The locals swore they hadn't killed him, and although no one really believed them for a long time, sure enough, a few years later, he did turn up many miles away, living on roots and berries up Cuenca direction. That was when I got to know him. His mind had become pretty scatty by then. Some of his most fanatical devotees said he had ascended so high he couldn't talk to us normal folk any more."

Rory told me that Johnny was still living in the forest about eighty miles away. He was seventy-five years old now, and Rory even offered to bring me in to meet him; but it was a two-day ride away, and I never got around to it. I've regretted it since.

Rumour had it that both Demofilo and the Merry Prankster had been involved with Johnny back then, but I could never find out whether they were actually part of his commune or not. Although I tried to get them to talk about it, they never wanted to. There was a sense of shame among the ex-pats about how the first commune had ended. It had been an unfortunate incident which coloured the high enlightenment they had been seeking. Other than the fruit trees, the only obvious legacy of Johnny's teachings were his gospel translations and Demofilo's devotion to colonics. Johnny had advocated daily sessions to clean out the toxins on the path to enlightenment, although instead of buckets of coffee, he favoured swallowing a cloth and passing it through the intestine. I never tried this, but I did try reading his translation of *The Healing God Spell of St John*, which was fascinating and, if accurate, threw light on all sorts of inconsistencies in the other gospels and revealed Jesus' teachings on diet and yoga.

Of course the foreigners in Vilcabamba had joined many other cults and crazes since Johnny's time. Even the Screamers had been there for a while. They had considered moving down from Colombia at one point, but decided it wasn't remote enough. I suppose everyone was searching for the same thing: all after love, in one form or another. And no doubt most of them, like me and the Screamers and the IRA, had become confused and ended up with some warped version of it. That's what was hardest, keeping the love pure, not distorting it, not letting the mind get in the way. Maybe Eve was right. Maybe the best thing to do was not to think about it, to just trust your impulses and let them guide you. Although I still wasn't sure whether that was as likely to lead one to kneecapping young Protestant boys as it was to any genuine spiritual enlightenment, at least you wouldn't end up swallowing rags and pulling them through your intestine. That was what happens when you spend too much time trying to work stuff out.

I was becoming ever more disillusioned with paradise, but it was only when war broke out that I knew I would have to leave. Peru and Ecuador had been fighting each other over their border for years. It was largely an academic exercise, as much of the forest through which the border ran had never been mapped. As no one except Indians had ever even been there, they were basically arguing over imaginary lines on old conquistador charts.

Having squabbled over it since Inca times, they fought a full-scale war in 1941, ending with the "Rio Protocol", which was basically a lucky bag with neither side knowing what they had got until they had mapped the area. The US Air Force came along to help with the mapping, and it was soon clear that Ecuador had got the bum deal. They lost more than half their territory, a region rich in uranium, gold, oil deposits and whatever other resources would be discovered in the future. Ecuador had been stewing over this ever since. They went back to the protocol to pick through it forensically and discovered to their delight that it was full of holes. It referred to entire topographical regions that didn't even exist, as if the US cartographers had dreamt the whole thing up on drugs. The maps featured an imaginary mountainous watershed where there was in fact a river, and as a result, an eighty kilometre stretch of border could never be finally pinned down.

Unfortunately for me, this disputed area was just up the road from Vilcabamba, and for a whole series of reasons, the idea of another war was beginning to appeal to both sides. The Ecuadorian vice-president had recently fled the country to avoid prosecution on corruption charges, and his government was looking for a distraction, while Peru was experiencing an economic downturn and wanted to boost morale somehow. Peru had always had the strongest and best equipped army in the region and was itching to show it off. Since no one could give me a straight answer about the level of risk, I couldn't decide whether I should leave immediately or not. Everyone was hoping for war, but few believed it would happen. The farmers imagined that it would bring better prices for their sugar, the shopkeepers hoped to get rich selling things to soldiers on their way to the front, and the local priest was looking forward to a surge in devotion. Ministers started visiting barracks and overseeing parades, and brass bands buffed and polished their instruments.

Troops were flown in to try and find this nebulous border once and for all, but it was proving difficult since the location was so remote and hostile that it was difficult to get to, or even to move in once you were there. Helicopters dropped troops into clearings or on riverbanks, where they were then trapped. The jungle was impenetrable, a cat's cradle of vines and leaves, shrouded in mist and overrun by snakes and monkeys. No one really knew where they were supposed to be going, and with only fictitious maps, how could they ever be sure where the border was, where they should start fighting? And even if they thought they found it, communications were so poor they couldn't tell anyone else. Satellite phones were the only thing that worked, and neither army had enough of them. Once the soldiers were dropped in, they were swallowed by the green abyss and not heard from again, like astronauts on the far side of the moon.

The threats and name-calling from parliament seemed to go on for ever. It was such a fuzzy thing to be fighting over – a line on paper which, although it claimed to be a map, was really just a series of squiggles, some of which bore a certain symbolic relationship to reality and others which were just spirals across a page. Something more clear-cut – a decisive act of aggression – was needed to get things up and running. But with Latinos being so phlegmatic by nature, there was little chance of this. The wait was getting embarrassing for everyone, because by this stage the attention of the world was on us. We were the latest international war. Clinton had been briefed; the UN were preparing a statement; the news networks were deciding whether to send in crews; and meanwhile, forty miles south of me, Peruvian and Ecuadorian soldiers were wandering blindly through the forest, hoping that by pure coincidence they might bump into each other and there might be some shooting. All anyone had ever wanted was a bit of shooting and killing to sort things out, one way or the other. The uncertainty made everything more tense, and Vilcabamba wasn't a place I wanted to be any more, but I had promised Nadine I wouldn't run away again, at least not until she came back from Seattle. Her mum wasn't getting any better, and it wouldn't be fair to leave now.

It was on a Sunday – malaria tablet day – that war was finally declared. No one really knew what the trigger had been. Some say it was a shot fired during a football match that the two armies were having in the jungle, others that soldiers from one side had discovered a cocaine processing plant belonging to the other and they couldn't agree how to split the profits. Maybe it was simply a lack of communication: one thought the other said they were at war, so they were.

Either way, an army corporal turned up at Caravanserai to explain that foreigners wishing to leave would be allowed to, but any who remained were expected to assist the war effort. I discovered that the work visa Demofilo had arranged for me committed me to certain obligations to the state: I would not be eligible for combat, but I was to be put in charge of overseeing the recruits from Caravanserai. Every community was expected to organise and equip its own reserve battalion. As part of this, the hostel was to provide ten men – to feed and clothe them and arrange a time and location for their training. The army would provide a drill sergeant and weapons, but it was up to us to house the sergeant and store the weapons. Demofilo said he would oversee preparations for putting the hotel on a war footing and make arrangements for the protection of any remaining guests, but it was my job to carry out most of the work. There was a fear that Peru, which was far richer and bigger than Ecuador, would pour troops over the mountains and annex the whole region, and as a result a few people were panicking and smashing up everything they owned so that the Peruvians wouldn't get it. My first job was to make sure no one harmed the hostel.

This was all I needed!

To be annexed and end up a prisoner-of-war on Peruvian soil: how the hell had I got myself into this? It's what happens when you listen to angels. It reminded me of the feeling of flipping around in the shower tray, except that this went on day after day, and no one was going to come along and switch off the power.

Choosing which of the staff to send to war was the hardest thing I've ever had to do. I was a child, a deluded dreamer who slept in my Star Wars duvet back at home. How could I decide the fate of another man? And what sort of messed-up world would put me in that position? I wasn't even Ecuadorian, for God's sake. Demofilo had told me to line up all the workers on the verandah and together we would choose. It was like picking your team in the schoolyard, except I was more the grim reaper than team captain. We tried to be as fair as possible, knowing that in most cases the wives and children of these men would still be working for us. I hate to think what they must have thought of me, and yet there was so much to be done that I soon forgot all about it and spent the rest of the day sandbagging windows, battening doors and draining the swimming pool to make it into a bomb shelter. We used the tourist ponies to transport ammunition to an arms cache that we had dug in the same coffee plantation that Eve and I had spent our day sprawled in. I was delighted when the ponies were requisitioned by a battalion on its way to the front and we had to abandon the work. It was a crazy, nasty time, but sickly exciting too.

We sat up that night waiting for the pounding artillery, the burning sky, the long lines of weary, blood-soaked men, but nothing happened.

Gradually both governments realised that their troops weren't ready. They weren't even in position since they hadn't been able to build camps or trenches. They could hardly move through the mud and still weren't even sure where the border was. To their horror, both governments realised they would have to bring out their air forces. It was the last thing they wanted. Neither had very many planes, and the few they had were still being paid for by instalment. They would have to keep up the repayments even if the planes were destroyed, and there was no way they could afford to replace them. They had only bought them for ceremonial occasions – fly-bys at parades and such – certainly not for fighting over treacherously misty areas of jungle. Whatever little training the pilots had was for air acrobatics, not combat. Everything was getting terribly messy; both sides were keen to call it off, but they couldn't lose face now that the world was watching. Secretly they started peace talks even before a shot was fired.

The situation was particularly grave for Ecuador. It was far poorer and had fewer planes than Peru, and the few it had were cheaper and older. Demofilo managed to get access to the internet terminal in Banco del Andes before soldiers decided it was a strategic facility and smashed it up so that it couldn't be used by Peru when they annexed the area. The information he downloaded made it clear why the army was being so defeatist. Peru had a squadron of super-nimble Mirages and Matra Supers, all fitted with the latest airborne-intercept radar and air-to-air missiles, while Ecuador had basically bits of old scrap. Every night the news showed glossy footage of Mirages and Kfirs but I could see no Ecuadorian markings on them, and they were probably just shots from the company promo videos. The Ecuadorian president, Sixto Duran-Ballen, boasted that we had the largest cache of Blowpipe Manpods in the world, but only because every other army had got rid of theirs after they had proved so useless in the Falklands and Afghanistan wars. Rumour had it that President Sixto bought them up on purpose *because* they were useless: he needed to lose the war as he had an interest in a cocaine factory on the Peruvian side.

The radio crowed day and night with jingoistic, rabble-rousing speeches, while the television news showed triumphalist, Rambo-like scenes of sweat-smeared soldiers, with bandanas and brave smiles, trekking in slow-motion through the forest, sharpening their bayonets and reading love letters from home. Everything was played to a soundtrack of stadium rock: U2, Dire Straits and Metallica. It was all so crass. Great action sequences of swarming helicopters and battalions of tanks were shown speeding through the desert, filmed using gyroscopic camera sweeps and overdubbed with lush, orchestral sounds, but it was all a lie. The war was being fought in the jungle, and I can't imagine anyone was fooled by this old Desert Storm footage which had been carefully edited and given a new voice-over. All I wanted to do was get the hell out, but by that stage the airports had been boarded up and the runways blocked.

The morning that we blew up a Chinook helicopter (which must have been donated by the US for drug enforcement work as it had the DEA insignia on it), we got drunk and made up a song about the captain and his crew. I remember his name was Garcia Rota because we made it rhyme with *puta*. He was with the 5th Jungle Division, and I got the feeling people thought it was a bonus when it was learnt that he had a young family. We all became malevolent, misanthropic. That same day we were told a Peruvian plane had crashed into a mountain in bad weather, and we felt invincible.

Bombers were forever tearing overhead on their way to the jungle to drop their payloads. Since the troops couldn't find each other on the ground and the pilots weren't skilled enough to fight in the air, all they could really do was carpet-bomb the old-growth mahoganies, brazil nuts and podocarps. Somewhere in there were a few soldiers, and by blindly blasting the place they hoped to hit one or two. The forest burned day and night as more trees were lost than in any forest fire. I thought of how the place had swirled with life and consciousness that first day I was cycling out from Baños and again on the day with Beth and Mordechai taking San Pedro, and it just broke my heart.

Poor Rory was in despair, on the verge of insanity. He had resorted to shooting at our own planes with his shotgun in fury over what they were doing to the trees, and for this he had been beaten and placed under house arrest. He would have been put in jail, except Luna was already in an internment camp on the coast under suspicion of spying and there was no one else to mind the children. It turned out that Luna was half Peruvian, although she had always claimed her accent was from a mysterious Spanish father. She had been arrested by a vindictive officer on the first day of fighting, and that was the end of my massages. I rode back and forth to Rory's house a few times to check on him during the first few days of fighting and to bring him food. He was literally losing his mind, and he didn't trust himself to be around his children any more. He asked me would I bring them to Caravanserai with me, to have them stay there, and I agreed. Lana, with her stoic, bright smile, seemed to know for certain that everything would work out okay, but poor Cedar's spirit had sunk as low as his dad's.

I got up one morning to find a Peruvian Mirage droning heavily over the farm, hanging menacingly in the air with no real objective other than to frighten us. I was about to go back inside, not to give it the satisfaction of my fear, when suddenly two Ecuadorian fighter jets came clawing towards it from the horizon. The whole thing was so surreal, like paper airplanes or conkers. Both sides rushing at each other, firing and missing by miles, then whirling round to try again. Why did they do it? Why try so hard? It must have been so beautiful up there, with the trees stretching to the horizon, the same view that had made the Huaorani man cry when the missionaries had brought him up. Could they not just fly off somewhere else? Surely there was enough room for them all? It was such a big, silky sky. Although the Peruvian's plane was faster and better-equipped, it was still two against one: why would he risk it? At most it would take ten minutes to get back to the border. If he turned now, he'd be back at base for breakfast, no doubt earning kudos for making direct contact, maybe even a medal for surviving enemy fire. But instead he kept on going, coming round again and again. I couldn't believe that the guns and missiles were so inaccurate. It was just as people had been saying. The government had barely afforded these things, and there certainly had been no extra money to maintain them or train people how to use them. That was why there were so few casualties so far. None of the weapons really worked.

I was just about to go inside again when the Peruvian plane flew directly into the line of fire of his own flak and its fuselage started spinning. The pilot managed to right himself for a moment and began gliding downwards, but then, with a flash of flame, the plane turned and tumbled, spinning like a sycamore seed. I could hear the cheering from people in town, as though we were spectators at a hunt or a beagling event.

A body ejected – the pilot I presumed; the second crewman must have died or been trapped – and as the parachute floated down, I could hear the pickups gunning-up in town, ready to track him down and finish him off like in a real hunt. He was still 200 metres up when a wind rose, sending him blowing over the forest, and we lost sight of him. At some point, he must have crashed through the canopy, and there was no way anyone could follow him there. It was virgin cloud forest, and few, other than Johnny Lovewisdom, knew their way around. I imagined the silk sheath stretched across the branches and the pilot dangling somewhere beneath. Could Johnny possibly be near by? The last I had heard he was based a hundred miles away, but I was told he wandered a lot. Was the pilot still conscious after smashing through the leaves? Could he cut himself out of the harness, and if so, would he survive the fall through the branches? Did he have a radio to call for help or was he slowly bleeding to death, his blood dripping on to the forest floor alerting panthers? There was no way of knowing for sure. No one would ever find him, unless somehow by sheer coincidence a logger or oil worker might look up at just the right point and see his skeleton dangling from a branch; that is, if it hadn't already been ripped apart by vultures or clawed at by jaguars from a nearby branch.

Perhaps the strings had tangled, twisting him up against a trunk, and he now lay breathing his last breaths against the cool, crisp bark of a mighty tree. Right at that moment, he may have been whispering his last confession to it, feeling that evanescent sense of love that only trees can give you. Eventually the bark would grow around him, knitting a scab over him or swallowing him whole, so that only later, when the trunk was felled and being milled into planks for patio decking, would his bones be revealed. The planks would most likely be discarded as unusable and milled into paper instead. Perhaps he would become a map, a more accurate and harmonious map.

The war was over within a week. Peace was declared and everything returned to normal. But when I heard about the Indians, I knew I had no choice but to leave: how they had been press-ganged into being trackers by both armies and found themselves fighting their own relatives; how Peru had used them as decoys to check for land mines and Ecuador allegedly used them as human shields. All those bombs dropped on the forest hadn't landed on soldiers but on the Indians, the few hundred communities of Shuar and Aguarana living there. It was they who owned the thousands of acres destroyed and poisoned. It was through their hunting grounds that the hundred thousand mines had been laid, the same mines that would be blowing them up for years to come.

I had to get away after that. It had all been a great mistake. I should never have come. This was a pathetic place. To think I had thought I'd find the answers here. It was a land in which every potential and high hope invariably turned to dust, a place known for its magic realism, only because reality was too grim to bear.

Chapter 10

BACK IN IRELAND, I did what everyone did there in those days: I stagnated. It was endemic. The muggy climate engendered lethargy, mildew spread through the mind, and one's hopes mouldered. Back then the whole island was a composting chamber in which enzymes in the rain mixed with fear and alcohol leavened inertia. All the new ideas stirred up by the shaman, by Rabbit, by the dog and even by that burning light in the sky were moribund in the wasteland of pre-boom Ireland. They simply perished on contact, suffocating in the clamminess. I did try to remain open, I really did, but this was a place for preserving tradition, not imagining new ones. Only cynicism really thrived, and I soon learnt to keep my mouth shut.

Beside my bed, ribbons of job applications had been cut out and left for me. My family thought it was time to begin my life, to dust down my BA in cretinhood and get on to the ladder. Instead, I went back to the farm to work in the fields again, digging potatoes for the summer – praying the soil as old Diarmuid used to say, each potato a bead on the rosary around my neck. I spent the winter pulling leeks, growing strong and learning from Diarmuid (whose gout had cleared up) what the world was really all about. He regarded it as his personal mission to stitch my frayed mind back together, back on to the weave on which this world is embroidered, taking care to trim any remaining dreams off at the edges. And I must say it worked for a while. I was happy working during the day and going to the pub at night. Life was simple and good;

there was a relief in stagnation, in knowing that fomentation was arrested. But it couldn't last for long.

I tried desperately to hide it from myself, but secretly I knew I was back where I started, without any of the answers. And now I didn't even have Rabbit any more. I hadn't missed him until I got to the farm, but while digging away at the drills, I came to notice the absence of his running commentary, his insights, his mild mockery. I remembered how we used to be closest when I was weeding my herb garden as a child. The back garden was our safe space. We knew no one would find us there, find me talking to myself. It was our world outside the world. Now I wanted him back, but I had no idea where to start looking. All I knew for sure was that he hadn't disappeared entirely. He'd never do that; it's part of our deal. This wasn't the first time I had banished him, and I knew that if I really wanted to I could get him back. When I was eight, I was transferred from a largely girls' convent school to an academic boys' college run by Jesuits, and my life fell apart. The college was Neanderthal. In the convent, I had let the boys get on with their inane ball games while the girls and I lost ourselves in sophisticated make-believe worlds. Suddenly, at age eight I found myself in a place where the only thing more important than academic excellence was sporting prowess, and I hated both. They put me on a high stool, interrogating me about why I wouldn't play sports. When I told them it was because playing with balls was remedial and if they could think of a game which didn't involve balls I would be the first to join, they pinched me. I suggested swimming, and they pinched me again because they didn't have a pool.

I knew I couldn't survive there, and even if I could, I didn't want to. So instead, I decided to contract an illness, a serious one that would kill me off, but not too quickly, so that, if they really wanted to, my parents could recant, repent and make things better. That was when I had shut down contact with Rabbit: he didn't agree with the plan, so I simply got rid of him. It was easy. I just wished him away from the very core of my being, and when I was sure he was gone, I dug up all the herbs in my garden and stood them upside down so that the wind choked their roots and burnt the oils out of them to further clarify my intent to the world. The leafy ones – sorrel, Corsican mint – rotted into a sludge, while the dry Mediterranean ones – sage, verbena, tarragon – crumbled to dust. The feverfew and angelica were rare specimens from a castle garden belonging to the Guinness's and I was never able to replace them. Some weeks later I contracted glandular fever and spent months going from doctor to doctor with various real and phantom symptoms. Eventually I came to a compromise with my parents: as long as I agreed to turn up at school each day and passed my exams with average marks, they would allow me to continue drifting along in my own world. It was an acceptable solution in an imperfect world, but Rabbit, being a purist at heart, wouldn't go along with it, and he simply abandoned me for a year. It was at the time I needed him most, but I was in no frame of mind to go after him, to make space in my head for him. The fears had crowded in too close, and I couldn't connect to his world.

Now almost twenty years later, here I was on the farm, racking my brain to remember how I had got Rabbit back all those years ago, until suddenly it dawned on me that all I had to do was call him. Intention, that was all it took, like Dorothy rapping her heels together. I thought of Don Luis and how he said everything was there, beside us, just in other rooms we couldn't see. So I closed my eyes and wished as hard as I could, and sure enough one day as I was trimming leeks in the shed, Rabbit snuck through the tear in the fabric of time, popping back as though he had never left. To my surprise, he wasn't at all snotty about what I had done to him; how I had treated him after Eve; nor was he overly judgmental about what I had been doing since. I was sure he would say the whole thing had been a waste of time, a treadmill that brought me back to where I started, but instead he insisted I was right on track. I felt he was just sweet-talking me, and as if to prove it, he spent the next few weeks undoing all of Diarmuid's careful work – unpicking the stitches that Diarmuid had so patiently darned and setting my mind back wandering again. Around about Halloween my sleep became haunted by a series of dreams involving the spider again, but this time I wasn't so afraid, and I could hear that he, too, was talking about *Ame Rica*. Everything was to be found in Ame Rica, he claimed. Rabbit took up the chorus, and I knew they wouldn't give up until I took notice. Since I had been so wrong about South America, I thought I ought to check out the North. I owed them that much at least, and once I had enough money saved, I gave in my notice to the farmer, said goodbye to Diarmuid and headed back out on the trail again.

I couldn't decide whether to head east or west in America, and after finding a cheap flight to Seattle, I chose the latter. The fact that Eve had made her last movie in Vancouver, just across the border, and that the little pebble she gave me had come from the Queen Charlotte Islands nearby influenced me a bit, too. I wanted to bring the pebble with the tiny turtle painted on it back to where it had come from. Also, I had met someone in Caravanserai who had invited me to visit them if I was ever in British Columbia, which was just north of Seattle.

Arriving at Sea-Tac airport was a revelation. Stepping out of the airplane into the mystical light of the Pacific – that aureate glow that had lit every Hollywood movie – made me realise I was in the right place. This was what Rabbit meant when he talked of sweetness, of Rica. It was the light of dreams, the splendour of promise. I had no idea such light even existed before. I always thought it was make-believe – a phantasm of klieg lights, filters and deflectors. The air felt so pumped full of ozone, full of such latent possibility, that it uninhibited my inhibitions, and I resolved to give myself over to this place entirely.

This would be a success.

Taking a bus into town, I went to a coffee shop which shimmered with handmade tiles in burnt sienna and dark stained wood and a huge plate-glass wall that brought the street right inside. It was exhilarating. Outside were the custard cabs, the chrome-sequined trucks and brownstone buildings I had grown up with on the screen. Inside was a line of happy, sallow people in soft cottons, oozing insouciance as they queued up for their terracotta bowls of coffee, their faces lit from the side by gentle spotlights bathing them in the umber and ochre of a Renaissance altarpiece. So much love had been lavished on a simple coffee shop, which was not just for the elite but for everyone. Behind them was a bank of lavish pastries backlit for dramatic effect. It was when I realised that these people were actually queuing to pick one out for their *breakfast* – that in fact the pastries were a plausible morning meal – that my mind awakened fully to the new world I was in. The muffins and cookies and brownies weren't snacks or elevenses or dessert; they constituted an acceptable meal in themselves. What a concept. And then it struck me that, of course, North America is the New World, and that if I were to reinvent the world, I too would start out with only the very best.

I phoned my friend Fabian from outside the café. He remembered me from Caravanserai without too much prompting, and after some initial hesitation invited me up to his farm in the Canadian Rockies. He was preparing to build a yoga hall out of bales of straw, he said, and could do with some extra help.

He gave me directions from Vancouver, and it was the moment I crossed the border from the US into Canada that I realised Vancouver was going to be even more startling than Seattle. On stepping out of the bus station, I was shown the way by an incredibly helpful pickpocket, who got arrested only seconds after guiding me. The staff at the youth hostel were even more charming. In fact I thought the whole thing was a setup, that I was on Candid Camera, or something. They practically hugged me when I came in, asking me all about myself, what I was up to, what I was interested in – and not in any fawning, insincere way, but with what appeared to be genuine interest. As they talked, a queue built up behind me, none of whom seemed to be bothered by the delay. Everyone was happy and relaxed. Everyone buzzing on coffee and cookies: fulfilled, sanguine and satiated. I hoped anthropologists were recording this. This was a whole new breed of humanity. It had been hard enough to explain the Shuar to Diarmuid, but West Coast Canadians . . . I couldn't even begin to make him imagine such people. Where was the greed or desperation or suspicion? What evolutionary leap had these people made, and how did the rest of us miss out? The staff weren't the white Wasps I had imagined West-coasters to be, but Polynesians, Asians, Latinos, all of them sharing an endearing ebullience and speaking the most animated English, like bells tolling in celebration. Posters on the walls announced what each of them were doing that evening, in case anyone was feeling lonely and wanted to join them. Where was the ennui, the cynicism?

I thought of the apes in *2001: A Space Odyssey*; how the movie had traced their evolution from lone hunters who, over time, formed societies once they overcame their fear of each other, and how the societies had begun to fight and learned to use sticks as weapons. The film had shown their lives continuing more or less unchanged for generations, until one ape, daring to imagine what lay beyond his environment, had thrown a stick up into the sky. The stick had spun and spun out into space, until after millennia of further evolution, it led eventually to space exploration. I remember how disquieted I had been at the time that the spaceship had an American flag on it; I thought it was crass and jingoistic. Only now did I realise that it could only have been American. America and Canada were the apogee of the evolutionary process, the bravest and most innovative of all races, who had come together to form a new society. It was the optimists, the dreamers and visionaries who had headed west, while the pessimists stayed at home scratching a meagre existence from the exhausted soil. I realised that I was one of those sluggards. The inhibition and suspicion that defined me had been discarded by people here as antiquated relics of a harsher time, no longer necessary in this new world, this world of abundance, of double-chocolate-chip brownies.

Ame Rica. This was what Rabbit had been talking about.

I spent a few days in Vancouver, mesmerised by its affluence and, in spite of myself, becoming infected by its miasma of nonchalance. Soon I started to believe I had as few cares as the locals did, who, if the papers were to be believed, were concerned only with finding somewhere big enough for the gay pride rally, deciding whether yet another warehouse should be converted into a public arts space and choosing how many Greenpeace flags to put on each lamppost. Like dolphins, everyone seemed to spend their time playing. People of all ages were jogging, rollerblading, playing Frisbee, hackie-sack and other games I had no names for. Girls in bikinis on rollerblades pushed old people in wheelchairs; distinguished old men in shorts and long hair pulled trolleys full of multicoloured toddlers, who all whooped and cheered at the sight of flowers and trees. Fat people didn't try to hide their weight, and old people didn't hide their years. The bay was teeming with canoeists, nudists, scuba-divers, smiling children in yachts and tiny water taxis that ferried you around the city. There were no hobby fishermen because that would be harming fish. Above me, a zero-emissions Sky-train slid between spectacular modern buildings, and right in the centre of town was a park with ancient rainforest dense as any jungle and rose gardens and beluga whales, too.

I knew for certain I was in the right place: somewhere where even old people were young; somewhere expansive and buoyant. South America had been a bad idea from the start. It just wasn't the place to go looking for life or love. I knew that now. After my time in Africa, I had seen enough war, enough death. I was looking for somewhere young now, somewhere fresh and brave. North America had always been a light in the dark. A place where people chose to reimagine their world, to take a fresh canvas and dare to fill it with their dreams. "The frightened never set out. The weak died along the way. Only the bravest and greatest survived," I read on a sign celebrating the pioneers. This was where I needed to be: among a people who dared to believe in their own potential.

I booked myself on a Greyhound heading up into the Rockies towards Nelson, where Fabian lived. The journey took fourteen hours, and as the road snaked endlessly through a carpet of cedar and hemlock, I imagined the whole of British Columbia must be one great forest, broken only by lakes and rivers of pristine clarity. It was so sparsely populated you could scream without disturbing a soul, and I could see why it had become a haven for loners ever since the first reclusive immigrants who couldn't fit in with other settlers on the prairies had arrived a hundred years before. There was nothing but trees and water for miles around to disturb you. During the Vietnam War, the first misfit, loner immigrants had been joined by American draft dodgers, and ever since it had been the place of choice for the eccentric and alienated: Trotskyites, Buddhists, naturists, tree-huggers, drag queens, freeway fighters, alternative artists and animal rights activists. A lush haven with a sense of wilderness as potent as any desert.

The bus driver was a woman, admirably obese, with thighs as wide as basins and a forehead pumping sweat. She wore shorts and sandals with Velcro straps that crunched from the strain of staying on, like ballet pumps on a battering ram. Uncle Sam's wife. She was incredibly able: at stops outside malls and diners, she hauled her massive form up and out through the narrow metal door to load and unload crates on to waiting trolleys. She was like a human crane and gave no sign of resenting this extra stevedoring role on top of steering her whale of a bus through the mountains. In fact, she was irrepressibly vivacious, and after each stop, once she had manoeuvred herself back behind the wheel and wiped the cascading sweat from her face, she would make sure to tell us – still panting and in a speech parenthesised by gees, whizzes and darns – when the next "coffee 'n doughnut" break would be. Instead of the Jean-Claude Van Damme movie that had played on the bus in Colombia, she showed Sidney Poitier's *Guess Who's Coming to Dinner.*

Around midnight, the bus pulled into an ocean of concrete outside yet another Wal-Mart in the town of Nelson, and I saw Fabian there waiting for me. He was sitting in an old crimson pickup parked in a pool of floodlight, and he shouted to me to throw my bag in the back and hop in. He looked as Van Goghian as I remembered – the same haunted eyes burrowing into his skull, the close-cropped orange beard and a face that was always in semi-profile. One eye was better than the other and so he rarely looked front on. There were two others in the cab with him, and they slid up to make room. They looked spaced out, their eyes either turned inwards or gazing blankly through the windshield. Fabian reached across and kneaded my shoulder by way of welcome.

"It's good to see you again, my friend," he said. "We're in the middle of a mantram workshop in Cold Creek right now. I've paid for you; it's my treat. It's a three-day thing. Started today, but you'll easily catch up. We've all been mantraming since dawn. We're pretty spaced, actually."

The others nodded in agreement.

"Thanks," I said.

I had no idea what he was on about. What was mantraming? I had come across Fabian with his partner Melanie and her daughter Llael in the plaza in Vilcabamba a few weeks before Eve arrived. I couldn't have missed them. Fabian was dressed in a Renaissance chemise and carrying an easel, while Llael, who was almost four, was wearing what looked like a Mexican wedding dress. I told them if they came to Caravanserai I'd give them a good rate. We had got on well together. Melanie had chandelier eyes and a smile that made me smile; she brightened up everything. I used to wake especially early just to sit with her as she breastfed Llael on her knee. (It was quite a spectacle. I had never seen an almost four-year-old breastfeed before.) Fabian travelled with an espresso pot and made a big ritual of brewing dandelion root coffee each morning with water he fetched from the spring. They told me that they lived in a simple cabin in the woods in western Canada and grew all their own fruit and vegetables. This was all I had known about them. I had been so touched when he handed me his address when they were leaving that I never really thought to ask much else. Now I was beginning to regret it. Travellers were always exchanging addresses, but no one had invited me to actually come stay with them before. What had I landed myself in for?

I was racking my brain, trying to think of a suitable way to find out what mantraming was without sounding stupid, when a deep whine started up from nowhere. It was the sound of a drill in a far-off tunnel, or a beehive in a hollow trunk – neither industrial nor natural, but somewhere in between. First I thought it was the pickup which was creaking and rattling as Fabian threw it around the bends on the forest road, but then I realised I could actually feel it reverberate through my stomach. It was getting louder and louder, but when I looked around it seemed the others couldn't hear it. They were staring straight through the windscreen as if in trance. I turned around trying to track its source, but it seemed to bounce off the side panels of the pickup. Then the pitch changed and it grew even louder, like an approaching biplane. I looked to Fabian, and it was then that I noticed that all three of them, like monkeys, had their bottom jaws jutting out. The sound was coming from them.

I sat back and waited politely until eventually it began to quieten. It ebbed away for a second, before each of them took a deep breath and began again. It was a good twenty minutes later that Fabian turned to me saying, "It's trippy, yeah? But beautiful. Feels like you're disembodied."

"Oh," I said.

"And it makes your chakras spin like nothing else – like caesium atoms," his friend added.

I couldn't think of a suitable reply . . . *How interesting!*

"You're really lucky to find this place, you know?" Fabian said.

"Yeah, I know," I replied, relieved to be on more solid ground. "I never thought it would be so remote. I'm amazed there was a bus here at all."

"No, that's not what I meant," Fabian corrected. "I mean, finding yourself in this place, at this time. This is a special place. It's powerful. People come here to process their shit. To stir it up and move on. You get drawn here. It's like a vortex. The Sinix't Indians never stayed: for them it was a place of transmutation, transcendence. It had been abandoned for centuries until the Doukabours – Russian renegade pacifists – discovered it; now more and more people are heeding the call. You don't choose it, it chooses you and you never regret it."

"Oh," I said again.

I was beginning to realise how little I knew about Fabian. These days it seemed everyone was an alchemist, everyone after their own alembic. Although part of me was open to all this, another part wanted to run a million miles away. I had had enough. In my mind I was already preparing myself for the long ride back to the coast.

"You've sure picked an interesting time," one of the others on the bench said. "They're taking the old-growths down, and we're just beginning to get organised. Stuff is happening."

The bus ride had cost me $75, and I was already kicking myself about the waste. I should never have come. I should have headed east to New York or south to New Orleans.

Fabian pulled the truck into a clearing in the forest which was empty except for a large log cabin built against a stand of hemlock firs. We all piled out and made our way into a room crammed with people dressed in earthy colours: men in plaid with beards and women in loose halter tops of ochre, burgundy or the white chocolate colour of organic cotton. I was winded by the smell of candles and eucalyptus. There were people everywhere – lining the walls, sprawled on the floor and even perched up on the joists – and everyone was holding little cups of herb tea or apple juice. In the centre of the room was a massive wood stove like what you'd imagine the boiler of a ship to look like. It was swelteringly hot, and sweat was running down the log walls like a sauna. I could hear noises similar to the ones Fabian and his friends had been making coming from different parts of the room. It reminded me of the buzz of a pylon or a washing machine stuck in spin cycle. Someone somewhere was playing a didgeridoo, and four women in shorts and bras were dancing and trailing long muslin veils that appeared ghost-like in the candlelight. One of the women was shouting spontaneous prose:

". . . draping Spanish moss, clockwise spinning and into my breast her hand rubbing my heart of flowers: pink, purple, parting my legs, red ones in my vagina, nosegays between my thighs, daisies and peonies. Open the lily, cream petals with peach-blushed innards. I smell, I moan – I will go deeper . . .”

Fabian dragged me across the room to meet his friends. A litany of new names: Fire-cat, Sophia, Frost. All of them gave me long meaningful hugs and congratulated me on making it this far. They were bubbly with excitement about what they had been learning in the mantraming class and were trying out the new nasal and throat sounds that Portia, their “awesome” workshop leader, had taught them. It sounded like morning in an old folks home, everyone expectorating uuhuughs, aayaahs and eeaayes.

A girl called Yashmack said I looked drained and began to massage my shoulders, while her boyfriend took my feet and pressed hard into them at different points. Fabian looked on, proud of his friends and proud of himself for having brought me to such a special place. From either end of me, the couple stared into each other’s eyes, winking kisses. I know I was supposed to feel cherished by this, but actually I felt more like a condom between the two of them. I imagined myself a nineteenth-century adventurer stumbling upon an isolated community of Aryan pioneers somewhere remote like Ceylon or Mauritius. Everyone in the room was white, and quite a few had the spiky crown and wispy facial hair of Teutonic ancestry. These people were of European extraction but behaving in a completely new way.

Although I was intrigued by this glimpse into Fabian’s world, I couldn’t get Diarmuid and the farm and our evenings in the pub out of my mind. That was what I needed now, a drink, a stiff one. It had been a long day and this was all too much. I mean, I’m open to new things, but there’s a limit. I had the sense not to ask for the drink; it was a strictly herb tea sort of place. The young couple finally gave up pawing me when Fabian explained to them that I must be exhausted after the ride, and he went off to find me a space to lie down in up in the attic. He returned with a meditation mat as a bed for me.

Yashmack's partner said, "Yashmack and I made love on that earlier
– our sleeping bag was just too noisy. I hope you don't mind. I think we
cleaned it after . . . it'll be infused with fire energy anyway."

I ignored the comment and went off to lie down, but I could smell
the semen from it, and it made me feel more like a condom than ever.

Next morning I was woken before dawn by a girl walking through
the web of mostly naked sleeping bodies that had formed around me in
the night. She was banging a gong. Everyone was sticky from the heat
and dancing that had continued long into the night, but as there were
no showers we all just pulled on our clothes and headed down to the
main room, where I saw the workshop leader, Portia, for the first time.
She was a huge Japanese woman who spoke in a heavy Québecois
accent. She must have managed to find a shower somewhere as she
smelt immaculate and even had flower petals in her hair. I sensed she
got off on this mark of delineation. She was breathing in deeply as
though revelling in our staleness.

"Consciousness is not in man . . ." she said to us by way of
introduction and the others replied in unison, ". . . man is in
consciousness."

"Goood, goood," she intoned in her nasal Québecois whine.

She repeated the same thing ten times, and we answered her like the
rosary. Then she got us to do a warm–up exercise: slapping our own and
our neighbours' knees and bum. I couldn't get Diarmuid and the farm
out of my head. I wanted to know what he would make of it. I wanted
to know what I had let myself in for.

Portia lined us up against the wall, telling us to breathe through our
base chakras, but before she could go any further, Fabian put his hand
up and was passed the talking stick.

"Portia," he said, pushing me forward, "I have brought someone
new to the group."

Portia was squatting sumo–like on top of the stove, and as I wobbled
towards her she scanned me searchingly.

"Yes, I could sense your resonance," she finally said. "It's out of synch with the rest of us, but don't worry. Do you understand the principle of entrainment?"

I shook my head.

"Of course not," she cooed and went on in the sing-song, turgid pedagogical-speak North Americans are prone to, "Entrainment is the process in which harmonious sound when projected at disharmony brings it into resonance. Mantraming is the sustained, vibratory sounding of single tones to open portals and stimulate sympathetic vibration, just as Aum, Amen and Abracadabra are keys to releasing stored knowledge."

I found it hard to follow her. The sound of her voice was so odd that it was difficult to concentrate on the meaning. Either one or both of her parents must have been Japanese, but there was no trace of this in her voice, which was the alluring but discordant blend of French, British, Creole and American that makes up the Québecois accent. I could see how she would have become interested in sound. Every vowel she spoke was a mini mantram.

"Joy will demonstrate for us," she said.

I didn't hear her the first time, but all of a sudden I became aware that she was looking straight at me, and that she had stopped talking.

"Sorry?" I said.

"Joy will demonstrate," she repeated, and a girl who must have been Joy came and knelt in front of me, letting out a spontaneous, intuitive, primal sound straight into my bellybutton.

"Your cells are beginning to move," Portia said approvingly. "I can feel it. They're harmonising. You may feel light-headed."

When Joy had moaned into me for a few minutes, Portia got up and put her arm around her and said, "Good girl, Joy. Excellent."

Poor Joy was panting from the exertion, and as she went to sit back down, Portia stopped her, saying, "Joy, love, it's you who needs energising now. Mocha will do you in return."

I looked at her, just to make sure she wasn't kidding, but she was quite straight-faced. I glanced around the room to make double sure, but all forty faces were staring back at me expectantly. Fabian was beaming with pride, basking in the reflected attention. I realised there was no way out. And so, kneeling down, I aligned my mouth with Joy's breasts, while Portia got her to hold my belly and told me to find the resonance portal inside myself and let it free. The room was focused entirely on me now.

"You need to find your inner zip," she said, "and release it."

I wished I had listened more to the Screamers. If I had allowed them work their juju on me, it would have made all this so much easier.

Opening my mouth, I forced out whatever sound I could, but it was nothing like the great bellow Joy had mustered, more like the tremulous *aaaghh* you give the dentist when he asks you to open wider. Portia was unimpressed. She told Joy to rub my belly clockwise, and got Fabian to stand behind me while I lent back into him. I knew the humiliation would continue until I got it right; I had to do something. So I imagined Eve. I imagined the moment she had walked out of Caravanserai and thought to myself, *If I could have at that moment made a sound, a sound of such transcendence that it would have lassoed her and pulled her back to me, what would that sound have felt like?* I saw it as much as heard it, a surging ocean swelling into the room, and all I had to do was open my mouth to let it out. I could feel it spewing up inside, rising through my diaphragm, and soon I realised it was going to come out one way or another. I wasn't in control. There was no way I could stop it now, and so I just freed my jaw and let it gush into the room, so loud and passionate it set the windows rattling, so loud that the folds on Portia's tent-like smock began to waft, and I feared the log walls might unseat themselves from their thick-carved grooves and we would all be crushed. The sound just poured on and on, out and out. Once let free, it proved impossible to dam. I found myself able to breathe in through my nose and out my lungs like a bagpiper, so that I was able to carry on until eventually everyone in the room broke into wild cheers, and Joy hugged me to her body. They had all felt it; it had seared them all, and still its echo continued to reverberate through the room like the burr of a beaten anvil. Poor Joy was clinging to me in floods of tears, and Portia reached out and stroked my cheek. She told me to stay sitting beside her for the duration of the class: I was the golden boy now, and all my cells and organs were buzzing like they were newborn.

The rest of the day raced by. Portia was like a magician; she could make sound physically appear and float in different parts of the room. She would let out a low rattly tone which gradually increased in pitch until a scraping sound came from the ceiling. It was like the noise of a passing truck, but it was in fact resonance, and its pitch remained fixed as hers ascended. When she added subtle overtones to it, bringing out the octaves and fifths, you could hear them hanging at different heights: the highest suspended close to the ceiling, the middle ones a few feet lower and so on down. It was spine-tingling.

After a lunch of seeds and leaves with whole-grain quiche, Portia brought us outside, leading us through the forest to an old water tank. We climbed into its steel shell and did more mantraming – boomeranging she called it. The tank made every sound become a never-ending song that came back louder and louder each time, so that we felt we were creating something that would last for ever, that would echo out through the universe until it eventually looped back to find us again.

Portia kept us in the tank most of the following day, training us to shake loose the rivets that held the steel panels together, in much the same way doctors use sound waves to break up gallstones. Our lack of success with this disappointed her, and on the way back to the cabin to prepare for the final ritual, which was to take place that evening, she told us to spread out into the forest and find a tree we felt drawn to and to touch it with our eyes closed. I picked out a cottonwood, because it was the only non-coniferous one I could find. She asked us to feel its energy, to hear it.

"If you know the right sounds, you can shut down the neurones that keep you focused on reality, on the film projector running before your eyes," she said. "You can get to see the frames between the images, to see how nature sees things. These are the sounds you used to use before the Tower of Babel, the ones babies still use.

"The trees are speaking to you," she went on in a slurred hypnotic tone. "They love you. They love *you* more than anyone else, because *you* are the wise ones, the ones who nourish them."

She went on like that, about how we were more aware, more attuned than other people, and that the trees loved us more because of this. I did my best to go along with it for a while, but it was hard going. I thought of Esteban's idea of using techno to manipulate people's brain patterns so that they would start caring for trees. I wondered was she up to something similar.

"You are the chosen ones."

Rabbit was shouting at me that you just can't go around saying trees love some people more than others. It's ridiculous; it's verging on racism. It's elitist at the very least. Rabbit said I had to challenge her – I couldn't just stand there and take it. He wanted me to rebuke her or at least walk out, but the others were so deep in communication with their trees – caressing them, staring hard into them – that I was reluctant to break the spell. It's hard finding anything to believe in in this world, and I didn't want to be the one kicking their sandcastle. I tried putting up my hand for the talking stick, but no one noticed. Even Portia had her eyes shut and was rattling on about the powerful effect we had on each branch and leaf. Finally I felt I had no alternative, and I cleared my throat.

"Wait there just a minute . . ." I said.

It was like I had pulled a plug: everywhere people grudgingly looked up, dazed and disorientated. They shook themselves reluctantly back to reality. Portia stared at me, startled. I could see she wasn't used to being interrupted. She pulled a grimacing smile to hide her impatience.

"Yes?" she enquired superciliously.

"Are you saying, trees prefer us to other people?"

"Not just us, my dear, all enlightened beings," she said patiently. "It is we who feel their life-force, who heal them, who know their pain. Our voice soothes them; our touch caresses them."

"Okay," I said, "but so does everyone else's, surely?"

"You are from an old country, Mocha, a dark one," she said. "Some things are difficult for you to understand. Not everyone is enlightened, you see? It is not their fault, but nature gets very little from them, only their anger and sadness. Its true strength comes only from us – not just the few of us gathered here, oh no, there are others, more of us, around the world – but very few I'm afraid. We must be strong. Mother Nature needs us now."

"You're talking about some sort of Über-race, are you?" I said.

"Don't look at it that way," she cried. "Just ask yourself, is it true? Feel it inside. The trees cry out for you, and only you can know if you are ready. We know you are – we all heard your cry."

Portia turned to the others.

"Remember, Mocha is from another place," she said, "a place of old energy. For him these things are hard to accept. He has come to us and we must help him."

She turned to me and asked, "Will you let us?"

I didn't know what to say. It was all so new to me, but I didn't make any protest when she gathered the others into a tight circle around me and got them to raise their right palm and point it at me. I listened detachedly as she went up and down the scale a few times, searching for just the right mantram before finally settling on a low cooing tone which she got the others to copy. The sound was dove-like, and when it was picked up by the other thirty people, it became so powerful that it made every hair follicle tingle and my middle ear twirl like a gyroscope. To have that much sound, that much attention, focused on me was incredible. So much good will. I could feel how keenly they wanted to help. They would have done anything; well, almost anything. (They weren't quite as devoted as Gina.) I found myself swaying back and forth, surfing on the vibrations.

"How do you feel?" Portia murmured in a silky tone, and I couldn't lie.

"Beautiful," I said. "Really beautiful."

She got them to continue mantraming for another while, and I hoped it would never end. Finally, she asked, "Now, do you see where we are coming from? Is it any clearer? May we carry on?"

I nodded. I was on a cloud far away. The film reel had stopped, and I was already out of the cinema, drifting heavenward. I scoffed at my backward ways which had tried to fight against the wisdom of these people, people infinitely more evolved than I would ever be. They went back to their trees, and I closed my eyes and reached out to mine, to the soothing bark of the cottonwood, waiting for more of Portia's lulling words. But before she had even opened her mouth, Rabbit was back.

This is shite, he said. *And you know it.*

I clenched my eyes to block him out, but he just came back louder and I knew he wouldn't let up. I had no choice in the matter. There was only one thing I could do now. It was one of those times when having an angel who thinks he's looking after you is a real pain.

"Look," I said to Portia at last, "I don't want to screw anything up for the others, or burst anyone's balloon or whatever, but none of this feels right. It just doesn't. I'm leaving."

"Of course," Portia cooed in a syrupy tone. "I understand. We all do. You're just not ready yet. That's okay."

The implied insult was cutting, but overall I was surprised at how easily she had let me go. Zealots are rarely so willing to let their acolytes slip away before they've converted them to whatever dodgy psychological Band-Aid had worked on their own personal disorder. As the others stared at me with obvious condescension, I made my way through the trees back to the lodge. I could tell Fabian wasn't pleased. I had let him down. He barely acknowledged me as he handed me the keys of the pickup truck and told me to come back and collect him after the ritual that evening.

Chapter 11

THE PICKUP, A four-litre GM beast with crude steering and a hiccupping engine, wasn't as easy to drive as I had hoped. But after a few false starts, I managed to get it out on the road and drove as far as the local diner, the Greedy Loon, which I had spotted on my way in on the first night. After two days of barely cooked grains, nuts and roots, I needed a dose of coffee and cake, and although the diner looked the sort of place that served dishwater coffee, it would be better than nothing. In fact, it turned out to be one of those great womb-like sanctuaries you find in remote areas: a diner with aspirations to being a hunting lodge, with a roaring stove and cosy banquettes.

Snuggling into a corner, I ordered hash browns and blueberry pie and gorged on mug after mug of decent coffee. I had an hour or two to waste before heading back for Fabian, and I frittered away the time writing my diary and racking my brain trying to think where I should go next. I should bring Eve's stone back to the Queen Charlotte Islands first, and maybe track down the native artists who painted it, then head south to Oregon.

Despite waiting two hours in the diner, when I got back to the lodge the final ritual wasn't over yet. I sat outside in the pickup listening to them, imagining them growing closer and feeling as one. I felt left out. Rabbit said I was back where I belonged, on the margins, just like in San Agustin and in the zoo in Baños and on my tree stump at school. As usual, it was him who had put me there.

Around about eight the doors flew open, and everyone piled out singing and shouting and hugging. Most of them avoided me like I was tainted, and I could tell Fabian was still annoyed. But he was so stoked from the final session that he couldn't help but smile. He was with Sophia and Frost, and they all had their arms around each other and were humming one of Portia's tones.

"We're going back to my place," Fabian told me a little curtly, "to smoke some spliff and do some more mantraming."

"You can drive," he added, with a hint of command in his voice.

I didn't feel like I had much choice in the matter. It seemed this was my punishment.

They all slid in beside me on the bench, and I pulled the pickup back out on to the gravel road. It was still twilight, but the heavy curtain of pine rising up on either side made it seem darker. It took all my concentration to keep the pickup away from the flood gullies and logging tracks that forked off the road at odd angles. A few times I took the wrong track and had to manoeuvre back again, which was hard on such narrow roads. Finding reverse at all in the shattered gearbox was a matter of luck, and after shunting back and forth a few times, my arms were aching and I was feeling miserable. A night of mantraming and dope lay ahead of me, and I had no interest in either. But it *was* only one night after all, and in the morning I could hitch into town and catch a Greyhound bus going somewhere, anywhere.

I was caught up with these thoughts, trying to decide what I'd do in Oregon and at the same time blocking out whatever rubbish the others were talking about, when Fabian turned to me, saying, "I've gotta clear the air a bit, you know? You let me down in there today. You did bad. I trusted you, I introduced you to my friends, and you let me down. You could have ruined the whole vibe. Luckily, we're all pretty balanced here, and it was cool, but . . . I treated you as one of us and you went all slumburbia on me. Maybe I shouldn't have expected so much – you come from a different place."

I saw immediately that this was the perfect get out clause for me, a way of leaving with honour intact, and I was about to explain that I felt so badly about what I had done that I was determined to leave the next day, and there was no point in trying to stop me. But I didn't get that far. A battery of shimmering light came charging around the corner at us, and I found myself completely blinded. The light was so disconcertingly bright and expansive that there was no way of seeing beyond it to where it began or ended. I immediately thought back to the alien light I'd seen in Baños, and I suppose I must have panicked. I remember stabbing for the brake, but it must have been the accelerator I hit, as the pickup jolted even faster forwards. Squinting my eyes, I stared as hard as I could ahead, but all I could really see was an incandescent white-out. I could hear the others gasp in shock as I went for the brake again and this time got it, but it was almost too late. The back tyres skidded on the gravel and I had to ease off. The meteor-like mass was still bearing down on us, and only when it was right in front did I make out the strip of spotlights above and below. It was a truck with all its beams on full. A logging truck. I swerved hard to make room for it on the road and it did the same for me, and we slid along each other's flanks. It had two trailers attached that stretched on for ever, like a train. The road was barely wide enough to hold us, and my right wheels only just skimmed the margin. Both our vehicles held tight and we made it safely through, with only my wing mirror smashed in the process. Everyone let out a sigh of relief, and I eased off my death grip on the wheel.

"Logger assholes," Frost said. "They really don't give a damn."

Glancing in the rear-view mirror, I saw the truck's tail lights sway from side to side, but I didn't dwell on it. I was sure he would slow down and right himself. But he didn't, and suddenly his back trailer jerked a good two feet across the road and we heard the screech of airbrakes fighting to regain control. He had swerved in too fast on passing me, and the back trailer had lost its grip. It was swerving now, imposing its control, wrestling with the cab for dominance. Suddenly, both trailers were wavering behind the cab, and I knew it couldn't hold. Fabian and the others, alerted by the screeching brakes, looked back.

"Bloody logger assholes," Frost said again.

In shock, we watched the rig fish-tail across the road, the second trailer plunging off into the ditch and we heard the clash of timber against metal echoing back at us as the logs came loose and tumbled off. It must have been the noise that set the caribou off. I was concentrating too hard on what was happening behind me. I know that. I should have slowed down, or even pulled over, but part of me wanted to get the hell away.

It was Sophia's shout I heard first.

"Oh my G . . .!" she cried.

Before I knew anything, the chassis jerked violently, and I heard the bone-jarring thud of my undercarriage hitting something big. We were hurled from side to side as the wheels rolled over it. A cloud of fur flew into the headlights, and I jammed on the brakes, but not in time to save the second one, a caribou doe, too shocked to run. The bumper hit her just below the knee, sending her feet buckling under and her torso lunging forward on to the hood. Her antlers came to rest just in front of the windscreen. She was alive, writhing and flailing on the bonnet, her forelegs battering the radiator grill for grip. I sat there watching paralysed as she got herself up, fell down again, and then up once more on her forelegs, dragging her hind legs across the highway, her hide matted with blood.

The four of us were frozen numb, my foot still digging redundantly into the brake pedal. It was Fabian who summoned the strength to get out first. Through the drool- and mucus-spattered windscreen, we watched as he walked in a pool of blood across the road, leaving a trail of red footprints over to the animal which lay exhausted in the far ditch. Fabian stood staring down at her through his weaker eye, before finally taking her crown in one hand and jaw in the other, and after steeling himself a moment, he jerked his arms swiftly, snapping the spinal chord. The doe fell limp, lifeless except the odd twitch of nerve endings denying the inevitable.

It was just as Fabian was straightening up again and turning to make his way back to the pickup that we noticed it. All four of us at the same time. Somehow we knew to look ahead, and there, standing proud on the forest road, right at the limit of the one unsmashed headlight, barely bathed in its beam, was a buck: a massive, noble caribou buck standing in the centre of the road, primordial and proud, with a rack of maybe fourteen prongs gleaming beige against the curtain of cedar behind. He stood there staring at us for maybe a minute until he was certain we had seen him, until he was certain we had realised who he was and what he was doing there. Then he turned and made his way solemnly down the logging road, his tines gleaming sporadically as they picked up shards of headlight. We were left with the rhythmical clicking of hooves on gravel and a feeling of disconnectedness, of rawness – and of having been somehow forgiven.

"My God," Sophia whispered. "You know what that was?"

She looked to Fabian.

"I know. I know," he replied.

"Are you sure?" Frost said. "You really think so?"

"What does your heart tell you?" Fabian asked.

"My heart," Frost replied with a tremor rising to his throat, "says yes. Says, of course. Says you know it is, you stupid sonavabitch! It really is."

"What?" I cried. "What is it?"

Fabian walked back across the road towards us. He was giddy now, and reaching in through the window, he mussed my hair, saying, "After you had your hissy fit and stormed off, Portia told us about an animal, a spirit animal, that would come to us. It would come to a few of us at once and would point the way, reveal our destiny. There would be no more ambiguity, no more grasping in the dark. From now on we'd know exactly what to do."

"So?" I said.

Killing caribou hardly seemed a worthwhile destiny.

"*That*, my friend, is what we must find out," said Fabian with a laugh. "The *so* is exactly what we need to know."

He opened the cab door and the rest of us poured out excitedly. The first deer I had struck, the one I rolled over, was tiny, the doe's fawn perhaps. It lay now in a heap, its lifeless eyes shining red in the glare of the tail lights, its neck twisted unnaturally, exposing a long tongue and smooth white throat.

Frost and Fabian hauled it into the ditch. They said we would return in the morning to bury them both. Meanwhile, we walked to the logging truck, which was a few hundred metres back, its cargo of a dozen logs scattered like a toppled temple.

Seeing the trunks so huge and lifeless, their scent intense from the upheaval – as though they had released their smell as a panic response – made everyone fall quiet. It was Frost who spoke first.

"I fuckin' hate it, man!" he said. "I fuckin' hate it. The carnage, you know? How can they do it? How can they kill these beauties?"

Sophia came and put her arm around him, saying, "After all the mantraming, after all we've felt, it seems even worse, doesn't it?"

"Bastards," Frost agreed.

Fabian had gone further up the road, and suddenly we heard him scream, "Oh my God!"

"What?"

"Come here, come here! Look at this!"

We ran up to Fabian, who was standing beside the first trailer, which had been covered in a tarpaulin that was now ripped, revealing beneath it just one single tree, a tree so large that it took up the entire width of the trailer. It was bigger than all twelve of the others put together, and was taller than the cab. The pinchers which fastened it down were stretched to their full extent, and even at that they were barely able to clasp a tiny section of it. It must have been a thousand years old.

Sophia vomited right there on the spot. Frost came and hugged her. He too was winded with the shock, with the pain. It was known that the government was going after the big trees now. The economy had collapsed a year or two before and it had decided to liquidate some of its assets. Canada, which had always been a paragon of responsible forestry, had turned suddenly merciless, but no one imagined they were taking out the really ancient ones.

Frost went up to the cab. There was no sign of the driver. Both airbags had been activated and lay spewed like spiders' webs across the dashboard.

"He must have gone to get help," Fabian said. "He's got to get himself a new rig fast, or else. If he's caught with that tree he's screwed. That's totally illegal; they could never have sanctioned it. It's probably why he was hauling it at night."

"We should get his name," Sophia said, pulling aside the airbag fabric and rooting around in the cab. A minute or so later, she stuck her head out, looking slightly awed.

"Come over," she whispered. "Come over here."

We followed.

"Take a look," she said.

It was just a normal trucker's cab with gaudy decorations and thick upholstery. We looked to Sophia.

"Do you notice anything?" she asked.

We didn't. "The colours. Look at the colours!"

I could see nothing unusual.

"Remember what Portia said?" Sofia thrilled. "'The answers will come on a platter. A platter made of gold and draped in crimson.' Remember?"

They nodded.

"Now look again," she said.

And sure enough the cab was a sort of crimson-purple. Everything inside was as gold as a tabernacle; even the carpet strands glinted with tinsel.

"Don't you see?" she said. "It's all here. This is what we have to do. It's about the trees. We've got to fight. It's what they want from us, what they *need* us to do."

Fabian found this so profound that he made no reply. Instead he climbed up on the cab and hugged Sophia. Then Frost began a long mantram, a keen for the tree, to let it know he understood, to let it know they all did, and that its death would not be in vain. They all joined in, and after a while, so did I.

I think we may have mantramed for about half an hour, and when we finally drove off with the smashed bumper clanging along the road, we headed straight to the police station to report the logging truck.

That was the moment at which everything went ballistic. Up until then it had all been a simple series of events. I could trace it on a linear map: from getting off the Greyhound to going to the workshop to getting to the police station, but after that everything took on a life of its own and I was just swept along.

First of all we went back to Fabian's house and spent most of the night ringing his friends, organising a vigil to make sure no one touched the tree trunk. Someone had obviously put an order in for that tree, and they would already be planning how to salvage it and get it out of there. Fabian was determined this wouldn't happen. From now on it would be under permanent guard.

His house was amazing. Half of it was of notched logs and the rest made of bales of straw coursed like bricks and plastered. It felt like a cocoon woven from its surroundings. The walls were undulant and hand-plastered with frescoes of wild circles. I slept that night in a cave-like corner surrounded by sacred signs.

At dawn, I found myself back at the crash site, building a blockade to stop other logging trucks getting through. The story had spread quickly, and people started arriving with food and drink for us, but once they saw the tree, this pillar of life, wide and tall as a cottage, as a whale, as the passage through the Red Sea, many of them burst into tears, pledging help and funds and whatever else was needed. The tree was dead now, the world's largest tombstone, but still it had power. The way the locals shuffled gently up to it, laying their hands on its bark, looking up in wonder at the endless length of its thousand-year timeline, reminded me of volunteers at a whale-beaching or children at Santa's grotto – that sense of awe mixed with impending loss. They were hoping beyond hope for an ET moment, the moment this alien consciousness would shake itself awake and stand slowly up again, creaking and groaning as it stretched out its few remaining stumps and stunted branches, grabbing whatever leaves it could find and finally stretching out proudly to the heavens in a triumphant sun salutation. Nobody wanted to leave, to face the fact that it was dead for ever. There was enough sap left in it to infuse them with an indeterminate conviction that they would feel emptier the moment they stepped away. The local paper ran a front page spread that afternoon, and from there things really snowballed. People switched from shock to anger. They began arranging community meetings, local government lobbying and a revival of the local watershed campaign. Within a few days, fundraising drives were being held, mission statements printed, blockades mounted at the entrance of the two major logging areas and a picket outside the timber mill.

I couldn't believe the whirlwind around me.

Opposition to the logging had been increasing for months, but seeing the size of this monster lying felled on the side of the road seemed to catalyse people, to galvanise them and provoke a whole new wave of outrage. Fabian was at the heart of it, and so, in spite of myself, was I. I certainly didn't choose it, but I couldn't just leave after creating such a mess. Somehow I had to find a way of paying Fabian for the damage to his truck, and in the meantime he seemed to presume that I would be willing to help out with a camp that was being built in the forest. It was to be situated right between the two main logging areas and would become the command centre of the whole campaign. Food donations and equipment were already being dropped off there, although it was still just a clearing in the trees with a water pipe and a shack which bears had been trying to raid. Fabian wanted a proper storeroom built and an office space, too. And I felt I couldn't refuse to do my bit. So every morning I found myself hiking up into the woods with my measuring tape and lunchbox for what became a crash course in building. I had always wanted to learn carpentry, and within days I was using skill saws and nail guns to knock up sheds and deer-proof fences. (It was pointless making the fences bear-proof, since the bears knew how to open gates.) After the first week, we had two buildings up, and we went on from there to build a full-scale campaign kitchen to feed the activists who were turning up in greater numbers every day.

I was amazed by the passion these people had for the forest. Sometimes, when we were up near the logging area, I'd see them crying, just from watching the lumberjacks at work. What to the loggers was a normal day's work was tantamount to murder to the campaigners: stabbing the trees with chainsaws, burying the whining engines to the hilt. The noise always brought me back to the Amazon, to that trip in to meet the Shuar. It was a sort of chorus echoing through the Americas, like how birdsong follows the dawn around the planet forming a ring of constant song. A song cycle of falling trees, like the keening at a wake.

I watched as a logger tapped a wedge into a fir one day, transfixed at the skill, the intuitive precision involved. When the tree let out a roar and tore through the last fibres and whooshed over, sucking in air as it went, I heard a scream. I was sure someone had been crushed. I ran through the undergrowth to help, and found Sophie there, unharmed, but standing over the ghostly trunk sobbing breathlessly. She was inconsolable. Beside her was a logger with his arm around her comforting her. A vision in red dungarees and spike-soled boots, his chainsaw and jerrycan dropped a short way off in his rush to reach her. He, too, had heard her cry and come running.

The idea at first, I think, was just to bear witness: to let it be known to the logging companies that people weren't prepared to turn their backs any more. The Doukabours were the first to come out in support of Fabian and his friends. They had come to Canada from Czarist Russia fleeing persecution in the late nineteenth century and were well used to such Davidic struggles. They had suffered imprisonment and even death to protect their belief in pacifism and vegetarianism back in Russia, and even on reaching Canada six hundred of them had been put in prison for three years for simply parading in the nude. For a few days, Fabian's house rang with the sound of their Cossack-glossed voices as they shared ideas on peaceful strategy with him, but that all changed the night a jeep full of loggers turned up in ice hockey gear and steel-tipped hockey sticks to frighten a group of locals protecting a watershed. Things ratcheted up after that. Everything turned nasty, and I was less keen to stick around than ever.

The whole thing was a minefield. We had almost shut down the timber industry, and as far as I could tell, most of the community were dependent on it in some way, either as mill workers, loggers, licensers, planters, surveyors or transporters. This was a remote community made up of the sons and daughters of immigrant trappers, lumberjacks and homesteaders, who had long ago lost touch with whatever crumbling part of Europe they originally came from and had never lived anywhere else. They wouldn't survive a day in the city and were just doing what they had always done, making a living from the land.

I began to realise that Fabian and his mantraming friends were completely isolated from these people. There was a virtual apartheid between the old community and the New Age blow-ins that had been bridged only to a small degree by the logging issue. They both realised that without the trees protecting the watersheds the area would become uninhabitable, but other than that, they were miles apart.

Fabian was part of a new crowd of maverick artists, spiritualists and back-to-the-landers who'd come to the area and built homesteads in the woods over the last twenty years. They all socialised together, arranging endless potlucks and workshops, and over time had built the equivalent of a parallel universe within the town to cater for their needs. Right beside the burger bars and drug stores of the regular community were two health food shops, each as big as a supermarket. There was an organic bakery, organic chocolate maker and organic coffee roaster. There was a hemp clothes shop and three New Age bookshops. The regulars walked past these every day without ever daring to set foot inside. These were frightening, bohemian dens, where everything smelt of incense and women didn't shave their armpits and people hugged in the aisles. The hugging was the biggest problem of all: whenever you met anyone you even half knew in town, you gave them a long meaningful hug, which meant the aisles were forever blocked by clinging couples.

It was only when I joined the picket outside the timber mill that I came face to face with the divide. The segregation was so thorough that it hadn't even impinged on me before; I had simply airbrushed the regular community out. Now, seeing them turning up each day at the mill in their scrappy clothes and beat-up cars, their faces grimy from decades of sawdust and resin, I realised how deep the split went. These locals were all completely bewildered by the protestors: by the girls in sexy tops and combat pants who hugged them and whispered beseechingly into their ears, the boys mantraming in support behind. I was uneasy with the whole thing. I thought of Diarmuid and what it would be like for him, on top of all the shit he faced digging trenches and spreading manure each day, to face this ordeal going to work in the morning. Meeting Steve made things even clearer.

I only got to meet him because of my need for coffee. It gave me a chance to slip across enemy lines. The alternative community didn't *do* coffee. (I don't know how the organic coffee roaster stayed in business, but from what I was to learn later it may have been a front.) They had their own juice bars and vegetarian sushi cafes so that they never had to set foot in the fast-food joints and diners of the regulars, never had to be tarnished by them. (When Fabian had picked me up from the bus outside Wal-Mart on the first day, he told me he had never been inside the supermarket, and none of his friends had been more than a couple of times at most. Either the neon lights gave them headaches or the merchandising made them nauseous or the injustices of foreign trading practices and slave-wagery of the shelf-stockers made them too angry. Some admitted, like recovering addicts, that they feared that if they saw the Frosted Cheerios and Oreo cookies of their childhood, they might suffer a relapse. In my time in the area, I was only in that supermarket once, and it did indeed appear an alien and sinister place in comparison to the small rustic health stores and artists' homes around it, like the set of a futuristic horror movie, a world of price smashing and frozen walls, only humanised by women called Bonnie and Yolanda who smiled as they scanned your items, and moms who slapped their bawling children in the aisles.

As it was, I was the only one of Fabian's friends who drank coffee, and although they were prepared to overlook this at first only because I was from a primitive place, I could see how offensive they found it. After a while I started going to the Greedy Loon on my own instead, so they wouldn't have to smell that oil tar aroma arising from the roasted grains.

It was at the Greedy Loon that I met Steve. I was ordering my daily 16oz mug when he heard my accent and came over to tell me about his cousins from County Cork. Steve had spent thirty years planting trees above and below the 60th Parallel – Canada's near-mythic line dividing the harsh southern territories from the even harsher northern ones. He started telling me about some of the Irishmen he had worked with, and what amazed me most was how many of them were now dead, killed by falling trees, snowdrifts, badly placed wedges, cougars and grizzlies.

"I even seen a young Belfast boy bitten to death by black flies," he said, "and that's why my wife, she got down on her knees and prayed the day I landed the job at the mill. The wages ain't a patch on before, but she knows she'll have me home each night, bringing my two arms and legs with me. That's worth something. It's worth anything. And yeah, the winters are bad, but nothing like up north. You wanna go North o' Sixty sometime, my friend; you wouldn't believe it."

We chatted on and gradually he brought the talk around to what was on his mind.

"Tell you truthful, them hippies is our only problem here. You have the same back in Ireland – the tinkers. It's the self-same thing. They don't eat like us, don't drink like us; they stays apart, but they is always around. Always hanging out, smokin' their dope, doin' nothin'. They don't send their wee 'uns to our schools, nor pay their taxes, but they use our roads all right, our water, our lighting, our everything, and none of us ever showed no heed. We let them have their fancy festival and rituals and *Bealtaines* – believe you me, you wouldn't wanna be here around equinox time. Wooo, man! No chance you'd get sleep with all the whoopin' and cooin' and cryin'. None of us, we don't ever say a thing. They come to our Thanksgivin' Parade bombed out of their trees on psilocybin mushrooms and march behind our union banners, our fire brigade floats, our lumberjack displays, and we can feel them jeering at us – surely to God we can. We know what they think of us, and what they think of our schools. My wife is on the school board, see? They had to let go a teacher just last year, 'cause of not enough kids. Meantimes them hippies have now wangled themselves some form of a therapist for their weirdo school!"

I sensed Steve knew exactly which side I was allied to. Although I mightn't have dressed in the same baggy hemp clothing as the others, my shaggy beard (which Fabian insisted I grow so people wouldn't think I was an undercover Mountie) gave me away. I had been coming to the Greedy Loon every day, and Steve had never once said a word to me before. If his plan was to influence me, he did.

But, it was Rabbit who really set me thinking: he had always told me not to get bogged down in duality, in wrong or right, black or white. The world was grey, he said; a mystery, not a problem. He got me to look at stuff from different angles, wider ones, and from there the idea of harassing loggers and mill workers didn't look so great.

Although it felt good to have a cause, to be fighting for something – not to be on the outside looking in for once – ultimately, I realised, there was enough fighting in the world already. I remembered how back in the Amazon, just before the dog had bitten me, I saw the whole thing was so much bigger than me, that somehow everything in the world had speeded up and was having so many unforeseen consequences, both great and terrible, that it wasn't for me to judge any more. This wasn't my fight, and anyway a fight wasn't what I was looking for. I was looking for love. I would have walked away right there and then, but I still felt I couldn't leave Fabian without paying for the pickup. To do that I would need a job, and finding one wasn't so easy. It seemed the alternative community rarely used money any more; everything was based on bartering. I was offered as many eggs as I wanted to build a compost heap for a cosmic palaeontologist, and free Reiki massages in return for apple picking, but no mechanic was likely to accept payment in eggs or Reiki. A Swedish family did offer me actual money to work as a facilitator in a New Age birthing wing they had built on to their cabin for natural home births, but they couldn't say how much it would be.

"We leave that to the discretion of the moms," the babushka-like wife had told me. "If you touch them deeply, I'm sure they'll respond in kind."

But that was hardly a guaranteed wage, and I thought the last thing the expectant mothers would want was to be touched deeply by me. In the end, it was Melanie, Fabian's bright-eyed partner with whom I had spent my mornings in Caravanserai, who came to the rescue. She was no longer going out with Fabian and instead was studying to be a Buddhist monk on an island off Vancouver and needed someone to help mind her little girl, Llael, who was now five. Llael was staying with her uncle, Hugo, who lived on the far end of an abandoned ski track and ran a transport business which took him away from home a lot. He needed someone to stay at home and look after Llael, and he was willing to pay me in real Canadian dollars to be a live-in nanny. It sounded ideal, although, of course, Fabian didn't think so. He wanted me to forget about the money and focus instead on the campaign. I was the catalyst for the whole thing, he said, and I had a vital role to play, a shamanic role, whatever that meant. I was intrigued that he had used the word shaman, but I explained that my Catholic conscience wouldn't rest until I had paid him every cent I owed, and a week later I moved to Hugo's.

Chapter 12

LIKE EVERYONE ELSE in the area, Hugo lived in a remote cabin with a large woodstove, no shower and an outside lavatory. The only difference was that his was even more remote than usual, perched high above Kootenay Lake with the snow-covered Valhalla Mountains soaring behind and forest stretching as far as the horizon. Hugo was strong and quiet. He reminded me of Robinson Crusoe, with that same reticence and far-distant gaze. Melanie told me he had spent some winters fishing salmon off Alaska when he was young and had been treated fairly coarsely by the crew. It left him with a wariness, an emotional bruising that never healed. Whenever he did talk he was equable, nothing ever seemed to upset or rile him, but I always had the sense he was holding back. Before he would utter any word, he would chew over it, fingering his beard methodically, until he was certain it was adequate and necessary. I was always prepared for something profound from him, but over time I began to realise that the amount he thought about something, vacillated over it, generally had no bearing on its importance. And although it was impossible to connect verbally with him because his only form of conversation were terse monologues, I liked him. He was easy to be around: solid, implacable and very generous. I couldn't believe how much he was willing to pay me.

Llael was another matter. Melanie had warned me before returning to the monastery that her daughter was no longer the angelic little girl I had watched being fed each morning in Caravanserai. First off, she was now fully weaned – she had stopped breastfeeding on her fourth birthday – and had developed a complex persona of her own. Yet, seeing her at the time, snuggled up on her mother's lap, I wasn't overly concerned. Admittedly her face had come to look a little sterner: it was thin and strong-boned, and her skull, which was bald, throbbed with veins. I presumed she had shaved to copy her mother, who was shorn for her novitiate, but in fact Llael's entire school had had their heads shaved rather than use chemicals against an outbreak of lice.

Melanie went back to her monastery once she had introduced me to Hugo, and it was only when she was safely cloistered away from the world that I learnt what she had meant about Llael. For the first five days I was there, the girl simply refused to acknowledge I existed. As far as she was concerned, Hugo had a ghost staying in the house which only he could see and hear. No matter how hard he tried to get her to listen to me or to let me help her, she just beamed back at him as though he were senile and needed mollifying.

"There's no one else here, Hugo, I'm afraid," she would say, in a reassuring tone.

Hugo would take a while to ruminate on her reply, to think over its various interpretations and implications and how best to respond to them each in turn, before normally settling on repeating the instruction in a firmer tone. The ball would then be back in her court, and she would slam it straight back with great force, insisting with her sweet, angel eyes that she honestly had no idea what he was on about. There really was no one else in the room, but if he wanted her to play "pretendy friends" she would. This always floored him. It was her inviolable assuredness more than anything. Hugo was a solitary individual, with an ever-questioning, amorphous mind, whose grip on the exterior world was intentionally kept slack, and he had never encountered the incontrovertible conviction of a five-year-old before. I think he began to doubt himself, but to his credit he never let it show, and to her credit she never once let her guise slip. I had to admire her resolve. I even picked her up in my arms once and hung her from the ceiling, and she reacted as though thoroughly mystified, as though a force of nature had suddenly cast her heavenward.

"Look, Hugo, I seem to be floating," she had cried.

The whole thing would have been merely amusing if not for the fact that the moment Hugo left us alone Llael changed entirely, and she no longer made any attempt to hide her awareness of me, or her contempt, for that matter. If I dared even make a noise or interfere in any way with her life, her face broke into a scowl of such ferocity that it chilled me. Llael was the first child I had known, and I found her intimidating and intriguing in equal measure. I longed to know what was going on inside her head. Her dedication and perseverance to the ruse were awesome, and it certainly was having what I reckoned must have been the desired effect: my dreams began to become haunted with dejection, with my own inefficaciousness. My self-esteem crumbled. Over time, her disdain managed to corrode right through me so that I found myself trying to avoid her at some points during the day, at least until I was feeling stronger. She had succeeded where the Screamers had failed. I was seriously thinking of leaving, but I needed the money and I knew I would never find another job. Cleaning up placenta in the Swedes' birthing room in the hope of tips was a non-runner. I knew that if Llael ever got to me when I was feeling weak or tired I would crack. I just hoped it wouldn't come to that. I tried talking to Hugo about it, but she was so careful never to reveal herself in front of him that he doubted my sanity.

He muttered reassuringly, and with great pensiveness, about how: "These things, yes . . . these things are . . . *difficult*, at first. Difficult . . . All of us, we have . . . by and by . . . to, to get, *well*, used to each other. To accustom ourselves. Yes."

I got the sense he didn't believe a word I was saying. I asked him had others had any problems with her, and he assured me to the contrary. Llael was always charming, if a little roguish at times, he said. I told him what Melanie had said, about her not being as angelic as she used to be, but he said that it was the first he had heard about it and that, frankly, he was surprised. I became ever more convinced it was my fault. Children tend not to lie, and I reasoned that if Llael saw me as invisible or contemptible, it was likely she was right. Why else would she do it? What motive could there be? Was I as contemptible as she thought? And, if the whole thing was a pretence, then why? And how could she keep it up so persistently? If it hadn't been for the stabilising influence of Hope, Hugo's dog, I know I would have cracked. He was an old collie and he reminded me of the old Shuar shaman; he had that same sense of rootedness and was somehow able to reassure me, to keep me sane.

I don't know what would have happened if Llael hadn't finally let her guard slip one day at dinner. It was at the end of my first week: Hugo had asked her to give me a taste of her butternut squash as I had never heard of such a thing. He said it was such a Canadian delicacy that it would be a sin to remain ignorant of it any longer, and she had replied, as sweet as anything, "But pretendy friends can't eat, Hugo. They are only pretend. Remember?"

Hugo, who had been out working all day and was tired, was in no mood for this. He repeated the request in a firmer tone, and after much arguing back and forth, she finally cut me a slice. Although an enormous scowl was spread across her face, I was delighted. I felt real progress had been made. I put out my hand, but instead of handing it to me she stuffed the squash into her mouth and chewed it up well and then spat it out on to my lap.

Had she actually struck a flint over a petrol tank the mood of the room could not have changed more radically. Right before my eyes, Hugo switched from torpidity to animated mode for the first time since I had met him, and it was terrifying. He didn't say anything, or even do very much, but he turned puce and began breathing through his nose, somewhat dragon-like. I gulped in concern. This was what the Screamers had talked about, how repressed anger if not released would eventually erupt, devouring everything around. I could see Hugo was simmering towards the boil, and Llael and I just sat there stunned, not quite believing that this man who was always so moderate could have such a force within him. We could feel the air grow turbulent around us. Finally, Llael burst into tears, into paroxysms of uncontrollable, deep-sequestered tears, as though she were a sprinkler valve triggered to dampen the flames. I breathed a sigh of relief to see her mask finally crack, but an instant later her tears froze and I gulped hard again. The atmosphere in the room had dropped too cold for tears. We were both staring straight at Hugo, and it was dawning on both of us that his fury was only just beginning.

There was no obvious show of violence from Hugo; in fact he had hardly moved a muscle, hadn't lifted a finger. He seemed incapable of it – simply too furious to coordinate. But underneath the still exterior, he was erupting into a mushroom cloud, sucking in and wiping out the sound around him, turning the room into a vacuum. Every drop of energy was feeding into him so that I genuinely began to feel afraid. But still I did nothing, just watched numbly on, waiting for the inevitable, hoping it wouldn't wipe us all out.

I had heard enough already about the tragedies that happened in remote cabins in Canada; about cabin fever and about whole families wiped out by one crazed member. Diarmuid on the farm had had quite a temper, and certainly after the Screamers I thought I had seen anger at its epitome, but it was the force Hugo was using to restrain himself that was so terrifying, suggesting, as it did, the extent of its opposing force – like a volatile chemical reaction of which only the smoke and sizzle reveal the true turmoil underneath.

My internal Geiger counter was beating into the red.

"Hugo," I whispered. "It's okay. It's okay, man. It's fine."

But he was too far gone to hear me.

It was only seconds before meltdown when he finally stood up and charged out of the cabin, chasing off into the woods to save us all, like something out of the Hulk. I had a sudden new respect for what the Screamers had been advocating. Primal therapy, trauma release, anger processing. As the panic levels dropped, tears rose in Llael again, and she snuck off behind the log basket in shock. I was still sitting with my dinner in front of me, scraps of chewed squash on my lap, listening to Llael cowering somewhere behind me, crying, and wondering what I had got myself into this time.

"Mocha," I heard her whimper after a time.

She looked up at me, eyes pleading. It was the first time she had ever used my name. A tectonic shift. I turned around and looked her in the eye. Her arms stretched out, and I knew I had only the briefest moment of opportunity: if I reached out to her now I had a chance. I needed to say, to do, something so nurturing, so potent, that she couldn't help but melt. I needed to evoke in her the same sense of affection, of devotion, that the dead tree trunk had sparked in the people of Nelson. If not, I might as well give up and go back to the Swedes to try my hand at midwifery. I knelt down and clutched her to me, and incredibly she didn't draw away. Stroking her hair, I gathered her to me, squeezing her gently, whispering God knows what – *a mhuirnín, a ghrá mo chroí. Mo pheata beag gléigeal.*

"We agreed," she said at last.

"What, love?" I asked

"You and I, we agreed."

"Of course we did," I cooed.

I didn't understand. I knew that if she felt even a drop of my fear, my uncertainty, she'd clam up again. I needed to melt into her, to make her feel my heart was wide open, but I wasn't sure how. Nurturing, cherishing wasn't something I was good at doing for myself, let alone someone else. The Screamers had been right; in terms of emotional outpouring I was a failure.

I couldn't think what to say to Llael, where to begin, so instead I said, with only a hint of desperation in my voice: "Grumpy Oilskins is in the apple tree. He's old for a bear, and his fur is so matted he doesn't see the creepy crawlies in it. He doesn't know they all have names or that their families live in different parts of him. He doesn't know that today is the most important day in the creepy crawly calendar. The day

Princess Crawly from Grumpy's claw is marrying Prince Creepy from his armpit, and that all the creepy crawlies and ticks and worms have been invited. Everyone is excited, and none more so than the princess herself, Princess Crawly, who knows that when she moves into the armpit from the claw she'll never again have to suffer being cold and wet whenever Grumpy decides to walk through the mud or rivers or snow. Never again. From now on she'll spend her winters all cuddled up and cosy."

Llael was in my lap, her arms stretched around my neck.

"It was to be the perfect wedding," I went on, buttering my voice with wonder, but careful not to condescend. "The creepy crawlies had found an ant preserved in a drop of honey for the feast, and it was growing better and bigger as more and more creepy crawlies got stuck to it. If Grumpy hadn't suddenly decided to climb down from the tree and have a dust bath, who knows how big the meal would have got? Once it got covered in dust, it was safe, and the lice were able to roll it up to the armpit, to where the feast was going to be. This made the princess feel even more joyful. She hadn't liked to think of other creepy crawlies dying on her special day, especially since one of them had been her sister, and she would rather not have had to eat her. Although Princess Crawly was a cannibal, nevertheless she would rather not eat her own sister on her wedding day. Someone else's sister would be fine."

I glanced at Llael, she was open-mouthed. I swear I could feel her begin to purr and I plunged on.

"Unfortunately, no one told Grumpy Oilskins about the wedding, about all the preparations and excitement, about all the fuss and bother, so when he decided to go out fishing one last time before the lake froze over for winter – to be sure he had enough food in him before he went into his cave to hibernate – he had no idea of the carnage he would cause. If someone had warned him, if all the creepy crawlies had cried out, or bitten him at the same time and got his attention, he might have waited. He didn't set out to be a massacring tyrant. He was just a hungry bear. If he had only known, he wouldn't have been wading into the half-frozen lake just as the princess was making her way up and down the strands of fur towards the prince. She was feeling invincible and delighted that all the preparations had gone so smoothly. Of course he wouldn't, and the princess wouldn't have right there and then be suddenly experiencing the terrible panic of seeing a massive iceberg charging towards her and . . ."

It was at that moment Hugo came through the door, looking exhausted, his eyes bleary and shirt rumpled, but otherwise okay. Meltdown had been averted or delayed at least. Llael was slumped on top of me, melted into the contours of my body, her eyes locked on my mouth. As she glanced up at Hugo, her smile faded momentarily and a flash of anxiety passed across her brow, but he beamed so broadly back at her that she knew it was fine.

He opened his mouth to speak, and after a few false starts, various hums and hahs and the odd prevarication, said, "I'm . . . really sorry, Llael."

It took a moment for him to replenish himself, then he turned to me, "Mocha . . . em . . . I'm sorry."

Llael looked up smiling, then snuggled closer into me, and I went on with the story until it was time for bed. I carried her up to her room and stayed watching long after she had fallen asleep. To my great surprise, I noticed every cell in my body ballooning with love.

When I climbed back down to the kitchen, Hugo was sitting at the table hunched over a pot of camomile tea. He gestured for me to sit down, saying there was something he needed to tell me. I thought he was going to apologise more, but instead he said he had been waiting for this moment since I'd arrived – for Llael to get to trust me. He knew she didn't take well to new people; she never had. She had already managed to see off three minders, although he had thought it best not to tell me this before now. I had got off lightly, it appeared. I was the first that she hadn't rung the police to report for being mean or for pulling dolly's hair. Hugo explained that Llael had had an immutable policy since she was first able to speak that she would only relate to people who she had an "agreement" with. These agreements were pacts she claimed to have worked out with them before she was born. She wasn't able to remember them offhand, but the minute she met one of these agreed people she'd know. So far, Hugo had been one, as was Fabian and, of course, Melanie, but most of Melanie's other boyfriends weren't. Even Llael's own father, a yoga teacher called Joxer, from Manitoba, hadn't been and had abandoned her and her mother on her first birthday. It had taken her a while to decide whether or not I was one, and it seemed I was. From now on she would trust me for ever, which for Hugo was an enormous relief. He could finally get back to his real business full time, which he had had to scale back until he found someone for Llael. He was keen to get things up and running again as soon as possible, and it was this that he wanted to talk to me about. The first thing I needed to know was that his business wasn't in fact cargo transport, but bringing cannabis into the United States. He was one of the main exporters in the region. He explained how, for a few days each week, he would drive around the area buying up small amounts of cannabis. It seemed everyone in the alternative community had at least an attic nursery, if not a full-scale basement grow-room on the go, while most also had an organic plot outdoors somewhere in the forest. Once he had collected a few pounds of the stuff, he would pack it into a rucksack and hike it across the border to a contact on the American side, who drove it down to Los Angeles.

He couldn't believe I didn't know about the cannabis farming. Where else did I think they got their money? It was the second largest crop in British Columbia after apples, he told me. And, knowing how important it was to the economy, the government turned a blind eye. The power company even increased supply in the area just to feed all the metal halides and arc lamps. If you listened carefully, Hugo told me, you could hear the buzz of tungsten halogen mantraming through the valley.

I did feel a bit foolish that I hadn't twigged it before. Although people lived spartanly here, in log or straw or mud homes, and grew their own food, I had wondered where they got the money for all the expensive organic goods and the hot tubs and the Ski-Doos they used in winter, and even the camper vans many of them used to escape the winter entirely. Any alternative community I had been to before was always penniless, with everyone on welfare and bitter about it. I just presumed that somehow all the "creative visualisation" and "abundancy" workshops people attended must actually work; that the affirmations they chanted were in fact as powerful as they claimed. I realised I had been naïve. On my first day in Vancouver, the front page of the *Globe and Mail* had a cartoon of a farmer in Saskatchewan looking up at black clouds over his cornfield, saying, "I've got to get the crops in". Beneath him was another hemp-tunicked man with a scraggy beard and sandals standing in a field of hemp in British Columbia looking up at the black American drug enforcement helicopters and saying the same thing.

Hugo told me that Fabian was one of the top growers in the valley and that he had even won awards at the prestigious Cannabis Cup in Amsterdam. The region frequently won prizes as their seed-stock was more bountiful and the buds more crystal-drenched than others. It was for this that Hugo got such high prices in Los Angeles; only the elite of Beverly Hills could afford his product, particularly the outdoor organic crop which was seen as a real delicacy. Suddenly, I understood why Hugo was prepared to pay me so much for babysitting: basically, he was buying me off. At first it worried me. Was I an accomplice to the crime? But Hugo assured me there was no chance he'd ever get caught. The authorities would never interfere.

"Why else do you think they allow the garden centres to stay open," he said, "with only a few poinsettias out front and warehouses of hydroponic equipment and grow-lights in the back? Everyone knows the local economy would collapse without us. They'd all be out of a job."

The only problem, it seemed, was with the American DEA officers who crossed the border from time to time to snoop around. Hugo told me that it was vital to assume everyone was possible DEA, except for him and Llael. Even some of the tree campaigners were undercover US officers, he said. But without jurisdiction in Canada there was nothing much they could do, except fly overhead in helicopters during the harvest season, which was more of a nuisance than anything, as the noise they made disturbed what would otherwise have been a pleasant day in the countryside. Recently, the locals had even found a way around this minor inconvenience: influenced by the scene in *Star Wars* where Obi-Wan Kenobi sends mind messages telepathically to storm-troopers with the words "You are not welcome here" (which caused them to turn around and leave), they had adapted it. They telepathically beamed white light at the black helicopters until they, in turn, were forced to turn around and leave. It worked every time, Hugo assured me, although I wondered was it not just that they ran low on fuel. I thought back to the black CIA helicopters that had accompanied the spray planes over the Screamers, and reflected on how much like a Rorschach blot the Americas were, with everything folded on the fulcrum of the United States.

I assured Hugo that I understood and that he could trust me, and the following day he went back to work full time. Somehow I managed to fool myself into thinking that I was in no danger, mainly because I was already so fond of Llael. I didn't want to give her up, and I knew I was unlikely to find another job.

It wouldn't be accurate to say Llael was adorable and cherubic from that moment on; of course, there were periods of sullenness, but few and far between, and I regarded them as good for me. Character building. Already I was finding myself loving her, and what good was love if I couldn't keep it alive in the face of a bit of hostility? One of the reasons I had stayed so long with the Screamers was to test myself, to find out whether I could take everything they threw at me, to be sure I could let it wash over me. A test of endurance. Rabbit always said that love was something you shared with someone, not got from them, and I wanted to be sure I wouldn't stop sharing just because the other person did. It had to be unconditional or else it wasn't love.

Yet, no matter how much I pulled the wool over my eyes about the nature of the situation, part of me was constantly waiting for the door to be kicked in, and it was only through sheer good fortune that I happened to be back in Ireland by the time America finally managed to tighten the screws on Canada enough to precipitate a raid by twenty Mounties, who came bursting through the door on Hugo and Llael on the one and only day he happened to be minding six times more cash and cannabis for a friend than he had ever had before. He had been right about the spies after all. They had been watching all along. It was one of the tree campaigners who had set him up. He was just lucky that it was the Canadians who got him and not the Americans: if the Feds get you, you never see your family again. It was this that scared me most of all, the thought of having to make my way to the monastery to break the news to Melanie, to tell her she'd never see her brother again except through Perspex.

Over and over again, Hugo would reassure me that the forest tracks he used – a warren of abandoned Sinix't Indian trails that wove along the border which were never used – were so remote that no one could ever find him. Nothing could ever happen. Like the border between Ecuador and Peru, the region had never been mapped in detail, and there were still some routes that only the coyotes and bears knew.

The simplicity and relative safety of his plan brought me a certain degree of reassurance. I realised that it would have taken a lot of bad luck for things to go wrong. Without giving too much away, the plan was more or less that at around ten at night he would drive south into the Selkirk Mountains with Hope, the dog, and after making sure he wasn't followed, he would hide the car in a forest clearing before hiking about six miles through the mountains, using GPS to find his way, to a drop–off point about a mile on the American side. It was that simple – just a long Sunday afternoon walk, except it was pitch black and through vegetation somewhat denser than the average city park. Yet although it was dense, it wasn't as bad as the Shuar hunting grounds. He kept the trail relatively clear, and only in summer when the sap rose in the thorns and they became aggressive did he come back with scars from the briars in the thicket. The whole run took less than five hours if everything went to plan. His partner on the other side would come by on a quad a little while later and pick up the package. It was a form of hunting, I suppose, except more like a treasure hunt, with Hugo as the indulgent parent hiding the treasure. He had only ever seen border guards once, and Hope had smelt them so far off that it had left him plenty of time to ditch the gear and turn back towards Canada. The guards were suspicious, of course, when they finally came across him, but there was no way of proving he wasn't just a hiker out with his dog. He had lost about $10,000 in the dropped bag, but it was mostly other people's money, and he had soon earned it back for them. (I still worry that the DEA may have come across that bag and found a trace of Llael's fingerprint on it which they input into a computer, which might be churned up fifty years from now and she'll be interrogated about something that happened when she was five years old. Maybe the bag is sitting on a shelf in Langley, waiting to be scanned through some frightening futuristic machine which will reveal the DNA of anyone who was ever near it.)

Most of the time I preferred not to think about the work at all. My job was to mind Llael; the rest was none of my business. And after a few weeks of worry, I got over it and the whole situation became absolutely normal. On run nights I'd cook Hugo a big dinner of wholewheat pasta with beetroot and seeds to keep his carbohydrate levels up, and once he had read Llael a story and waited till she was asleep, he would pull on his black skiwear and Gore-Tex boots and head out the door with Hope. I wouldn't hear from him again until he rang me to say he was back on Canadian soil having made the drop-off. I would then fall back asleep assured and wake up the following morning to hear him driving up the laneway, or if things had gone really smoothly, he'd be at home already and preparing buckwheat pancakes and maple syrup for us, for yet another celebratory breakfast. Llael and I were always sent out for a long walk after these breakfasts to give him a chance to rest. During busy periods, we helped him with the work, stuffing the zip-locked packs into turkey-roasting bags as an extra security layer to throw off the sniffer dogs. On my advice, he even went and got child-sized surgical gloves for Llael so as not to leave any fingerprints.

Within a few weeks, I was able to start paying Fabian back what I owed him, but he was reluctant to accept it and instead wanted me to come back and help him with the campaign. He said things were going really well. Sophia was now living full time up in a tree, the Joan of Arc of the Kootenays, the local television station had christened her. She was attracting a lot of attention from radio shows, and overall she was in good spirits, despite a few stormy nights which had caused her to confront her demons and make her bawl with fear. But she was glad of the experience and was now considering running a workshop on "tree yoga" to teach other people what she had learnt. It would be a full residential week's course with everyone living in trees and confronting their demons. I reckoned it would go well. Demons were the one thing that united everyone I had met over the last two years. Everyone was either avoiding or confronting them. For Sophia the worst thing about tree life had been the journalists. They only ever focused on whether she was missing sex or not, and how she managed to go to the lavatory. She had been asked the same questions a hundred times, as if she were some kind of animal, but she had kept her cool throughout, reminding herself that they were at a different level of awareness and couldn't understand anything beyond that.

I explained to Fabian that I wasn't ready to come back to work with him. I was having far too much fun with Llael, and was finding the remoteness of Hugo's cabin addictive. Being on the far edge of wilderness was a natural high, and in case I ever needed more stimulation, Hugo would bring me on road trips around British Columbia with him at the weekends. I lived for these trips. The land was just so pristine, so untrammelled, with swathes of spruce and maple broken only by flashes of silver rivers and looking-glass lakes that reflected every mountain and tree-line in crystal clarity. I could see the region was as much about water as trees. A third of the world's fresh water lies in Canada, and the people seemed to make use of it as much as they do the land. Every second car had a kayak on the roof. Hugo told me the definition of a Canadian was someone who knew how to make love in a canoe. Suddenly I understood the sense of well-being Canadians emanated; it came from owning this estate, this paradise. I couldn't get enough of it: watching ospreys soaring over lush forest and beavers desperate to finish their dams before the river froze over; the poignant call of a loon rising from a mist-clad lake (another cliché); the skeletons of old trees floating hauntingly by – all this with Llael snuggled up against me and Hugo calmly driving, cogitating over a possible future remark.

Hugo tried convincing me that these trips were for my benefit, that they were sightseeing trips, but that was just a joke. In truth they were about money laundering. Every few weeks someone would drive up from LA with a roof-box of US dollars which had to be distributed to growers throughout the valley. It was all done with amazing trust and good manners. The only problem was that at some point the money had to be converted into Canadian dollars without alerting the suspicion of the banks, which in a town the size of Nelson wasn't easy. Fortunately, some of the health food shops and vegetarian cafés sometimes accepted American dollars, but the rest of the money had either to be given to Hong Kong immigrants in Vancouver, who would launder it at a high commission, or else stashed somewhere in one's cabin. Hugo came up with a third method, which was to drive around little dairy and logging towns changing small amounts in each bank along the way.

At first I was determined not to get involved, but perhaps I came to realise that considering all the kindness Hugo had shown me and the pleasure I was getting from the life, it would have been churlish to refuse. Having a foreign passport would have made me invaluable to him after all, as I could have changed as much as I wanted without raising suspicion. If anyone ever commented, I could have always simply remarked that while I found their country very beautiful, it was also incredibly expensive, and insist on changing another few thousand, just in case. Not for one second am I saying that I ever did anything illegal, of course. I'm merely extrapolating a potentiality. If such a thing had happened, it might have attracted funny looks at times, particularly when the tellers noticed the Colombian, Peruvian and all the African stamps in my passport, but my face was too soft to arouse much suspicion. Hugo promised me that if I did what he asked of me, he'd buy me a slap-up meal afterwards, so that I'd feel just like a gangster's moll.

Llael could get pretty cranky on these trips, refusing to allow me sit up front in the cab, and I'd have to cower in the back with Hope. I didn't regard this as bad behaviour, more that she was expressing herself and her determination to influence her surroundings. I thought it was a good thing and secretly wished I could be as strong as she was. I could understand why she wanted to retain control: her mum had more or less abandoned her for Buddha, and in the year since I had met them all in Caravanserai, three different men had passed through Melanie's bed. I still wasn't sure who Llael's father was. She swore blind it wasn't Joxer, and when I asked her who it was, she told me that she had a few dads. Fabian was just the most recent. It was no wonder she wanted me on a tight rein.

What I liked most about Hugo and Llael was that they weren't as alternative as the others. Although they ate the usual leaves and sprouts, and chanted over their food to infuse it with something or other, they knew about the real world, too, and didn't hate it. They had a television, for example, and Llael was allowed to play with Disney toys. I liked the compromise they had struck. Llael didn't say she hated sweets like some of the other children, and Hugo was prepared to have the odd coffee if no one was looking. But it was my connection to Llael that really anchored me there and made me risk arrest. I had never really known any children before, and Llael was a revelation. I felt more understood and free with her than I had with anyone before. Somehow, her world was so unfettered and malleable it felt like *home*. Like I had been out of synch all these years and suddenly had caught up. For the first time since I was her age, I found someone who saw life on my terms, whose grip on the imaginary world was as strong as on reality, who judged life as much empathically as logically. Empathically, the opposite to emphatically. With no one keeping us tied to reality, we flew away to wherever we wanted to go and often it took an effort to refocus when Hugo appeared.

We would be lost in some imaginary world, but, notwithstanding this, part of me would always remember my responsibilities as guardian. I knew it was vital to remain the responsible one and managed to balance the two roles most of the time. I used to beg her not to play her version of tip-the-can, which involved running from the cabin to one of the apple trees and back without being mauled by the black bears that climbed into them and stayed there until every apple was eaten. That the bears were willing to risk coming so near the house was my first intimation of how harsh the encroaching winter would be. The first snows had already focused people's minds, and in homes throughout the valley I saw people redoubling their efforts: chopping and stacking firewood, bottling fruit and hoarding sacks of rice and beans.

Llael's and my favourite game was "blind man", in which I closed my eyes and mistook her for various things – a toothbrush, an umbrella, soap, a bicycle. I would pick her up and use her as the item until she convinced me otherwise. We played this for hours on end, until eventually we would be laughing so much it began to hurt. This was the game we were playing the night the phone didn't ring. The night Hugo had gone out earlier than usual, saying he'd ring when he had made the drop–off around ten.

Llael hadn't been able to sleep that night. She said it was because Hugo hadn't read her a story, and so we had stayed up playing. When the phone didn't ring at ten, I was only a little bit worried because the battery on his chunky old mobile phone was forever acting up. Llael must have picked up on my concern, though, as it took another hour for her to fall asleep. By eleven he still hadn't called. He had never been late before. It was the clockwork nature of the thing, the regularity, that had always reassured me more than anything. I had come to accept it as foolproof. This was the first night he had gone out in snow. He had said that, if anything, it made things easier. At midnight there was still no news. Even if the mobile was broken he should have reached a pay phone by then.

At 1 a.m. I decided I had to do something. I knew that even if he had been arrested, he would have called by now. We had discussed at length how I was to set off for the coast and bring Llael to her mother if ever there was any trouble, but he had never mentioned what to do if he just disappeared. What if he was perhaps in need of help, if, say, he was hurt? Surely I had to go help him? Bears were my biggest worry. There was little chance a bear would eat him, but if he got injured in some way, a curious or startled bear could easily pull his arms off, just out of curiosity. I owed it to him to do something. I knew exactly the spot where Hugo parked his car; he had pointed it out to me when we had gone for walks in the forest. The least I could do was drive there and see what I could find.

I left it another hour, just in case, going over in my mind what my responsibilities were, where my loyalties lay. Basically I was a nanny, and nannies don't normally go rescuing their drug-smuggling bosses, but if the alternative was to have to tell Llael I had done nothing to save her uncle, I knew which I'd choose. I had to do something, and so after wrapping Llael snugly in a blanket, I carried her out to the pickup and gunned the engine. It took less than two hours to reach the entrance to the forest trail where he parked. The burning eyes, emerald and wise, were recognisable the minute I saw them in the headlights. It was Hope, loping towards me at full pace, barking. I stopped the pickup and got out. We were in the forest about a hundred yards from where Hugo usually parked, and I walked along the track with Hope to where his car was still parked, same as always. There was no sign of Hugo. I thought I could make out his tracks in the thin layer of snow that had fallen, heading off through the trees, but I could see none returning. Why wasn't Hope with him? I half hoped the dog would bound off, leading me Lassie-like to my injured friend, but I could see she was as confused as I was. And anyway, even if she had been the ultimate tracker dog, I could hardly have followed her very far with Llael in my arms. I hung around aimlessly in the clearing for a while, not knowing exactly what to do. Finally, I headed back to the pickup and, after locking the wheel hubs into four-wheel drive, I drove up an old logging track which ran roughly parallel to the trail Hugo must have taken.

There had been no logging in the area for a long time, and the track was overgrown. At times it spread-eagled into arteries which were difficult to navigate. I kept as much due south as I could, but the trees blocked out the stars and it was hard to tell where I was. A few times I got out and called for Hugo, but there was never a reply. At one point I came across a wide fire corridor cut between the trees and a series of quad marks running along it. It was perpendicular to the track, and I thought it might possibly be the border line. I got out, carrying Llael in my arms, and ran along it, back and forth, calling Hugo's name until Llael became anxious and cried so much there was no need for me to call any more. I soon realised how futile it was. There were miles and miles of uncharted forest around me, and Hugo could have been anywhere. I carried Llael back to the jeep and we drove on, hoping to come across the drop-off point Hugo used on the far side. Perhaps his friend would be there and would know something.

"Hugo can't die," Llael said.

"No, of course not," I cried. "He's not going to die. No way."

"But he can't," she said again. "He's going to mind me. We agreed."

"He will be fine," I said. "I promise."

"But we agreed – even before I was born, we agreed."

I stroked from her forehead right down her back like a cat, hoping with all my heart that I was right. Secretly, I grew ever more despairing, but she seemed convinced, or at least reassured, by her assertion and quietened. I resolved to do whatever it took to bring him back, to make her words come true. Her words had that potent, incontrovertible quality that the Pacific coast accent gives to things – it had always been able to melt me, to drive me to strive harder. Every syllable seemed to ooze encouragement, empowerment. It was the peel of hope ringing with potential, and coming from Llael it could make me walk through walls.

I don't know how long I had driven before I noticed the Stars and Stripes and Stars and Bars flags in among the trees and the chain-link fences and cabins nestled behind. I was on American soil for sure now, an eerie, backwoods region similar to where the Unabomber's hideout had been. Considering I had no passport with me, no vehicle documentation and no papers for Llael, this was not necessarily a good thing. It would be hard to convince anyone who saw her wrapped in a blanket on the bench, anxious and tear-stained, that I was her rightful guardian.

I saw how stupid it was to risk going any further, and I pulled up beside a wood stack to turn around and head back to Canada. It was only then that I noticed the flashing red light. There was hardly any propane in the tank, definitely not enough to get us back through the forest. It didn't seem like too big a problem at first. I had some money on me, Canadian dollars for once, but I felt sure someone, somewhere would accept them. All I had to do was find a petrol station and fill up. If I drove a little deeper into America, I was bound to come across something. The homesteads were probably the first signs of habitation, and there'd be a town up ahead for definite.

Shifting the pickup into drive, I crawled onwards into America, only beginning to start worrying when it seemed the road was stretching on forever with no sign of a town anywhere. The tank was growing visibly emptier. It was around five in the morning at this stage, still dark and very cold. Without the heating on Llael would have frozen. If the propane ran out now and we lost the heat, I didn't know how long we could survive. At the next spangled banner we came to, I pulled off the road and hiked down a trail towards the house that I knew must be hidden in there somewhere. I came across a US mailbox nailed to a tree which reassured me that I must be on the right trail, but seconds later a Dobermann pinscher came bounding dov 1 the track at me, barking furiously, and I turned and ran back to the pickup, slamming the door only just in time to save myself. Seeing its slavering mouth against the window brought me back to Ecuador, and I wondered what the hell it was about me and dogs.

Revving the engine, I sped away, forgetting all about trying to conserve gas, and kept on going until we came to a house with a strong, secure fence all around. Even then, I didn't risk getting out. From inside the pickup, I beeped the horn as loudly as I could, but no one stirred, and I heard nothing except a coyote calling in the far distance. Tentatively, I got out of the pickup and edged my way towards the gate, which had an old brass bell hanging over it. I swung the clapper, but still there was no response. It was only when we were inching off again that I saw a light come on in an upstairs window. I threw the pickup into reverse and sped back, shouting out the window as I went, but the light went dead and no one else stirred.

My anxiety was mounting. Although there was no snow on this side of the border, it was freezing cold and we hadn't passed a vehicle all night. The region seemed barely inhabited. I don't know how far into America I was, but as far as I could tell it was largely abandoned, a mountainous tract of trees and rivers with only the odd scattered homestead hiding here and there. It was pointless going on, the engine was going to give out at any moment. I pulled over into the ditch and shut it off, pulling off my jumper and wrapping it around Llael to keep her warm. I was cradling her in my arms. My hope was we could somehow make it through until morning, but it was a risk. In my mind I could already see the front page photo in the local paper of the two of us clasped together at the wheel of the truck, rigor mortis adding a statuesque quality. Seeing her clasped like a limpet to my chest, I had the uncanny feeling that I was the giant spider looming over the Inuit, and this chilled me even more, because I remembered Rabbit saying that those were the people I hated most, and I certainly didn't hate Llael. I was sure that this was the event the dream was predicting. The Inuits related to the cold we were fighting and to our location in Canada, up near Inuit country. I was the spider, but I certainly didn't hate Llael.

Rabbit, I said, *I don't hate Llael. I love her.*

Llael bridled, sensing somehow what was on my mind. I thought I could see the translucent form of an Inuit woman like a mask above her face, and the more I stared the more it resembled Portia.

Rabbit, I said, *I don't hate her.*

You didn't hate any of them, Rabbit said. *Can't you see that? A spider doesn't hate its own eggs, but maybe it doesn't like the shell so much. It's like the grain of sand that makes the pearl: the oyster loves it despite it being an irritation.*

Looking down at Llael now, I realised there was nothing I wouldn't do for her. I had known her only a few weeks, not counting the early mornings in Caravanserai the year before, and we would probably part again soon, but she was part of me now and that would never change. She had freed my mind, given me some of her strength, reminded me of the complicated inner psychology of people, their limitless imaginings. I thought about her "agreements". Who knows, maybe we had agreed to come together, to enchant each other for a while. I thought of Gina's baby back at the Screamers and wondered whether it was because we didn't have an agreement that I hadn't tried to help him, that I had been willing to let him die. Was our agreement for me not to interfere? Was that what Rabbit was trying to show me in the octagonal library? Those volumes: were they the same as Llael's "agreements"? If so, I wanted to see the one between me and Eve. I wanted to read the fine print.

I hugged Llael closer to me. It was a strange kind of love I had found. I hadn't imagined someone else's child could mean so much. I didn't think I had it in me, but I was proud of the fact that I wanted so little from her, just to care for her, to help her. I was happy to curl up in the back of the pickup with the dog if it made her feel a bit more secure about the world. Love was not about finding joy or completion, but sharing it, and I imagined that although we would both cry when we parted, we'd know it wasn't really the end, just time to move to the next agreement.

Chapter 13

HEADLIGHTS APPEARED IN the rear-view mirror, and I got out and waved madly until the vehicle slowed down and pulled over. Inside was a Native American woman with a grey ponytail.

"Get inside that truck of yours, right now," she chided in a warm voice used to giving orders. "You'll die of the cold. I'll pull up aside you."

She pulled her camper van level with ours.

"Now," she said. "What's with all the fuss and bother?"

I asked her where the nearest petrol station was.

"*Petrol*, as you call it," she said in a cheery, singsong voice, "there ain't none of that here, hon. This here is a reservation. The Colville Indian Reservation. No *petrol*. There's a casino if you want, open all day, all night."

Then she saw Llael.

"Oh, my," she said, "that little mite ain't looking for a casino; are you, pet?"

Llael shook her head.

"You run out of gas?"

"Almost," I said.

"Oh, my," she said with a nod which continued unconsciously as she mulled over the situation. "What you best do is follow me. My sister-in-law, she has a campsite aside the casino. We'll get you some food, and you can rest there till morning time, till people are up and about. Then we'll find you someone to fetch you gas."

Her name was Desiree, Desiree Beareagle, she told us as we pulled out on to the road again and she guided us a few miles along the road to an old shack with RVs and tents around it that looked out on a lake. Across the road was the casino Desiree had mentioned. It was set in a field of tarmac overlooking a giant dam. Desiree got out of her van and knocked on the door of the shack, but everyone was still asleep and the place was all locked up. She came across and got into our pickup and we swung back across the road to the casino. The casino was a huge barn-like building with a roof sign the size of a juggernaut lit up in flashing lights and wooden poles around the entrance to give it a native feel. A flag flew from the tallest pole showing a baying coyote surrounded by eleven feathers. Desiree gestured us to follow her, and after whispering something to the guard on the door, she led us into the steel hangar, which was carpeted inside with rich paisley and had aluminium ducting blowing hot air down on us. The flashing machines stretched from wall to wall like an army of robots. There were fewer than a dozen people gambling, none of them Indian.

"By rights, no minors are allowed," Desiree said, "but who'd be raiding us at this hour, huh? At least you'll be warm here, and there's plenty of free food."

She pointed over to a trestle table beside the video poker games. Llael pulled me across to it and began to gorge indecently on potato twists and spicy chicken wings. People must have thought she had never eaten before, and I tried to explain that it was only because she had actually never tasted some of these foods in her life. In an office that hung from the roof girders above the gaming floor, Desiree introduced me to the night duty manager, another relation of hers.

"Gas or diesel?" he asked.

"Propane," I said.

"Whoooo weee. Propane!" he replied.

Most of the alternative community in Canada had converted their vehicles to hemp oil or cooking fat; at least propane, natural gas, was a little more widely available.

"If it was anything normal I could siphon you out some straight away. But propane! You'd be as well off looking for rocket fuel around these parts."

The New Agers felt terrible guilt for driving pickups. They would have cycled everywhere if the distances weren't so far; converting them to the least-damaging fuel was a way of assuaging this guilt. I've never seen a Native American on a bicycle. The idea reminded me of the Salasaca Indians staring in wonder at the condor in Baños.

"But, all's not lost," chimed the night duty manager. "Hang around here an hour or so and give the day a chance to start, then we'll ring around, see if we can't rustle you up some of what you need."

He reached into a drawer beside his desk and pulled out a little sack with a dollar sign on it.

"Here's a few chips to keep you busy meantimes," he said, adding with a laugh, "but try not to bankrupt us . . . then again, with your luck, you probably won't!"

I left Llael at the food table and, after borrowing a few dimes from Desiree, I rang Hugo's mobile and the home number, just in case. But there was no reply. I was doing my best not to worry, at least not until I had got Llael and me out of our present mess. I thought about ringing Fabian to ask his advice, but then I remembered Hugo's warning to not trust anybody. It might in the end turn out that everything was fine, that Hugo was safe and there had only been some slight hiccup. In the meantime, I would have grassed him to a DEA spy without knowing it. I couldn't take the chance. It was better to keep quiet as long as I could.

At the gaming machines, although I kept losing, Llael, to my embarrassment, was on a winning streak on a game called Texas Tea. She racked up $78 in chips, $78 of badly needed Colville Indian funds which would have otherwise been spent on the adult literacy and drug recovery programmes that, according to billboards on the walls, were fully funded from the casinos takings. I was trying to convince Llael not to cash in her chips when the duty manager called me back to his office. There was a phone call: it was Hugo.

The phone number of the casino had come up on his mobile. I grabbed the phone like it was an oxygen mask. He was fine, he said, a little shook up, that was all. He was stuck somewhere. He didn't know where. In the forest on either the American or Canadian side – he wasn't sure. But he was fine.

In slow, deliberate phrases, his articulation as amorphous as ever, Hugo explained to me what had happened: how he had come across a bunch of hunters near the point he usually made the drop-off, and how he had managed to hide before they saw him. But, despite taking inordinate care, he had inadvertently stood on a dead twig or something, which they heard. Thinking it was a deer, they set their dogs on him and gave chase. Hope hadn't been there to warn him in advance of their presence because Hugo had already sent her back to the car for barking too excitedly at the snow. The hunters were just a bunch of good-old-boys out for a bit of fun, and at first Hugo had been able to outrun them easily. They didn't even know what they were chasing – they were just following the dogs – but as Hugo kept having to wind his way through half-frozen streams in an effort to throw them off the scent, he lost pace. Eventually the hunters spotted him in the distance and, seeing his backpack, they guessed what he was up to.

"Narco-fucking-commy," they had screamed.

It had just been a bit of fun for them up until then, slugging cans of beer as they ran, but when they realised who they were after – a real-life drug smuggler, a reactionary menace trying to pollute the minds of America's young – they redoubled their efforts. And fuelled by this indignation, they picked up speed. The old hunter-gatherer sap came to the fore again. But they were well out of shape, and it wasn't long before they began to flag. A quarter of a mile on, there were only two of them left, and soon they too gave up and called the dogs to heel. It was all over then; he was safe. But for some reason one dog had refused to accept the order. No matter how much they whistled and screamed, it ignored them, continuing relentlessly on as though it were laser-locked on to Hugo. Whatever obedience training it had been given was cast aside in its single-minded devotion to the chase. Hugo realised he could never out-run it, and he eventually climbed up a tree to escape.

All of this was told to me in excruciatingly protracted snippets, prolonged by infinite pauses and ponderous sighs, and although I tried interrupting at times to fill in the gaps and speed up the story, he somehow was able to control even the pauses by elongating the last word before taking an endless intake of breath for the next.

Finally I managed to interpose, "But it's all over now? You're okay, aren't you?"

"Ohhh, no! No, no . . . No, that wouldn't be the case at all. . . I'm far from okay, far from fine. I'm still in the tree, you see."

"You're in the tree?" I said.

"I'm ringing you from up in the tree."

The dog hadn't been dissuaded by Hugo's climb and had settled itself down to wait, growling and glowering up at him. Hugo was ringing me from one of the upper branches, and when he pointed the phone downwards, I could actually hear the dog's growl. It was suitably menacing, and I could feel the old leg wound tingle.

"Can I help in some way?" I asked.

"No, no. There's nothing you can do. There's nothing anybody can do. You'd never be able to find me. Just you take care of Llael for me, that's all. I'll sort this out one way or another. I'll ring you as soon as I can."

I got Desiree Beareagle's mobile number and gave it to him. Meanwhile Desiree herself had come into the office, saying it had just dawned on her where we could find propane. There was a massive gathering being held up the road a few miles, and there was sure to be some there. We headed out to the car park, and after tying the pickup to the back of Desiree's van, she towed us east towards Spokane to a huge sports field with hundreds of cars and trucks parked outside. As we approached, I saw what looked like antlers sticking into the air at skewed angles, hundreds of them, as though a herd of deer had been corralled in the field. As we got nearer I realised the peaks were skirted with cream cones, and it was only when we had parked and were zigzagging our way through the trucks and camper vans that I could make out what they were: tepees – hundreds of them, spread out around the field.

"It's the Fall Powwow," Desiree said. "I don't know why I didn't think of it before. They'll have propane here, for sure, for all the cookers and heaters. We're not allowed to have fires any more; can't get a permit – too dangerous. Some of the richer tribes even bring propane fridges with them for their drinks and stuff."

The central field was empty, but in the campsite all around it people were waking up, sticking their heads out the corseted openings of tepees, looking unsettlingly like bones poking from badly sutured wounds. A line of women were queuing up to wash their teeth at a tap, and behind them Desiree pointed out a huge propane tank on a flatbed truck with a row of gas cylinders beside it waiting to be filled. It was still locked up for the night, but Desiree assured us it would be open again soon, and she steered us towards the canteen to have some breakfast while we waited.

Llael thought she was in paradise: after dinosaurs, Indians were her favourite thing. She had even done a project at her Steiner school on the Trail of Tears – the Cherokees' forced march to Oklahoma. And knowing her, she probably knew as much as anyone here about what hides were used to make tepees and what dances were performed on which occasions. She had even once led me through the death rituals of the Heida Indians, the tribe whose turtle stone Eve had given me and which I still hadn't returned to the Charlotte Islands. From her I learnt that the Heida were revered in British Columbia; their stark, zoomorphic designs were everywhere. Llael insisted on going to see one of their totem poles as a birthday treat each year. Melanie's monastery was on an island not far from the Charlottes, and I think Llael liked to imagine her mother was training to be a Heida shaman rather than a Buddhist. She begged me to find out whether there were any Heida at the powwow, but it seemed to be mostly the Colville and Coeur d'Alene bands.

Inside, the canteen was a riot of noise and colour. A few hundred people, all in various bits of regalia, buckskin, beaded breastplates and deer-hoof bandoliers, were tucking into big dishes of bacon and eggs, hash browns and greasy biscuits. I could see Desiree was respected. Everyone waved when she came in, and she was ushered over to sit beside the elders at a table that was only slightly less raucous than the others. After greeting everyone with varying degrees of formality and respect, Desiree introduced me and Llael to them, and platters of gravy and biscuits with all the trimmings were set in front of us. Llael looked saucer-eyed at this new food.

I found myself sitting beside a heavy-set man with huge dark glasses like the Pyrex mugs in the Hungry Loon. On his fingers were orange plastic rings that matched a feathered brooch pinned to his waistcoat, which was white with fawn tassels. Desiree had introduced him as the elder of some tribe. His brow had a pained expression, as though he were suffering from an ulcer.

"Which side are you on, anyway?" he asked me gruffly. "Noble or hostile?"

"Sorry?" I said.

"Which bullshit side are you on? Do you think we're noble savages or hostile savages? You look like a noble, to me. That's the worst. Bloody New Agers, selling vision quests for $80 a pop, poaching all we have left. Fucking idolatry."

"Now there, Tom," Desiree soothed. "Go easy."

But Tom was in no easy mood.

"With a 20 per cent discount if you book early and a surcharge for Visa cards," another man added.

"What?" Tom scoffed.

"For the vision quests," the man clarified.

"They wave their sage around," Tom went on, "make a sweat lodge and wham-bam in comes the spirit animal – like a store Santa at Christmas. These people whose only contact with nature is through the windscreen of their SUVs suddenly see the spirit of a coyote soaring above them. And it speaks to them, and them alone; and not just about scavenging or humping some hot coyote bitch. No, it reveals the path to prosperity, to happiness. Bullshit."

"I wish they'd tell us those things, too," his friend added.

"Fuck them," Tom said. "Animals *are* sacred, they talk to all of us, and you can't *buy* access to them. You can't make appointments. It comes from inside, from who you are, your past, your people. Maybe these people should seek out spirit SUVs or spirit burgers instead of buying us up. They have their movies, their myths – why don't they go look to them for answers. Leave us alone."

"I'm only looking for propane," I said when I got a chance.

"Yeah, right," he said.

"But I do think that some people really are interested," I said. "Genuinely. Americans come to my country to kiss an old stone, but some of them know even better than we do what it means to be Irish. They see it from afar and so it's clearer."

"That's what I'm saying," Tom added, "learn more deeply. Try and help us instead of booking up our shamans so that they have no time for their own people. You people are every bit as linked to the land as we are. The animals and plants feed you too, sun warms you, air nourishes you, earth nurtures you. You people should remember who you are, who you come from, and not steal our memories. It's all we have left."

"On the Trail of Tears," Llael trumpeted suddenly, "the Cherokees didn't even have the strength left to cry."

We all fell silent and stared at her. Finally, someone else at the table said, "Amen, little child. Amen."

By the time we emerged from the canteen again, the scene outside in the central field had changed completely. A massive drum had been carried to the edge of the field, and around it young men were gathering, steadying their baseball caps, patting their groins, loosening their bandannas in readiness to chant and beat the drum. They looked like a bunch of rappers about to go on stage. In front of them, a master of ceremonies was arranging a group of dancers on the field, and all around them people were setting up easy chairs in readiness for the day's events: for the competitions, the songs and dances that would follow. The head veteran began a long monotone prayer before leading the ever-growing crowd in an initial chant, and then signalled for the drumming to begin.

It was incredible how on that first beat the scene changed so radically. The drum pulsed energy into the central circle, charging it for the day's events. Its palpitations, mixing with high-pitched chanting and dancing that was breaking out everywhere, seemed to bring the circle to life, as though a tear in the fabric of time had opened and suddenly we were all under its spell, a sort of alpha state with everyone on the same wavelength, focused intently on the dancers who seemed to shimmer like a mirage, undulating like viscous liquid. Our minds had been captivated by the drum, sent elsewhere. Wherever you looked, the same dissonant rhythm was being played out in the women who seemed to hardly move, yet whose feet were tapping and shifting, tilting their centre of gravity inwards like a jolting quadruped, like young buffalo adjusting to the earth; deliberately throwing the audience off-kilter; the scattered micro-tonal intervals of their chanting agilely bypassing conventional patterns, short-circuiting our circadian rhythms.

The men's movement was more jerky, with foot-stomping and sudden torso swerves reminiscent of frightened deer. The whole thing seemed designed to entrance us. I thought of a locksmith inserting his file and manoeuvring it just so, until the bolts clicked into place.

A group of younger men in eagle-feather bonnets and riding painted ponies passed through the circle. Their raffish tack – rifle bags and hand-stitched chaparajos – reminded me of hot rod cars. When I looked around I noticed Desiree had changed into a buckskin skirt with a shawl and a fan in her hand.

"I never miss a chance to dance," she said. "I'm a sucker for it – it's so rare nowadays. God, I love it! I always did." She stared off towards the circle. "The propane man might be a little while yet. I hear he had a late night."

I was feeling a lot more at ease by this stage. Now that I had made contact with Hugo and seemed to have solved the propane issue, there was less pressure to hurry home. Llael, of course, wanted to stay for ever.

"See those dancers over there," she said to Desiree, pointing to a mêlée of Mohicans and head-dresses quivering in time. "What are they up to?"

"I call it sticking the tomahawk in," Desiree said, "that moment of pure transcendence, of knowing exactly where you want to be and what you want to do. Your passion, your heart's desire. For me it's in that circle, it's dancing. It used to be tomahawking, although, of course, that's no longer acceptable, at least among the Turtle Island tribes. The People of the Condor – what you call South America – they still believe in the old ways."

"In killing people?" I said.

"In competing," she corrected. "In setting man against man in the ultimate dance. The dance of war."

"Yeah!" Llael cheered.

"What's yours?" Desiree asked me. "What's your passion – your version of sticking the tomahawk in?"

I wasn't sure I had an answer.

"What's he doing?" I said instead, pointing towards a whirling figure dressed from head to toe in rosettes of starburst threads, with so many orange-dyed feathers that he looked like he was on fire, like he was a phoenix dancing out of the centre of the earth. The question was as much to deflect Desiree as anything. I had no idea what I wanted to stick my tomahawk in. I remember in the jungle in Peru I had really wanted to be a shaman. I thought that was my goal, to find my spidermanhood. Now I didn't know any more.

Llael piped up, "He's bringing the eagle staff into the ring. It brings him strong medicine."

This was a five-year-old girl telling me this. Sometimes I was so proud of Llael I could burst. I really did love her.

"Do you know what medicine is?" Desiree asked.

Llael hunched her shoulders.

"Medicine is what you get if you follow your passion, if you listen inside and follow what you hear. Nowadays, soldiers kill for generals or for other rich people. I only ever used the tomahawk because I felt I wanted to inside."

"You've killed people!" Llael exclaimed.

"Well, not me exactly – my people. Nowadays we don't need to kill, but I still need to dance. Come on . . ."

Desiree jumped up, gesturing us to join the circle. Llael followed immediately, but I hung back. Noticing me, Desiree came back and squatted down beside me.

"You don't need to know the steps," she said. "Look at those people; all they're doing is moving back and forth. For an outsider it looks like the most boring thing. They look like zombies, don't they? And you wonder why they're not smiling, why they're not letting loose? In fact, that's precisely what they *are* doing. They are expressing themselves inside in ways nobody can see. They're connecting with themselves, their happiness, sadness, regret, whatever. It just feels great to be in the circle doing that in public. Like baring all, but without the messy entrails. Revealing yourself entirely but doing it from within. If people could just feel what it's like coming up to that drum. It's something I wish every human on Mother Earth could know. It's all I . . ."

Her words reminded me of something Eve had said, but Desiree didn't get to finish. Her phone rang. It was Hugo again. She passed it over.

"Mocha!"

"Hugo, is that you?" He didn't sound like himself. His voice was a decibel higher, his tempo quicker.

"It's not good news," he said. "I'm still in the tree."

He was more animated than I had ever heard him be. I could feel panic down the line.

"The dog isn't going away. I've been throwing branches down, and it just makes him worse. I figure he must be an old sniffer dog, trained not to give up until he gets his man. He must have smelt the drugs – that's why he's been so crazy. I think they train them by getting them addicted. He's like a junkie now, gagging for his fix. And he'll probably keep this up until one or other of us collapses. I'm so scared, Mocha. I really am."

I tried saying something reassuring, but he kept pouring on, as though a dam had burst and the reservoir of years of unspoken words were flowing out.

"My mind is going crazy. I'm getting a fever. I keep imagining I'm being hunted, killed, devoured – it's like a nightmare, except on a loop. First, I'm in the forest hunting, with the bow slung over my shoulder and I've a leather pouch crammed with sloes and dewberries . . . I can see it as though, as though, I'm right there. Then I find a huge puffball, but it falls apart and inside is all rotten. A boar comes and it stares me down before charging. I have no time to run, and it skewers me through the stomach, leaving me bleeding while it begins to chew my thigh. I can smell the boar, I can even hear the thing. It just goes round and round my head. I've gotta get out of here, Mocha. I've gotta get down."

"You're panicking, Hugo, that's all' I said. "Keep reminding yourself it's just fear. Breathe."

But he wasn't listening. He'd stopped talking, but he wasn't listening to a word I was saying. The minute I stopped he began again.

"Then I'm fine, I'm back in the tree and safe, until I drop the berries and the boar gets them and that makes me feel worse. Because those were the first berries after the snow, and Melanie is back at the cave, her belly concave with hunger, trying to coax milk out of her emaciated body, and suddenly I'm lying beside her and this time the fire has gone out and I see wolves, a pack of wolves, in the mouth of the cave, and I know they are going to get us. They'll get all three of us. And rather than grab a club and fight them off, I bury my head back under the goatskins and try to sleep until I hear the screams . . ."

The line went dead.

I tried hiding my concern from Llael, but she was always too able to intuit my thoughts. She knew there was something wrong.

"We have to leave straightaway," she said.

I looked at her in wonder. She couldn't have heard our conversation.

"Now!" she cried. "I want to see Hugo."

It was so out of character for Hugo to behave like that. He was always so rational, except for that one time with the squash. I wondered whether he might have eaten some of the cannabis or if it was just that the experience of being hunted had awoken the same race memories in him that Rory had talked about. I wondered whether my reluctance to go hunting with the Shuar had stemmed from the same thing, a memory of the fear and uncertainty of our hunter-gatherer past. I thought of Johnny Lovewisdom and the night he had spent in the tree, and also of the Peruvian pilot: did they face the same thing? I know Sophia, the tree campaigner, did. My life was becoming a fractal of repeating themes. A matrix of angry dogs and people in trees.

Overall, I wasn't too concerned about Hugo. As long as he stayed in the tree he was safe; if the dog tried to climb up he could always beat it down with a branch. I felt I owed it to Desiree to fill her in on some of the story, as she could sense there was something badly wrong, and when she heard she went straight to the master of ceremonies, asking him to lead the crowd in a prayer for safe hunting for Hugo. The master of ceremonies began a low guttural call, to which the dancers replied with a thin wail of their own that whined up through the octaves like mantraming. Desiree said it would send him strong medicine.

Meanwhile, the gas man had opened shop and was refilling the awaiting cylinders. We filled the car and then wound our way through the encampment one last time, through the waves of tepees which stretched on forever, their bellies billowing faintly in the breeze. I was reluctant to leave. I felt there was something here for me, but I knew it was too risky to stay in the country any longer without a passport, and anyway I'd be more help to Hugo back home. It was something the Pyrex-spectacled elder had said that got me thinking. Something about Turtle Island which reminded me of the whole idea of *Ame Rica* and of what, if anything, Rabbit wanted me to find.

When I asked the elder what he meant by the term Turtle Island, he explained it was a native name for North America based on their belief that the continent was built on the back of a giant turtle that rose up out of the water during the Great Flood as a sort of raft. This raft only managed to rescue a handful of the bravest Indians, who then rebuilt a better society upon it; just as the Europeans had done many centuries later, sending their poor and destitute to America to start again. South America, on the other hand, was the Land of the Condor. It had a completely different energy. I thought of the stone Eve had given me, the tiny landmass with a turtle on its back. Was it some sort of sign? Was I supposed to be here? Was I right on track despite all my sidetracking?

For North Americans, both indigenous and immigrant settlers, there was really only Turtle Island – the New World. Nothing else existed: the rest was all either washed away in the flood or left behind on the voyage across the ocean. The People of the Condor – South Americans – on the other hand, were aware of their rich Turtle cousins, but apart from them no one else mattered. Everyone I met from Colombia to Peru asked me what part of the United States I was from, how near to New York Ireland was. Rabbit's idea of *Ame Rica* was definitely closer to North America than South, and coincidentally most of the people I had got to know in the South were North Americans: Eve, Nadine, Guinevere, Fabian. It was Eve and Fabian who had lured me here. Maybe there was some pattern to it all, something I hadn't yet seen. Fractals only really ever reveal themselves from a distance: they impose order on what seems at first to be chaos. But I wasn't sure I actually wanted my life to be a fractal. Although I did want answers, I certainly did not want order. And definitely not an ever-repeating loop, a Möbius strip of dogs and trees that I could never escape from.

Chapter 14

WE FILLED THE tank with propane and said goodbye to Desiree, leaving her dancing solemnly in the circle like a peacock in heat. Llael and I headed back into the mountains along a remote road that Desiree had assured us was free of checkpoints. By mid-afternoon we were back at the cabin, and I rang Hugo's mobile straightaway. I found him in much better spirits.

"Hey, there," he said. "You got home all right?"

"Yeah," I said. "How about you?"

He was heading back to the car, he told me, and would be home shortly. He explained that after I had spoken to him last, he had managed to calm himself down: it suddenly dawned on him that there was a simple solution to his problem. If the dog really was addicted to drugs, all he needed to do was give them to him. Straightaway he had thrown down the bag, and the dog had leapt on it. Without its police handler, it was free to devour as much as it wanted, and it kept on eating until it could take no more. It then began to start digging into the frozen soil to bury the rest. It took an hour for the drugs to work their way through the dog's system and it dug until its paws bled, until eventually it keeled over unconscious. Hugo had tried ringing me back, but Desiree told him I was already gone.

"Weren't you afraid the dog would wake up and come after you?" I asked, thinking of those horror films where there's always one last attack left in the dying beast.

"I saw to that," he said.

"You did?"

He didn't say any more, but later he admitted that he had taken a rock and rendered the dog's skull a purée of crushed bone and frothy viscera, like a snail underfoot. I thought of the bowie knife Aviz had given me to gouge out the brains of my dog and was glad I never had to use it. I was glad, too, that Hugo had managed to get away from us before doing any real harm the night of the butternut squash incident.

The botched drug run changed everything. It was no longer safe for Hugo to use those routes. The hunters had most likely told the DEA, and they would be keeping surveillance. His traces must have been all over the dog's corpse. It was just too risky. He sent word to his American contact that they should lay off for a while, and finding himself suddenly with free time, he decided to take a trip south. It was the perfect time of year, what with the harsh winter looming and the cannabis crop long harvested. Like most people in the valley, Hugo owned a camper van for just such occasions. It was a converted orange and black school bus that had been painted magnolia and fitted out beautifully with walnut panelling, a cedar kitchen, heated shower and pull-out double beds. Despite being sumptuous, it wasn't as elegant as some of the buses others owned, which had Jacuzzis and surround-sound systems built in, but it would be more than comfortable for the trip he planned. It was to be his usual winter journey south to Mexico and possibly on to Guatemala if he felt like it, and when he asked would I like to join him, I jumped at the opportunity, especially as he said he'd keep paying me half-rate for keeping an eye on his niece.

We immediately set to work cleaning out the bus and packing up our things. I went to Fabian's house to pay him the last of what I owed, and he told me there was something he wanted to show me, something I really needed to see. It turned out to be a newsletter from a macrobiotic community north of Vancouver, which, in between long descriptions of its plans to build a new hexagonal vegetable garden and six columns of nostalgic recollections of a recent seed-gathering trip to Nepal, told of a weird incident that had occurred the previous year. The whole community had woken in the middle of the night to find their wooden shacks lit up like Christmas trees with light shining from everywhere, even up through the floor. The light had burned for fifteen minutes on and off, and had been so bright and such a vivid colour they immediately assumed it must be aliens. The incident had happened exactly three days before mine in Baños. Like me, they too had considered whether it could be that a power station had blown up or some freak lightning that had occurred. They went to huge lengths to investigate it, and after much work had found out that the HAARP research project which the US Forces was running in Alaska was conducting system trials at precisely that time. I had never heard of HAARP, but Fabian explained it was a government research programme aimed at manipulating the natural electrical frequencies that exist in the upper atmosphere by pumping millions of watts of high frequency radio energy into the ionosphere. It was kept top-secret at first and had only been revealed to Congress the previous year. The aim was to be able to fry a missile thousands of miles away or to heat up a region anywhere on earth so that they could temporarily manipulate its weather. The scalar waves they used were known to have a subtle effect on the neural system of humans, which would explain why we had all woken up at the same time, before actually seeing the light. It must have somehow triggered us, tripped our fuses. The phenomenon they were harnessing was basically the same as what causes the aurora borealis, and the light I had seen was definitely similar to that, only far brighter.

It seemed like a reasonable explanation for what happened, and I wondered whether perhaps I should write to the military to tell them of the unforeseen side effects: that it blasted whole communities with supernatural light. The technology was being devised as a stealth system – a way of destroying an enemy from thousands of miles away without leaving any visible trace – but if in the process the whole region ended up dazzled and disorientated, it would sort of give the game away. Fabian told me not to bother contacting the Americans. There were already reports that these new scalar waves were leading to huge disorientation among animals and were even killing dolphins, birds and small mammals. The army had just shrugged its shoulders, and so I reasoned the fate of a few isolated communities in the high Andes and the Rockies would hardly bother them very much more.

Anyway, Fabian wasn't convinced my experience had anything to do with HAARP. In fact, he had a whole different theory about what I and the macrobiotic goup had experienced. While he had been sceptical when I told him the story at first, now that he had corroborating evidence from the veggies, he was convinced it was far more seminal than simply military experiments. I'm not sure I can explain his concept, but as far as I could gather, he believed that the light was a broadcast from a higher consciousness blown to earth on the solar wind and sucked into parts of the Andes and Rockies in much the same way lightning finds spires.

"It's to do with polar magnetics and gravitational pull," he added when I looked befuddled.

I just nodded, not daring to ask any more.

"Light is information," he said, "a source of multidimensional communication. Those spectral flashes would have subtly affected the neurons of your mind, and its message would now be stored deep in your DNA, ready to play itself out in the course of your life."

He was convinced now that I was destined to follow a sacred path, and as a result was less upset that I didn't share his militant passion for trees.

"You have your own path," he said, "and you must follow it."

"Yes," I agreed, solemnly and self-importantly, mainly so he wouldn't be disappointed in me for abandoning his cause.

"What you saw that night was the omniverse coming to visit you," Fabian said, as he gave me a long farewell hug. "Remember it always. We play the game of being finite so well we forget that we are, in fact, infinite."

A week later we were all packed up, our passports in order and the bus cleaned out of any remains of cannabis it may have contained. I checked this myself as I didn't trust Hugo not to bring a few pounds along to make one last deal on our way through the States. He was coming under a lot of pressure from his contacts in Los Angeles to recommence supply. Their clients were beginning to feel the drought and were appalled at the prospect of having to go back to their old non-organic suppliers. Hugo didn't give a damn about the devil's whores, as he called the Hollywood crowd. It was the San Francisco Health Collective that he felt most guilty about: a charitable organisation that provided cheap cannabis to MS and Aids patients and which Hugo had always supplied at below cost.

We pulled out on to the highway south: Hugo, Llael, myself and Maud, who was an imposingly pert woman of German extraction with a forthright and artless character. She was Hugo's new girlfriend. Llael called her the Racoon because of her spiny, two-tone hair. Hugo had warned me that she could be abrasive and that she held strong opinions. He advised it might be wise to keep my distance. I had been hoping Melanie would come along, and so I was ill-disposed to Maud from the beginning. Llael had had little contact with her mother in weeks, and I knew how much she missed her.

The process of excoriation that Melanie was undergoing at the monastery, of peeling herself back to reveal her essence, was bringing up a darkness that she didn't want her daughter to see. She didn't trust herself. In what sounded worryingly like the Screamers, the Buddhists wanted her to let go of most of who she was so that she could open herself to her true Buddhahood. To achieve this, she planned on spending the winter scouring the front steps of the monastery with a hog-bristle brush and copying complicated *thangkas* into sand. Somehow, she believed, this would bring her closer to her goal.

The practice of passing through darkness before the light, of leaping the chasm, of enduring the dark night of the soul, was something shared by most of those I had met on the trip, from the enema junkies of Ecuador to the Israelis on Pedro and the Shuar shaman. In the old days, there were always places set apart for this process: pyramids, alembics, transmutation chambers – cocoons in which to metamorphose. Gardens of Gethsemane. Holy Sepulchre caves. Nowadays, it seemed you had to find your own cave. It was just a pity Melanie's was so far away from her daughter and from the warm beaches of Mexico. Considering those chandelier eyes of Melanie's, whose warmth I had bathed in every morning in Caravanserai, I couldn't imagine she could have that much darkness in her anyhow; definitely not enough to keep her away from her daughter for so long or to require a winter of scrubbing steps.

This inner despair was common among the people I met in the Canadian Rockies. Their workshops and rituals were all about facing, or overcoming, or avoiding it. They believed they were purer, more sensitive than the masses, and therefore more aware of the darkness. Like Portia had said, they were resonating at a higher frequency. To be honest, I didn't really understand: although I was introverted and self-obsessed, I was basically pretty content in my own little world; at least compared to them I was. No wonder I had been such a disappointment to the Screamers.

I wondered whether this darkness they were so intent on mining was the root of all the illness that was so common among them. Everyone was constantly sick with aches, allergies, sweats, nausea, energy depletion, etc., which they combated with everything from blue–green algae, bioenergetics, urine therapy, soya-only diets, soya-free diets, Bach remedies, ginseng, craniosacral therapy, Hopi ear candling. Their shelves were laden with more pills than a retirement home: vitamins, minerals, essences, extracts, Ayurvedic and homeopathic cures.

Llael and I played Blind Man and Rapunzel in the Dragon's Lair for most of the trip south. We used to leave the pull-out bed open as a sort of playpen. Hugo did all the driving. He had done the trip almost every winter since leaving school, heading south to some Aztec ruin in Mexico or else continuing as far as the Mayan pyramids in Guatemala, and from there heading to the coast to catch fish and surf. He knew his way along Highway 101 and the I-5 blindfolded and had friends along the route in Eugene, Berkeley, Big Sur and Santa Barbara who let us sleep in their yards and gave us showers and breakfast. Most of them were old school friends or distant relatives who had long ago cast off their bohemian ways and were always slightly alarmed to find Hugo and his freaky passengers pitching up on their doorstep. They found it hard to explain us to their corn-fed wives and Nickelodeon-reared brats. I did my best to fit in; making sure to smile and say thank you a lot, and not to leave the bathroom in too much of a mess. I hushed Hugo up whenever he started scoffing at the widescreen daises that commanded the centre of each home.

"You say yourself that we must always respect diverse cultures," I would remind him in a whisper, and he'd grumble and fall silent.

The only downside to the whole trip was Maud. Hugo had gone out of his way to warn me she could be full on. He said it was this abrasiveness that he loved most; she was a live wire, a voracious and veracious specimen. I think he must have told her to go easy on me at first, as she kept to herself for the first few days. A few times I noticed her staring at me gimlet-eyed, and I just assumed her behaviour was in keeping with the general dominance of her demeanour. It was only when we were entering the redwoods in southern Oregon that Hugo told me what Maud found so intriguing about me was my episode with the Screamers, which Hugo had told her about. She couldn't get over the fact that I hadn't had sex with Gina. To her it was astonishing, and somewhat creepy. It was why she behaved so strangely around me, he explained. I had noticed she had been keeping her distance, as though I were infected. She had even marked out three distinct zones on the bus, with Hugo up front driving, Llael and me playing on one of the beds in the middle and her on the floor at the back doing her exercises. From time to time she glanced up at me, bug-eyed with incredulity – I presumed it was because she couldn't believe anyone could get by without exercising like her.

Maud was a sports fanatic, a bundle of perpetual motion, taut and lithe. She had no *off* button. A human ping-pong, her energy had to be expended in some way, mostly through a punishing regime of exercises which she spent half the day on. She stretched out on the floor doing squat thrusts, tummy crunches and weight lifting, her racehorse body wheezing with the effort, the whiff of pheromones heavy in the air. I rarely saw her in anything other than spandex and a sports bra or bikini, which wasn't as inappropriate as it would seem, since the bus was like a sauna, hotter even than the mantraming workshop. It had been designed to ferry Canadian schoolchildren through the winter and had its eight-litre engine bellowing a back draft in on us like a smelting furnace. It was exacerbated further by the double insulation Hugo had fitted to convert the bus into a grow-room for the summer. It was fine when we were up north, but the further south we drove, the more we roasted. None of us ever bothered wearing very much – only throwing a dressing gown and a pair of boots on at petrol stations and diners.

It was the fact that I had never had sex throughout my whole time in the Americas that astounded Maud more than anything. She couldn't imagine how you would get through a week, let alone a life, without it. It was too vital, too central to everything.

"Surely you slept with Eve?" she asked. "How could you not? Tell me you wanted to, at least!"

I tried to avoid the question, but in an enclosed, metal cell moving on a straight highway at 60mph there was little chance.

"We . . . we just decided to wait," I bleated.

"No! No, you didn't!" she cried, genuinely upset. Her boob tube, echoing the point, had the word "orgasm" written across it in touchy-feely, bubble letters. "Never do that! Never! It's by far the worst thing you could have done. Can you imagine an animal waiting? Or an angel? People always say the saints and prophets want us to be like animals: lambs in the field, birds in the sky, fishes in the sea. Do any of them wait? Do they? It's ludicrous. Of course it is. You must have sex.

"You just must," she went on. "That's what went wrong with you and Eve, you see? You didn't fuse your souls. You didn't even bother to try."

Maud was incredibly tactile and stroked me vigorously as she talked, but not in a provocative way; it was just her way of relating to the world. She would never even dream of having sex with me because we weren't a couple. She believed sex opened portals that should only ever be shared with a loved one. It created a channel which, as far as I could gather, was like a wormhole to infinity.

"But I never did love anyone," I explained, thinking it would get me off the hook. "And certainly I didn't love Gina."

She ignored the last remark and just shouted, "Eve???!!! What about Eve?"

I knew I couldn't explain it to her.

"Let's just call that whole incident a wipe-out," she said. "Okay? But if you ever find yourself in love again, you must make love. You must broadcast your love through the channel in the form of an orgasm, a shudder of ecstasy that ripples out through the galaxy."

She called it a ripple in the fabric of time and went on with a pseudo quantum explanation for it which I couldn't catch. Each night, Hugo and she would broadcast to the world, and although the bus's suspension was hard enough so that Llael and I didn't feel it, we invariably heard the final exclamation: Hugo trumpeting like the rasp of the fighter planes over Vilcabamba; Maud's wail reminiscent of the prayers at the powwow. Llael would lie awake giggling, knowing something was funny, but not quite sure what. It seemed that Maud's panting was a constant presence – either under her weights during the day or under Hugo at night – and to my surprise I soon got used to it. It was really only when she began having her "menses", as she called it, that I began to feel uneasy – and only because she practically rubbed our noses in it.

"You must understand the blood," she told me. "It all starts with that. It's all in there: the encryption, the encoding, the DNA."

This was over muesli somewhere between Monterey and Santa Barbara, with nowhere to escape to on an eighteen-foot bus.

"We need to feel it, smell it, drink it. It's a living symbol, our connection to the ancestors, the ultimate codes of consciousness. We forget we are only genetic libraries, vehicles for our blood's journey through time."

"Indeed," I intoned as noncommittally as I could through a mouthful of seeds and grains.

"Listen, Mocha, you nourished yourself into being with the blood of your mother. Why reject it now? It's not a curse. It's the opposite: it's our power point – our genetic blueprint."

I was rescued on that occasion by Hugo, who had pulled into a petrol station and wanted me to fill the windscreen washer for him. I think he must have told her to go easy on me after that, as she was on her back doing her scissor kicks when I returned. A few days later I let slip something about Eve and it set her off again.

"Mocha," she said, "we've got to get you sorted. You're a mess. You can't go on hanging out with kids all your life, you know? You need to grow up, man. You need to have sex. By knowing a woman in her moontime, not only do you get to know her – her core, where the answers lie and all the future questions – but you get to know yourself. That is the greatest gift a woman gives.

"Are you with me?" she said. She was like a sniffer dog when she got on her pulpit, like Paddy Gish high on *pasta básica*. There was no way I could avoid her. "You've gotta abandon the taboos, man. Let it flow."

I nodded desperately.

"Remember when you praised my pasta dish the other night?" she asked. "How good you thought the sauce was?"

"Uh-huh," I said. She had brought a huge box of vegetables from her garden and jars of tomatoes and pickles she had made herself, and was cooking wonderful meals for us each night.

"The reason it tastes so bloody good is 'cause I feed the soil. I put the fertility back into it. The problem with farming now is we don't bleed into the earth any more. The link between us and the ground has been broken. We've choked and gagged the life source."

"You menstruated over the tomatoes?" I asked.

"Of course! Only a few drops mixed in water, but it's so potent, Mocha . . . it's sanctified. The most highly oxygenated blood of all, and the only way you can get it is as a gift from a woman. When your sperm comes in contact with it, it telepaths back to you everything you need to know about me. I figured that, since you don't have sex, eating it would really help you. Would open you up. And I think it's doing the trick. I think it's helping. I see results already. You've got to get with it, man. This stuff won't be around for ever – 'cause our fertility cycle is changing. Women don't need to be available to breed so often any more; we're cutting adrift from the moon, moving to a yearly cycle. Just watch. It's an agreement we have with the planet – check it out if you want, medics are already taking notice."

Hugo, who was only slightly less evangelical on the subject, added, "Men spend their whole lives chasing blood in wars and horror movies 'cause ours is hidden from us, lurking inside in dark tunnels, and when we find it pouring out naturally, it freaks the hell out of us. Go figure!"

"That's what's at the root of the whole vampire thing," Maud agreed.

Chapter 15

THE ROAD WAS a feast for the eyes, munificent in its abundance: from the apocalyptic wastes of Mount Saint Helen to the lush forests of Oregon and northern California, and on down to the bounteous lands further south, an Eden of oranges, almonds, olives, artichokes, pistachios, grapefruits, lemons, cherries and grapes, all in neat rows stretching to the horizon. Johnny Lovewisdom would have been in heaven. Apricots, strawberries, garlic, lettuce, walnuts, mushrooms and tiny, ebony Mexicans with raven hair and bright baseball caps working wearily through them.

What happened next has no logic to it. I really thought I was over Eve. I hadn't bothered dropping the stone back to the Charlotte Islands because I was certain there was no need to any longer. I had moved on. I was over her. Llael had opened my heart again, and the cloud that had shrouded me since the night Eve walked out and that followed me throughout my time in Peru and back to Caravanserai and to the farm in Ireland had finally begun to lift the night Hugo detonated. From the moment I started telling Llael about Grumpy Oilskins with her lying close to me, heart to heart, I began to sense the barest touch of enchantment. I knew I had turned a corner. At one point that night, she and I had both looked up and seen a meteor streaking past the window, a rainbow-coloured streamer burning up its cosmic payload, and instantly I realised the healing had begun.

Unfortunately it hadn't gone as deep as I thought. Sometimes we can hoodwink ourselves. We can scam ourselves better than any conman or card shark. The truth was that I was still as messed up about Eve as the day I first went tearing out of Caravanserai into the Peruvian desert, and the moment we crossed the Californian state line it all came unravelled. It was as if the Shuar or my time with Diarmuid or with Llael had never happened. As if Eve had just got the call from her attorney that morning and I was now sitting drinking rum with that old farmer on his porch with the moths fluttering overhead, except that a different verse of Dylan's song was playing. Something about being chewed up and spat out all over again.

Suddenly there was only one thing on my radar. It was her. Eve. This was her state. Somewhere amidst its thirty million people, she was living and breathing. My senses switched to red alert. I couldn't help it; the place was too charged with significance, everything about it rigged to trigger my memories. Like a vampire smelling blood, I could sense her proximity. Eve was somewhere near by, thinking, dreaming, beaming her effulgent smile. She was in the air I inhaled. I had read in *Variety* that she was shooting a road movie for Warner Brothers, and while most of the filming was being done on the lot, some of the exteriors were being shot around California. I was bound to run into her. Of course I was. It was inevitable. If the gods wanted it so, it would happen.

Every roadside cluster of trailers, honey wagons and generators I saw made my heart pound. Was it the film crew? I would be guided to her; I knew I would. Rabbit missed her as much as I did. He wanted me to find love. (How long could I stay hanging out with a little child for after all? She was bound to grow up one day.) If Rabbit was any good at all, he'd be able to rig up something: a passing glance, a chance encounter. It was not as if I hadn't made it easy for him. Hugo had business to do in Los Angeles, and we were going to be spending three whole days there. It needn't involve too huge a manipulation of space-time to whisk up something. Either she'd be filming somewhere in the city, or else she'd be driving home here every evening. I wasn't asking for a full-blown miracle; all I needed was a simple twist of fate.

It shocked me how desperate I became and how quickly. I suppose it was like those addicts who don't just step off the wagon but plunge headlong back in. If Eve weren't a movie star, would I be doing any of this? If she were a baggage handler in LAX or an accountant, would I still care? The movie business was just so alluring. It was about dreams. She was a bit player in the world's dreams, practically mythic when you come to think about it. Rabbit told me that people saw her movies in the same way that he saw my life: able to fast-forward and rewind to where they wanted – it made her seem somehow multidimensional. She could appear on thousands of screens all across the world at the same time. People knew what was going to happen to her before *she* did. That was really cool, but it wasn't the reason I was chasing her. At the core of it, it was still about love. I promise. No matter how desperate or warped I may have become, I still avow that I was simply fighting for a piece of magic.

The first two days in LA were hell: staggering bleary-eyed through the streets with every oasis turning into a mirage, every sight of her morphing into someone else, my nerves jangling from a hundred false alarms and dashed hopes, the torture of always being almost on the point of relief. My neck was in spasm from craning one too many times. Llael felt hurt that I wasn't playing with her any more, but *I* had a life, too. She had to understand that.

Despite not seeing Eve, or anyone from any of her movies, or anyone even vaguely famous during the first two days in the city, I never lost hope. On the morning of the third day, I took a taxi out to Mulholland Drive to the house where I had sent all those letters from the desert in Peru, even though I knew she wasn't there any more. I just wanted to see the manicured lawns, the double garage she had damaged with her agent's Humvee, the pool that her New Age friends had enjoyed so much, the gates that she had ordered new locks for over the phone from Nadine's kitchen. There was an elderly German woman on the lawn directing a Latino boy, who I guessed was Ecuadorian, where to point the sprinkler. What with her squeaky hearing aid and semi-fluent English, she thought I said that I used to live here when I shouted through the gates at her. Immediately she pressed a button around her neck and the gates opened, inviting me in. But I declined. It was all becoming too creepy, even for me. I was weirding myself out. What next – would I end up rolling around on her bed?

I tried telling myself that Eve had dumped me fair and square. She had made it abundantly clear that we had nothing in common, and, who knows, maybe she was right. I should have moved on; I promised myself I would. I blame it all on Maud. I really think I had begun to put my life back together until she started messing with my mind. During one of her interminable lectures on the journey south, she had said that when two "electro–magnetic beings" join frequencies in love incredible things occur; part of them literally leaves the planet. This part gets catapulted into the beyond and becomes a triangulation point forever measuring the distance and angles between them and beaming back at them all their love, like some mutant Pythagorean theorem. But if the couple break up suddenly and the triangulation point isn't realigned, it keeps on beaming back all the old love until it eventually drives the two partners insane. What Eve and I had shared was beyond words, Maud said, and when two people encounter love of such purity, the resonance of it can blow your circuits out. It trips the switch, and you both need time to replace the fuse and come to terms with the force. To feel the force and not be frightened of it. Your blood telepaths itself on to the other person's cells, and it becomes branded there for ever – at least that's what she told me. You can't just walk away from that kind of love, not when you're dealing with something so potent. Eve and I had drawn down too strong juju from the stars, Maud said. It would be wrong to just abandon it now.

Maud patiently explained to me that our sort of love doesn't often make it this far into 3-D, and if we were to just let it go, on a whim as it were, it could have unforeseen consequences for us both. Like a wizard casting spells when drunk; like dropping isotope 236 into water. It's the reason you sometimes see zombies roaming around nightclubs hollowed out by the intensity of a too–pure romance, left eviscerated for ever. For ever searching outside themselves for a potion of the same proof. Desperately seeking the next fix, the next tolerable relationship to cancel out the disappointment of the last one. To hide the emptiness inside, that bitter dandelion taste on the tongue. It was my duty to save us both from that. My duty.

After two and a half days spent in LA with no sign of Eve and only an afternoon to go before we left the city for ever, I wasn't completely despairing. I had a plan B, you see. A fall-back position that I had already prepared. I had taken the precaution of booking a Warner Brothers tour for the third day, but I didn't want to have to resort to it unless absolutely necessary – unless Rabbit had screwed up and failed me. I was reluctant to do it in case it might be construed as stalking, but if left with no other choice . . .

The problem with Rabbit was that I could never accuse him of failing until long after the event. He would always chance his arm and say, *Wait and see – it'll all turn out just as you want it in the end*. And there was no way of knowing if he was wrong. No way of knowing for certain that he didn't have some grand plan up his sleeve which he was only going to reveal at the last minute. That was the problem with being stuck in the present; I was never able to see the future like he was. He *had* me every time, and he knew it. If I ever did confront him about something which he had promised would materialise and hadn't, he'd just dismiss it aloofly, saying that it *was for the best*, or, *it wasn't meant to be*, as if he knew more about it than I ever would, and that if I saw it from his perspective, I too would understand. God, he was pompous at times. Really, the master of platitudes. But I could never stay angry with him for long. To him, I was like putty. All he had to do was flood my mind with dopamine, mix it with some endorphins and tell me how he and the angels and the universe and God all loved me beyond measure, and I'd swoon every time. Every time. I couldn't help it, I'd swoon like a damsel. He'd send my neurotransmitters tearing down the highway of universal love, and I'd be smitten all over again. For a guardian angel, he was one crafty devil.

No sooner had Llael and I got off the bus at the Taco Bell across from Gate 3 of Warner Brothers than my brain switched into overdrive: my ears scanning like echo-sounders, my eagle-eyes tracking the territory. I understood the term "eyes out on sticks" for the first time. I wanted them to be periscopes that could see around every pillar, into every upper window, beyond every security barrier. For me, this was a surveillance manoeuvre, not a tour.

On leaving the rangy, lamppost palms of Burbank Avenue and crossing into her place of work – *Hi, dearie, hope I'm not disturbing you* – I realised I was stepping on sacred ground, the ground on which Eve, my Eve, walked every day. Tread softly for you tread on my dreams. Only for the stabilising influence of Llael, I would have hyperventilated there and then, collapsing to the ground in a swoon. And maybe that wouldn't be such a bad thing. Maybe Eve would spot me there, lying unconscious on the Warner Bros tarmac, and come running. She'd cradle me in her arms, nuzzling me to her breast as the rest of the fatheads taking the tour looked on in awe, hearing her whisper the words, "Mocha! It's you I love! Only you!"

They would cheer and throw their hats in the air, and *Entertainment Tonight* would clear its schedule to cover "Live on air" the real-life romance of the movie star and the potato farmer on the Warner Brothers front lot. Perhaps Spielberg or Soderberg would happen by, and after grabbing a camcorder from some guy, would record the whole scene. And from then on, every tour would pause at this point, and the perky, foxy-faced steward would retell the story and everyone would go "Aahh shucks" and click their cameras at the bare tarmac. We'd sell the film rights and use the money to expand our donkey sanctuary.

I sat up on the stretch golf cart, breathing to calm my nerves, tapping into Llael's energy for comfort. I could hear Rabbit murmuring about how pathetic I was, how desperate. How near to becoming a stalker I had become. But I wouldn't listen. If he was any good at all, it would never have come to this. He would have sorted something out. No wonder angels are out of fashion. When it gets down to it, they're just not there for you. All I wanted was to meet her again, to wrap things up. Then I could move on . . . if I had to. But as long as she was on this side of the grave, the least I deserved was a proper goodbye. If Maud was right, then it was vital we cut off this unmoored triangulation point or we'd end up like the zombies on the dance floor. If Rabbit couldn't arrange it, I'd do it myself. This crummy chariot would transport me on winged wheels into her outstretched arms.

I had casually asked at the ticket office whether her film was shooting today.

"Information regarding current Warner Brother productions and its affiliates is confidential, sir," the woman had said, but I could tell from her eyes that it was, and what's more she wanted me to know it. She was torn between telling me and keeping her job, it was obvious. She was on my side. Maybe Rabbit was kicking in now, making up for his previous failure.

"Thank you," I said with my most winning wink. "Thank you, so much!"

Just before we set off, Llael was taken away from me and put sitting up front beside the driver while an overweight Texan was put in her place to balance the cart. He smelt of hot dogs and instant coffee and had a wad of foolscap paper which he kept jotting on and crossing things out. He was as jittery as me: I wasn't the only one hoping to have my dreams come true.

"We'll always have Paris," the brassy and breathless young guide said – a little wannabe star. "Who can tell me who said that? . . . Well, ladies and gentlemen, that portensheewus line was first uttered right here in the French Street back lot by none other than . . ."

"Humphrey Bogart," we all chimed.

"Rightee-o!" she chimed. "In the greatest love story ever told."

I saw it immediately for what it was: a nudge from Rabbit that he was on my side and everything was going to plan. A beam a mile wide spread across my face as our little buggy of dreams roved on into a tiny forest where parts of *Robin Hood* and the *Dukes of Hazzard* had been shot. It was strange to find these trees in downtown LA. They looked like they had been there for ever, the last indigenous trees south of the Redwoods. I thought of Fabian. Although he hated movies as much as television, he would have liked those trees.

On the far side of the forest was a city block built for the James Cagney movies and now with the "ER" El-track tearing right through it. But I didn't take much notice, because I was instead straining to see through the upstairs windows into the offices behind. I knew I'd recognise her from far off: that slight strain in the neck from an old whiplash; the trace of shimmy in her walk from her catwalk days. All I needed was a glance and I would have her. Her choreography was etched on my mind the way a gosling imprints its mother.

With Mount Hollywood rising disconcertingly in the background, the guide pointed out Mel Gibson's office and Steven Seagal's. Eve wasn't at their level, of course, but perhaps she had something too – a broom cupboard or whatever. She had talked of her PA, who presumably had to work out of someplace. I didn't want to ask the guide in case it aroused her suspicion. I knew that if I caught sight of Eve, I'd have to make a run for it, and I wanted to have made as little impression on the staff as possible, so that only my empty seat would reveal that I had been and gone. In the event of such a thing, I felt sure they'd take good care of Llael – probably show her a movie and fill her full of Bugs Bunny junk. She'd be so happy with herself that she'd probably sulk when I got back to her, either hauled between two guards or arm-in-arm with Eve. For what else were the Americans if not conscientious about their children? This wasn't the Huaorani; they didn't strangle them with vines.

Llael was by far the youngest person on the tour, and a few times the guide pointed out things especially for her – the Bugs Bunny tower, the *Little House on the Prairie* school – but she had no idea what these things were. Although she was one of the few people in the valley who watched television, she did so rarely and it was mostly Discovery. It was the sight of a huge animated grizzly bear in a props warehouse that got her most excited, asking me was it Grumpy Oilskins.

A sudden sharp intake of breath ran through the cart as we spotted Matt Dillon climbing up metal steps into offices behind an old *Gremlins* facade. It reminded me of a whale-watching trip I had taken, that same sense of group exhilaration. Dillon was a minke. I wondered would Eve have got the same reaction from us: she was not quite as famous – more of a beluga, or a porpoise. I tried not to think about it. I needed to stay grounded. There was too much at stake.

Just like the whale-watching trip, the first hour was definitely the most exciting: that sense of expectation before the adrenalin crashed again. And it certainly did crash: knocking on fake walls and roaming through warehouses lost its charm pretty quickly. What can you say about a musty hangar full of trees on wheels and fibreglass rocks?

The Texan, growing shifty beside me, began asking awkward questions.

"Ma'am, can we see the Ubu Productions office – 'Sit, Ubu, sit!'" he said.

"That's on the Paramount lot, sir, not Warners."

He jotted down the guide's answer verbatim, including a little sketch of where she had said it, and then continued, "Ma'am, in episode 19 of series 1, Frasier tries to disguise the new chair with a rug, but Martin yanks it off, and Eddie has to sit on the sofa. Do you have the original rug, or if not, a replica?"

"Frasier is a Paramount production, sir."

He jotted down a note.

"I see," he said. "Well, ma'am, perhaps you could tell us – the Fonze, he slides down the banisters of the school in *Happy Days*, but it's only a one-storey building. Could you bring us to the banister?"

"I'm not sure where that might be. I can research it if . . ."

"Ueh, ueh!" he shouted, mimicking the false buzzer sound of a quiz show. "Wrongarama! That was a wrong answer. In fact it was a trick question. *Happy Days* was a Paramount production!"

That was when I spotted her. Eve. She was coming out of a trailer with the words Star Waggon (spelt with two g's) on the side – a blue sky panel rising up behind her, painted that same aureate glow of Pacific light I had first seen in Seattle.

I steeled myself. Rather than running straight towards her, I held my ground. The cart was heading in her direction anyway. It was she! My Eve! She was here! My winged chariot would indeed convey me hence. I sent balloons of gratitude soaring towards Rabbit. I forgave him everything. The triangulation point theory was true, and it was just reeling us in now.

When we were still a few hundred yards away, the cart veered off a little, and I knew this was the moment. My moment. I leapt to the ground, only fleetingly aware of the panicked cries of the guide, behind me.

"Sir, sir! Siiiiiiiir!" the guide shouted as I bounded across the lot. I was oblivious. There she was, a hundred yards ahead, just as I remembered her. Oh how sweet! How sweet.

She heard me coming and turned . . .

No! It was uncanny – he looked so like her. He really did. At least from behind. That same long neck and lustrous hair. The height and everything. The same way of rolling his shoulders. I stopped dead in my tracks, just in time. Of course I did. I didn't hug him or anything. I promise. He stared hard at me for a moment, before shrugging those replica shoulders of his and going back to work. He was adding a cross bar to the blue sky panel – hammering in three-inch nails.

Meanwhile, the cart had swerved to a halt and was swinging around to scoop me back up. I just stood there, frozen in shame. God, I felt stupid. So stupid. Where was that wave of enchantment now? I could sense Rabbit trying not to laugh. The bastard. Poor Llael. She understood. I could see she did; there was such sympathy in her eyes. It was more than just pity.

The buggy brought us straight to the gate, and security guards escorted us off the premises. We went across to Taco Bell to feed Llael's new-found craving for junk food. It was the least she deserved after that, to gorge on Double Decker® Taco Supremes®, Nachos BellGrande®, Cinnamon Twists, MexiMelts® and Caramel Apple Empanadas. I tried not to think how I'd explain these newly acquired tastes of hers to Melanie.

Chapter 16

BACK AT THE bus, a bushy-haired young man in a smock was talking to Hugo. His name was Jedah, and he had the same suspicious halcyon haze I had seen often in Canada, the look of weak-willed, born-again types and cult members. His VW Beetle was parked alongside us with a ski box on the roof, and when I asked him where he skied, he hesitated before mumbling that the box was for his brother's crutches. He blushed as he said it, and it seemed so ridiculous that somehow it made me remember that Hugo's money was brought to Canada in a roof box, and then I understood. The guy – so pixie-faced and amiable – just seemed like such an unlikely drug dealer.

As I buttered up a cashew nut sandwich for Llael, I listened as Jedah complained to Hugo about the grief he was getting from his rich clients over the sudden ending of their drug supply. Some of them were so upset at being deprived of their organic weed that they had bribed their gardeners and their office maintenance engineers to sow a few seeds for them. Screenwriters and directors from all over Beverly Hills had been hassling Jedah for the last fortnight about the risk of emphysema they now faced from having to smoke Monsanto-sprayed grass. They were coming down with allergies, and it was all our fault. Or, in fact, it was Hugo's fault. He should never have made that last run without Hope, Jedah said. Now he'd ruined the route for everyone. There were already rumours that the DEA were building a hide and a lookout tower in the area. Jedah was angry. Hugo had messed it up for everyone, and by way of a favour and penance, Jedah asked us would we drive some of his mates to a rally near Barstow in the Mojave desert the next day. Hugo agreed right off; it was the least he could do.

So next morning, instead of continuing on south to Tijuana as planned, we folded up the beds, I helped Maud take apart her weight bench, and we scattered cushions on the floor in an effort to turn the bus back to its original function as a passenger vehicle. Then we set off driving around west Hollywood, picking up Jedah's friends. I sat on the transmission, cranking open and shut the accordion doors and calling out "Mojave" to anyone we met, just to make sure we got the right people. They were a motley crew of wannabe actors, studio gofers, internet hackers and macrobiotic waitresses for the most part. I felt like the conductors in Ecuador, circling the town and shouting their destination over and over again until the bus was filled.

"Esmer-aldas-Esmer-aldas-Esmer-aldas."

Llael would grasp their hands, leading them into the bus like the tattered-gown girl in Quito who had coaxed me to Vilcabamba.

The rally turned out to be further away than we thought, nearer Needles than Barstow. Hugo grumbled a bit, but I had no complaint. It gave me a chance to see more of the desert: the bleak, stone-strewn backdrop to so many Westerns; the familiar canyons and cattails and cottonwoods; the classic images of jackrabbits lurking behind smoke trees and mini windstorms churning tumbleweed into thickets of mesquite.

We reached the community hall to find a crowd of people outside singing songs and another group clustered around an unfurled bolt of canvas, painting a banner: "No Nukes for Wile E. Coyote," it read. The singers were Native Americans, and their songs sounded similar to the ones at the powwow – the same cadences and keening pattern – only this time they were wearing regular clothes. Other buses, *real* ones, were pulling up out front, full of cooperative-kitchen types and the concerned moms, as well as the usual student activists. There were mini-vans too, with the names of different Colorado River tribes on them. Jedah explained that this was a public meeting for the locals about a radioactive waste dump that was to be built in the area. The amount of plutonium they planned to bury was equivalent to several nuclear bombs, he said. There was nothing particularly startling in this – the Mojave had always been a handy place to hide stuff – except that this particular site was between three tribal territories and only a few miles from the Colorado River, which provided most of LA's water. This had brought the Indians and concerned parent lobby out in force.

Inside the hall, people were arranged in concentric circles. At the centre were the elders: women and men in their seventies and older, some as worn as the centuagenarians of Vilcabamba. Those that still could were singing and doing simple dance steps. One of the company men, an engineer with a doctorate in nuclear physics, stood up first and explained how the dump was to be the most modern in the world, designed in such a way as to make leaking impossible. He oozed expertise, and I was impressed with his ideas until another engineer stood up and read out the nearly verbatim assurances the company had given about their other four sites, all of which had leaked. Two of them had become federal emergency zones. She pointed out that the company's newest, state-of-the-art site in Nevada had already contaminated the ground hundreds of feet below the site; in another ten feet it would reach the water table.

One of the elders stood up.

"This is the place we call Silyaye Aheace," he began. "Maybe we don't come here so much any more, maybe we should . . . come more often, I mean. It's where we've always collected the fruit from the screwbean mesquite. For us, it's sacred; part of our medicine chest. It is here they want to put nuclear waste in a hole in the ground. We as Pipa Aha Macav, the Mojave people, the Keepers of the River, must stand up, because the land is sacred and because we sing about it in our songs and in our stories. The songs are maps of our mind as much as the land, telling of the birds that pass through, the seasonal and celestial cycles and the sources of rare food and water. That's why we called it

Silyaye Aheace, the Place of Screwbean Mesquite. For many years it was a staple food for us, and we would gather here in the season. I remember it fondly, this place. For my grandmother, it was a bounty of herbs found nowhere else. My sons today still come in the season to run the ancient trails. We hold ceremony and conduct spirit runs here, to gain strength. Every year I lead the young men here. This is Mojave land. Our church, our temple. We need to know our stories and songs so that when *they* come, we know which is ours and which is not: Silyaye Aheace is ours."

Some of his speech was spoken and other parts sung, and in between were lines that I couldn't make out. I imagined what the disaffected bureaucrats sitting on their stackable seats must have made of it. For them this deal was worth billions. They had already got George Bush Sr to rezone the area in his last days in office. Such things don't come cheap. The chasm between the two minds could never be bridged.

Things got impassioned fairly quickly: a young girl singing a song about plutonium's twenty-five thousand year half-life – comparing it to the three thousand years since the Pharaohs built the Pyramids – was told to shut up by an engineer. Her father lunged at him. A geologist was drowned out in the heckling.

Jedah signalled for Hugo and me to follow him outside.

"It's always the same," Jedah said. "It's always so fucking fraught. Let's go someplace – just wander. There's some cool stuff around here."

The three of us got back on to the bus, where Maud was squatting on an exercise mat teaching Llael pelvic floor exercises.

"You can never start too young," she said defensively when Hugo raised an eyebrow. "It'll save her years of cramps later on, trust me."

Jedah directed us back along the road a few miles through creosote bushes covered in a fibrous orange growth, a parasite digging its tendrils into the plant and sucking it dry. I couldn't imagine this being a bounty of herbs. It looked post-apocolyptic. Near Old Woman Mountain we got out and started walking up through a tilting valley of rose-colored stone with amphitheatres of piled rock scattered on either side. Rocks were the only things that were bountiful, and they appeared even more numerous as they were partially mirrored in parched ponds of water.

"It's as good a place for a dump as any," Jedah said, leading the way up through a ruin of boulders, "don't you think? What else are we meant to do with the stuff? No one's worked out how to launch it into space yet. And anyway, these days it's all done professional: encased in concrete; buffer zones for miles around. The plants, the dragonflies, the seeds, even the fucking dew: they are all monitored for hundreds of years to come."

"You mean you're not against it?" I asked.

"Them Indians will get millions in compensation," he said. "They'll get jobs, too, and recreation facilities, conservation areas, anything they want. They're on to a good thing, if only they could see it."

"So what the hell did you come here for?" Hugo asked. "What did you drag us out for?"

"I *have* to be here. I come to them all . . . It's, it's a long story," Jedah said dismissively, kicking a rock and sending a kangaroo rat scampering off towards some cactus. "Just up here is what I want to show you guys."

Jedah turned and led us straight up the side of the canyon, picking his way through the scree like a goat. He stopped suddenly, and there in front of us on the face of a boulder, perched high above the road, was a form scratched into the rock. A sign, a design, some ancient religious or artistic symbol, carved out hundreds, even thousands of years before as part of a network of petroglyphs the ancestors of the people in the community hall had left in the region. Their tattoos of entitlement. Simple linear designs. Geometric symbols that no one understood any more. Some were clearly animal figures: bighorn sheep and rattlesnakes thought to represent the spirit helpers of the shamans – their *Rabbits*. Like the jaguar on the giant's shoulders in San Agustin. Jedah told us that only once had he ever seen a rock painting representing a human being. It was just an outline like a gingerbread man, but with the same line repeated three times outside, as though made with three different sized cookie cutters. Llael said she thought it showed the figure's aura.

I wanted to stay there longer, exploring the caves and rocks more fully. It was so redolent of all the Carlos Castaneda books I had read, so mysterious and alien. But Hugo was paranoid about Llael. She was turning over stones looking for more petroglyphs, and he was convinced she'd get bitten by a snake.

"We should get back to the meeting anyhow," Jedah said.

"Why," Hugo asked, "if you don't support it?"

"I have to keep an eye on something. Some photos. That's why I'm here," Jedah said. "Did you not see them?"

Jedah had got on the bus that morning with a large black portfolio that he had opened when we reached the hall and taken out two black and white photos. These he mounted on a neat collapsible stand and set up at the front of the room. They were pictures of a mushroom cloud. Awesome, frightening photos; beautiful, too. Mesmerising. Like when they show God exploding from the firmament in Baroque altarpieces. The mushrooms (I couldn't tell whether it was the same one in both photos) were huge and still swelling, soaring through an otherwise cloudless sky towards the ionosphere. Their stalks were lined with horizontal strata like the face of the Grand Canyon at sundown, and their crowns were blotchy, with some parts as clear as tomato–smeared ravioli, or the surface of the cerebellum, and others as faint as ink in water. It was as though the explosion had not been completely confined to this dimension; not all of it was here; some of it had escaped and we were just seeing its shadow. It had ripped a tear in the fabric, as the Q'ero had said. In both photos a group of soldiers were silhouetted in the foreground, cowering before its omnipotence.

"That was my dad," Jedah now told us soberly. "The one on the left in the helmet. He's been lugging those same photos around with him to demos and rallies for nearly twenty years now: bearing witness, he calls it, sharing the story. Every weekend of my childhood I spent on the margins of angry crowds, waiting for him to pack up and come home. Last year, it finally got to him, the residue of whatever he'd inhaled that day. He got sick with the leukaemia, and I promised I'd keep up the work for him. At least while he's alive. It's what keeps him breathing, and as long as he's still sucking air, I'll keep coming. I reckon I owe him that much. He only took the army job 'cause my ma was pregnant and they needed cash.

"He lives just near here, just out past Barstow," Jedah said. "Runs a little goldmine, or at least he did until he got sick."

"A goldmine?" I said. It sounded crazy, a hundred miles outside LA and a hundred years after the gold rush.

"Yeah," Jedah said. "My uncle's got it now. We could drop in if you want? It's not far, and it would mean a lot to Dad."

Hugo wasn't keen. He had gone out of his way already to help Jedah. He wanted to spend the rest of the day hunting for datura.

"Are you out of your mind?" I said when he told me. I knew enough from the Castaneda books to know datura was bad stuff. Even that wily old shaman Don Juan had stayed clear of it.

"It could kill you as easily as get you stoned," I said.

I was relieved when Jedah backed me up, saying it was the wrong season anyhow.

"But I'm not after the flowers," Hugo had replied. "The leaves are good too."

"Yeah! But that's pure Russian Roulette," Jedah said. "Get the dose wrong and you're gone."

"So what? You go happy."

Jedah and I insisted we weren't going to help him look for datura. No way. And so, in the end he gave us the keys of the bus and told us to meet him back there at sunset.

Jedah's hometown was a fly-blown ghost town, with precious few remains of its old gold rush opulence. The only obvious signs were an ornate gilt mirror that stretched the full length of the bar and a 1930s soda fountain that had been shipped around the coast from Chicago and then carried up from LA port. The hardware store still had a sign outside saying dynamite for sale, but that was largely for tourists. At the back of a rickety old warehouse was Jedah's dad's place. I wanted to take Llael and Maud for milkshakes while Jedah visited his dad, but he insisted that we all come along.

"This has been his life: meeting people, talking to them. It's what keeps him going, battling on year after year. I know he'd really love to see you guys, to have an audience again. It would do him the world of good."

There was no answer to that, and we followed inside.

From the doorway, I could see him stretched out lifeless, but the moment he spotted us, it was like a jolt of electricity shot through him and he catapulted upright.

"Hiya, folks," he wheezed, extending a liver-spotted arm to us. "Welcome, welcome! Don's the name. Has my son shown you guys the photos? Did youz see 'em? Jedah, did you show 'em?"

Jedah nodded and Don spat contentedly into a spittoon of frothy phlegm. He reached for smaller copies of the same photos that stood in plastic frames on his bedstand.

"That's me on the right, there," he said, becoming more animated by the minute. "Did you tell 'em, Jedah? Marine Corps out of Fort Worth, and that baby there is Shot Bee, an eight kiloton tower bomb, about half the size of Hiroshima's 'Little Boy'."

He said it almost with pride. Then he lay back on his pillow, closed his eyes and began to reel out his speech, like a priest reading the liturgy for the millionth time.

"Arrived about 0400 – pitch darkness. Outta the bus and into trenches say about six feet deep. All of us had Q clearance – wha'dy-ya know? Ring-side seats. 'Kneel down and bury your heads in your elbows; eyes closed,' we heard over the speakers. Speakers! Yeah, for sure! The whole thing set up and ready for us like a Coney Island extravaganza. Countdown to zero coming at ya. Then silence, utter fucking silence."

Don stifled a cough and gasped with the effort, the passion, the drama of a story he must have told a thousand times before.

"First the light, the brightest I've ever seen – even though my eyes were closed and my arms over them. Then the noise: a blast, thunderous, rolling across the desert, pushing the fireball outwards. That was when I peeked. I had to. The first wave was just touching the ground and a second one ricocheting upward and outward, rolling and churning; destroying everything. I could see the bones of my hand, man!

"The bastard was coming right at me, and I pulled my helmet down and pressed hard to the earth. It was shaking – felt like a giant fly swatter whacking my ass. Everything was an overexposed X-ray; the stunted trees like veins reaching out of the heart of the earth before crumbling to dust, like a vampire, staked.

"Then it was all over. The longest ten seconds of my life, boys, I'm tellin' ya – and a lifetime of problems just beginning. Then came the wind, strong enough to take your head off, that is, if you were stupid enough to look up.

"The sun was just beginning to rise, turning the mushroom heliotrope. They loaded us back on to the bus then, and there was rumours of a full-cooked breakfast, all the trimmings, back at mess. Instead they took us in to ground zero, had us wander around for a while. All that was left of the tower were four stumps sticking out of concrete – tapered to a melted point, bent all skew-ways. Everything else had evaporated. There was a tank, still intact, but you touch it and it turns to pure ash. It was hard to see much or even breathe with the dust, dirt, sage brush, all incinerated and now drifting home to earth. All that shit had exploded right at us and was then sucked upwards by the vacuum. Now it was coming home to roost.

"When we got back to the bus, we swept each other down and someone read me with a Geiger. A few of us were borderline and were told to shower well when we got back. One idiot sent the needle off the dial. They found a squelched-up ball of dust on him. A souvenir, he said. It would have burnt right through his heart overnight. One of my friends was taken out of the tent in the dawn bleeding from his nose and eyes and ears. I never heard from him again."

Don collapsed into a fit of coughing. But he seemed revitalised by the story, by telling it one more time. I didn't know what to say. He must have had the same reaction a thousand times or more. Utter silence. I could see he was delighted that it had worked again. It couldn't fail to mesmerise, to anaesthetise.

"At least I got paid," Don said, when his coughing subsided. "My medical expenses taken care of. Them tribal boys weren't even warned beforehand. The government had said the land was uninhabited, but that didn't take into account all them Indians roaming around. Some of them went blind within weeks; others poisoned slowly over time. They never suspected nothing, thinking it was just another of the white man's diseases. The sickest joke of all was the names we called the bombs: Mohawk, Aztec, Apache, Dakota."

I thought about the HAARP blasts and wondered could I, too, have been a victim of US military testing. What were the long-term effects of those scalar waves?

Before Don could launch into another story, Jedah interrupted. "I wanted to show the guys the old mine, Dad."

"Sure. Sure, son. Great idea."

I approached Don to say goodbye but he waved me off.

"No, no. I'm coming, too."

"No, you're not, Dad. What are you thinking?"

"Sure I am, I feel better than ever today. Come on, we'll just go for a short hop."

And almost miraculously this dying man pulled himself out of the bed, and with Jedah's help walked over to the closet and pulled on a coat.

His car was a fishtailed barge from the sixties, an embarrassment of chrome-bending and panel-beating prowess. Jedah folded his dad into the front seat while the rest of us plunged into the low-slung sofa in the back. Don kept up stories all the way about his grandparents who travelled out by cart from Oklahoma, across arid Indian land to the uncertainty of this place, and how they had started prospecting first for borax and then gold until the government gave them a parcel of land which they were allowed keep if they built a house on it. As demand for Borax increased during the First World War, they did well, and afterwards his grandmother had rented out rooms to mustard-gas victims who needed the desert air. The goldmine had never made much money, he said, and by the time Jedah came along, there just wasn't enough to support them all. Ever since, they had been doing less and less mining. The price of gold had dropped so low in recent years that they could hardly cover the cost of diesel for the crusher. But they still kept the place just about ticking over

The mine was a ramshackle scaffold of stout planks hammered together a hundred years before and preserved perfectly in the dry air. Inside it was dark and dusty, with only a few shafts of light peering through missing planks that revealed the crust of rock dust covering everything. The original 1908 crusher was still working, its cogs and pistons greased and gleaming as though it had just left the workshop. Its piston rods soared towards the roof, while heavy chains hung down to carts on a track that were used to carry the ore from the mine shaft next door. It was all so incongruous, so unlikely a scene to find less than two hours from Beverly Hills, that it reminded me of something out of the Warner Brothers lot or the Holodeck.

The mine shaft itself – a four-foot square hole with a winch above it – didn't look all that impressive from above.

"Guess how deep it is?" Jedah said.

I shrugged.

"Over a thousand feet," he said, dropping a pebble which took an impressively long time to find the bottom. "My granddad dug the first two hundred feet alone using only a pick and whatever explosives he could afford. Then Dad and my uncle continued digging until my uncle's lungs packed in. The shaft would have been over eight hundred feet by then."

Maud was staring into it, mesmerised, with Don clutching on to her for support.

"I did the final two hundred feet on my own," growled Don, his larynx pumiced by a life inhaling grit. "There's probably another thousand feet of side spurs going different directions, following horizontal seams into the mountain."

I looked down again with new respect. The hole was the lifetimes' achievement of three generations. It was sad to think of it obsolete – just an empty cavity. As I was thinking this, Maud suddenly perked up, saying she was becoming increasingly excited by it. By its potential. For her it was a vaginal passage, a great birth canal leading into the cervix of the Earth Goddess. She wanted desperately to experience what it was like inside and begged Jedah to bring her down. He refused. It gave him panic attacks, he said, but she could go down alone if she wanted.

This didn't daunt her in the least, and grabbing hold of the ladder, she started down into the abyss, with us watching from above until we could no longer see her.

"It's sort of awesome, isn't it?" Jedah said.

I nodded, impressed by how the darkness had gobbled her up so quickly, shifted her to a fourth dimension. Looking into it you realised it had a power over you, like snake eyes.

Jedah agreed.

"I get the same feeling looking off a bridge," he said. "You know, the water charging by, luring you in – like that scene in the movie with that English guy in it when he's on the bridge, you know?"

"Which?"

"You know the one. I heard you were banging the girl from that movie – what's her name?"

"I wasn't banging her," I said through gritted teeth. "I just knew her, that's all."

How the hell did he know?

"Sorry, no offence, man. Just Hugo was saying . . ."

"I wasn't banging her, right? I loved her," I said staring down into the blackness.

"Yeah, sure," he said agreeably, then adding too eagerly, "I can imagine!"

"Fuck off," I said.

"No, seriously, she's hot. Did you see her in *Playboy*? Something else! Impressive, eh?"

"I didn't see it," I said abruptly.

"You never seen those pics? Oh, man! You've got a treat in store. I'm sure if you call into that museum, they probably have it on file. You know the one, Erotica on Hollywood Boulevard."

"Don't be gross," I said. I had noticed the museum all right, it was right next to the Celebrity Lingerie Hall of Fame, but it had never occurred to me that they might keep her back issues on file. Even if it had, I wouldn't have looked at it. No way. It didn't interest me. Well, whether it did or not, I wouldn't look, not so much out of respect, but because if I ever did meet Eve again I knew I wouldn't be able to hide my blushes.

"Hugo tells me you two fell out?"

"Sort of," I mumbled.

I didn't trust myself to say any more, but he was looking at me expectantly. I knew I wouldn't get away so easily.

"Yeah, we did. Right! Actually I was hoping to see her again in LA, but . . . but, it didn't work out. I couldn't track her down."

"Shame."

"Yeah."

"Real shame."

"Yeah," I said again.

Jedah turned to his father.

"You know who I mean, Dad, don't you? The girl from that Keanu movie – the feisty one with the hair?"

"Her? Sure! She was some piece of ass," Don cried.

"You should have asked me," Jedah said.

"Asked you what?" I said.

"Where she lived, dumbo," Jedah said.

"You?" I said derisively.

"Yeah, sure! She smokes a little, doesn't she? You know, of the good stuff, I mean? She likes the bit of blow. I'm sure I read that somewhere: something about a little late-night indiscretion that made it to the gossip columns. I might be wrong, now – it's hard to keep track. This town is so full of drugged-up bimbos."

"I don't know," I said, purposefully noncommittal.

"Well, if she does, I'm your man," Jedah purred smugly. "I know every two-bit star in town who likes a bit of the good stuff. Who knows, I probably have her details on file somewhere."

"Bullshit," I said.

"What?!" he said, sounding affronted. "How else do you think they score? You think it just turns up out of the ether? No man! There's a system. Deliveries. House-to-house calls."

"Are you serious?"

"Fucking A!" Jedah cried. "I've probably been to every jumped-up wannabe in town. What's the bet I've called to her pad a dozen times or more dropping stuff off. I can't remember for sure, but it would all be back home in the database. This business is based on trust, you see? Building up loyalty. It's like anything – pool cleaning, panic room maintenance – you build up your clients and keep 'em sweet. Most times I just leave the stuff with the doormen or the minder or whatever, but sometimes they invite me right on up.

"Tell you what: soon as I get back to town, I'll see if I can dig you out her details."

"Wow, Jedah. Thanks!"

I was so excited.

Rabbit, that mischievous bunny, had pulled himself out of the hat at the very last minute.

We heard another "Wow!" come echoing up out of the centre of the earth and Maud poked her big, eager head out of the rabbit hole.

"Wow! That was fan-fucking-tastic!" she roared, casting her arm around for help.

"That was, like, out of this world. Literally! I could feel it. Really, I could – the pulse of the earth – the harmonic frequency of the Mother Goddess. It was so profound. I've had this awesome idea. Like, I really should be running workshops there, you know? Like in the womb of the Goddess? A whole rebirthing thing. Bringing people in touch with their inner being: that sort of vibe. Weekend courses following the sacred path towards the darkness of the nurturing womb and at the end re-emerging born into the light. It would be so deep! We'd actually have our lunch in the vaginal passage! I'd make up uterus juice soup!"

She turned to Don, who was resting up against the old crusher, and asked, "Would you be on for it? Would it be cool to rent it out just for the weekends? If I got the right numbers, I could pay whatever you wanted. People would fork out big time for an experience like this."

Don didn't reply. His face remained poker still. I noticed a shiver pass right through him, but it might have been the draft that seemed to rise up from the centre of the earth. Llael, noticing him shiver, came over and held his wrinkly old hand, and we all bundled ourselves back into the car again. Maud told us that the wind was the earth's breath and it infused our cells with something or other, but I wasn't really listening, I was already imagining having Eve's address in my hands. Fantasising about ringing the doorbell and hearing her footsteps approach. Her mouth coyly, tentatively inviting me in.

The sun was just beginning to set as we rushed back along the dead straight desert roads to pick up Hugo, passing convoys of huge parcelled bundles being whisked at high speed through the wilderness on military low-loaders. The bundles, which from their shape appeared to be tanks and helicopters and rockets and crates, were wrapped in beige canvas and strapped on to the olive-green trucks. From far away they looked like huge cobs of unripened corn, and I smiled to myself, thinking how the Ray-Banned soldiers with their bronze arms hanging nonchalantly out the cab windows and their chunky silver watches dangling loose, had no idea how ludicrous they looked.

At the spot where we had arranged to meet Hugo, we could find no sign of him except a bouquet of freshly picked desert foliage, with radial lines of pebbles spreading out in different directions. He couldn't be too far away. Each of us followed one of the lines off into the desert until finally Llael found him lying spread-eagled on the ground. He had taken off his clothes, and the sight of him brought me straight back to the Israeli boys, though Hugo was in a very different state of mind. He felt no despair; to the contrary, he was ecstatic. He had found the leaves he wanted and was now happily surfing whatever realms they had brought him to. Fabian had told me once that certain species of mushroom and lichen had been carried to earth by solar winds as spores, which had been launched into space by inhabitants of the Pleiades constellation thousands of years before. These plants, while looking like earth–indigenous species on the outside, were in fact portals into the holographic mainframe of Pleiadian consciousness. They were tools through which the advanced beings could download enlightened ideas to developing species throughout the galaxy when the time was right. It was an ingenious idea: a plant that when ingested would take the user on a journey of discovery, while also distracting the mind so that alien cells could go about their business of rearranging the internal mental circuits and programmes of the brain. Unfortunately the plan hadn't worked on earth. They had never been able to make contact with our most influential leaders since it was only shamans and hippies who took hallucinogens. Fabian regarded this as one of the great lost opportunities of mankind. He had even led a delegation to the UN buildings in New York to lobby the General Assembly to consider holding at least one plenary session a year under the influence of psilocybins. The widened perspective that this would bring about would be enough to initiate a whole raft of global initiatives. The Assembly had accepted his submission and promised to review it, but they hadn't got back to him yet.

Anyway, it was clear that Hugo was enjoying himself too much to go any place right away. He wanted to spend the night camped out in the desert. Llael and Maud were keen on this idea also and, after talking it over, they decided that instead of heading back to LA as planned, we would camp here overnight and continue on down to Mexico through Arizona at first light. I tried suggesting we take one last trip back to LA before heading south, but Hugo insisted that he needed to be amidst Mayan energy as soon as possible. The United States soil was debilitating, he said; it was sapping his energy. They were all so excited by the idea of reaching Mexico that I didn't feel I could press them any further.

Jedah said he couldn't stay. He had to get back to LA for work in the morning. But he told us not to worry; he could easily hitch a ride with someone at the protest meeting. It took me only a couple of seconds to decide what I had to do. I had to go with him. I couldn't leave him now, not without seeing this thing through. Not when I had got this far. It was too important.

I told Hugo that I was going to head back to LA with Jedah, but that if things didn't work out I'd meet up with him in Mexico later on. He was drooling down the side of his face at the time and I don't think he was taking much in, but he nodded amiably. Maud told me it wouldn't be hard to track them down in Mexico. They would be hanging out somewhere around the Mayan ruins in the Yucatan – most likely Chichen Itza.

"Ride it out," Hugo said. "That's my advice! You've gotta follow your heart, man . . . Soon come, good fellow, soon come."

Llael was a bit upset about my leaving, but she was spending more and more time with Maud now, and I felt it was important for her to bond with a mother figure. She didn't need me so much any more. I wanted so badly to tell her what she meant to me, how much she had helped me, how she had opened my heart; but she was only five after all. It would only freak her out. And anyhow, if things didn't work out, I would be seeing her again real soon. Maud agreed to drive me and

Jedah back to the community hall to collect his photos. Hugo wanted to go with us, to see us off, but he was convinced that he couldn't leave the precise spot he had found. He had to spend the night there, he said. He was on a spirit journey: charging his soul with Joshua energy. If he left now the battery would be flat for ever.

He wanted to give me a big hug to say goodbye, but it was awkward seeing as he was still naked and the datura had given him a permanent hard on. Somehow, by standing stork-fashion, I was able to get close to him without being impaled, and we had a genuine and heartfelt farewell. If all went well, I wouldn't be seeing him again for a very long time; at least until he came to visit me and Eve at the donkey sanctuary. I would miss him. I wanted to tell him how much I appreciated all I had got from him and from the rest of them – from Fabian, Portia, Luna, Rory, Esteban, Demofilo, Nadine, Guinevere and even stupid Paddy. Somehow they were all connected, all characters bound together by the road. Bit-players who had come along to play their part. I loved them all. Yet now I knew it was time to walk away. To strike out alone towards my destiny.

We got a lift back to LA from some Mexicans who were driving a container of lettuce to the airport and reached Jedah's house by midnight. It was as modest as the houses of the people I knew in Canada; these were definitely the most unassuming drug dealers I had ever met. Jedah even had a day job in the local macrobiotic café to throw off the IRS. No sooner were we in the door than he opened a safe in the wall and dug out his address book. He did it with such éclat it might as well have been another Dead Sea Scroll – the lost Gospel of Mary Magdalene.

But unfortunately Eve's name wasn't in it.

Typical.

It was too late to get back to Hugo now. I was stuck in LA with nothing. I hadn't really thought about how I'd make it to Mexico on my own until now. After paying Fabian everything I owed him, I didn't have all that much money left, and I didn't fancy hitching the whole way through Mexico. I was thinking all this through, realising I'd be back on the farm with Diarmuid a whole lot sooner than I had expected, when Jedah got up and fetched us both a beer. He came back and just sat there watching me. He could see how messed up I was. As usual Rabbit seemed to be enjoying the mess, but Jedah had more heart. Out of pity, he said he'd make a few phone calls for me, if I liked. See what he could find out.

"Do you know who her agent is?" he asked.

"Something Dyson, I think."

"Not Diana?" he asked.

"Yeah, I think so. Diana Dyson, that's it."

"Man, I know her. That chick is one of my regulars. You sure it's Diana?

"As far as I remember," I said. "But she probably remembers me, too. I sent some pretty desperate letters last year. I might be on a list."

"No worries!" he said. "Diana is cool. She likes a bit of the good skank weed – no harm in that! She used to be more of an Acapulco Gold girl, but she's maturing, becoming more discerning, and now she's a strictly BC bud girl. Organic or nothing."

He dug out her details, saying I should go see her first thing in the morning.

"I can't," I said. "No way. When she hears my name, she'll get me arrested straight off."

"Well, then don't mention your name," he said. "Tell them at reception it's Pepe Le Pew – and just see what happens. Trust me!"

So there I was next morning outside Dyson Associates on Vine, and sure enough the words, "Could you tell Ms Dyson, Pepe Le Pew is here," got me ushered straight upstairs.

Diana Dyson looked at me suspiciously across her desk.

"You're not Pepe," she said coldly.

"No, Ms Dyson. I'm his consigliore," I replied.

Jedah had told me to say that, too. He had briefed me on everything and warned me most of all to be super deferential. It seemed to do the trick. She told me to sit down and offered coffee.

"I'll come straight to the point, Ms Dyson," I began. "I met a girl and she fell in love with me, and I with her. It was the sweetest thing imaginable: what both of us needed more than anything, more than air. It made sense, made us sane, made us stay alive. D'you understand?"

Diana Dyson looked somewhat startled, but to her credit, she allowed me continue.

Jedah had reckoned on this. As with all of his clients, Diana was suffering the effects of the cannabis drought and was desperate for a fresh supply. He knew she would be prepared to put up with almost anything I did or said in the hope that somewhere stashed on my person I might have a few ounces of prime, organic, Rocky Mountain bud.

"Well, sometimes, Ms Dyson," I continued, "the world doesn't support such love. It's too fragile. It needs incubation, you know? Like how a nurseryman frets over his seedlings: protecting against frost, breaking down clods of peat that seem too big. Like how kidney transplants don't always take – the merest, minor thing, unforeseen event, can cause upset.

"That's how it was with us, Ms Dyson, that's how it was with us. We experienced a shock, a fright; just a little one, but it was at the time we were most tender, and right there and then it withered. Right in front of our eyes, Ms Dyson.

"If you had only seen it! It was such a beautiful thing. And then it withered. It needed support and it just wasn't there."

I could see her glancing towards the phone, weighing up whether to call security or stick it out another minute. I upped the pace.

"Anyway, I shouldn't be concerning you with this. It's all in the past now. Right now what is crucial is that the two of us meet again. It's vital. You see, we both ran away. In different ways, we did the same thing. And as you know, Ms Dyson, that's never good. It's just not healthy. That's why I'm talking to you."

I could see a flicker of something other than suspicion pass across her face, possibly even sympathy. She was beginning to realise her chances of scoring were diminishing. I drove home my weak advantage.

"She's a client of yours, this girl," I said. "And although I don't know how the whole experience has left her, we both owe it to her to check. To make sure she's okay. To put it simply, Ms Dyson, I need to see her. You have to help me. You're the only one who can."

A flash of fury passed across her face.

"Who the hell do you think you are?" she said.

"I'm a friend of Eve's," I replied urgently, "and if you care at all for her, you'll allow me see her. It's what she needs now, whether she knows it or not."

"How the hell did you get into my office?" she asked, but the question was directed more at herself than me.

I just smiled.

"I'll say one thing for you, you're the most resourceful potato farmer I've ever met."

My heart catapulted, but I didn't dare let on. She knew who I was! She knew precisely who I was. Eve must have mentioned me, because I certainly hadn't mentioned anything about potatoes to anyone. Was this good or bad? I sat back and we both looked at each other for a torturously long moment. Then she let out a low sigh and reached for her Rolodex.

"Tell me at least that you've brought some grass with you," she said resignedly. "Please tell me that."

I think she already knew the answer. If I had had any, I would have given it gladly.

Twenty minutes later I was in a taxi winding my way into the Hollywood Hills, Eve's address on a scrap of paper twirling between my fingers. (The house was on Turtle Rock Drive! It couldn't possibly be more appropriate. It was the sign I had always looked for.) Suddenly, I was where I had always wanted to be. Driving towards her. Approaching. I was almost with her, believe it or not! It was too awesome to register.

In my mind I was already there. I could feel her beside me. I could practically smell her. And if I allowed myself, I could enter the labyrinthine tangled chamber of her blood and bones and hear the cacophony of gurgling, twitching drumbeats inside her body. Physically I was still sitting in the taxi, of course, but somehow I was also connected to her in her house a mile or two in front of me. She was walking around right at this minute – I was certain of it. I was inside her after all, I could tell. And as she walked so, I felt her thighs rise and fall like ships at sea. The memory of flipping around in the shower tray came back to me, that sense of electromagnetic energy surging through me. The phone rang and she went to pick it up. It was hard to make out what she was saying – all the internal sounds were making such a racket, an orchestra of flushing and flowing – but if I shut my ears to it and found a coding, a framework within the tumult – imagining how the words would sound from the far side of her larynx and rearranging them into their proper configuration, turning them inside out, as it were – I could more or less make it out. By concentrating on each syllable and breaking them down into vowel sounds and dental and plosive consonants, I gathered enough to be pretty sure she was talking to Diana Dyson. I could feel the effect Ms Dyson's words were having on her: the inner reactions, the contractions of the heart, the speed of her blood, the repercussions in her mind. Ms Dyson was telling Eve about me, telling her I was on my way, and although I could feel surprise, there was no fear, no dread or even anger. Interest. It was interest more than anything, and maybe just a hint of happiness, too. Just a hint is all I'm saying. Whatever, it was definitely more positive than negative. I was sure of that.

I was dangerously close to the edge, now. This was more than just hearing Rabbit – I had actually slipped through the fabric of space. The cliff of insanity lay straight ahead. Some would say I had overshot it, but if so, Eve was there, too, and that's all that mattered.

When finally the taxi swung into the driveway, I saw her standing there at the doorway waiting. And I swear I could see her smile. I could, I really could! My cells were stretching out from my skin towards hers, and so, too, were hers towards me – literally popping out as though they were opposite poles that wanted, needed, to be together. A webwork of golden-coloured thread was spreading out from both of us, wrapping us in its cocoon. It would be okay. It would all be okay. Rabbit whispered something in my ear, and I told him I loved him.

DRAGO JANČAR
Joyce's Pupil

The finest short stories of Slovenia's most prominent author

A young man learns English in Trieste in 1914 from James Joyce, who repeatedly describes an oil lamp. Years later, in 1941, this same man must flee his country, and he becomes the Slovenian voice of British radio. On his return to Yugoslavia, he falls foul of the new communist authorities.

The characters who populate the stories of Drago Jančar stand at the periphery of tragic histories; they see the ground open under their feet yet remain leaning above the pit.

Drago Jančar has been described as "the seismologist of a chaotic history". In this exceptional collection Brandon introduces the vision of the leading Slovenian writer of his generation.

Drago Jančar, born in Maribor in 1948, is a novelist, short story writer, essayist and playwright. His works have been translated into many European languages, and his plays have enjoyed a number of foreign productions. In 1974 he was taken into custody over alleged propaganda, and he was active in the democratisation of his native country as President of the Slovenian PEN Centre between 1987 and 1991. In 1993 he received the highest Slovenian literary award for his lifetime achievement, and in 1994 he won the European Short Story Award. He lives in Ljubljana.

ISBN 0 86322 340 0; paperback original

NENAD VELIČKOVIĆ
Lodgers

Lodgers is a hilarious, unsentimental report from the
front lines of the Balkan wars of the 1990s. All of the
folly and the horror of that time are revealed in the
sarcastic report of the novel's teenage would-be
authoress.

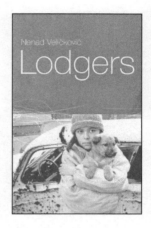

Maja lives in the basement of a Sarajevo museum,
enduring with equal annoyance Serb artillery and
vegetarian meals that taste like fried sponge. Her father,
the museum director, zealously guards the treasures
upstairs while their aged co-lodger Julio plots to trade
them away. Maja's mother copes with yoga while dour
stepbrother Davor endures the endless crying and
cravings of his pregnant wife. Floating amidst it all is Maja's grandmother, blind
and deaf, yet drawn to any conversation involving food.

Need and crisis propel Maja and her companions from one humorous situation
to another. Yet her pitch-perfect gallows humour makes it clear that the brutalities
of war penetrate these small moments of life – and even the self-centredness of a
teenaged girl.

Nenad Veličković was born in Sarajevo in 1962. He is the author of novels,
short stories, essays, tv and radio scripts and plays. He has received many awards
for his writing and he teaches Literature at the University of Sarajevo. He served for
four years in the BiH Army and in the early 1990s was Secretary of the Institute
for Literature in Sarajevo.

ISBN 0 86322 348 6; paperback original

BRYAN MACMAHON
Hero Town

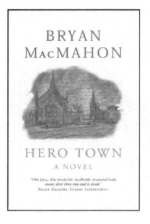

"*Hero Town* is the perfect retrospective: here the town is the hero, a character of epic and comic proportions. . . It may come to be recognized as MacMahon's masterpiece." Professor Bernard O'Donohue

"For the course of a calendar year, Peter Mulrooney, the musing pedagogue, saunters through the streets and the people, looking at things and leaving them so. They talk to him; he listens, and in his ears we hear the authentic voice of local Ireland, all its tics and phrases and catchcalls. Like Joyce, this wonderful, excellently structured book comes alive when you read it aloud." Frank Delaney, *Sunday Independent*

ISBN 0 86322 342 7; paperback

JOHN B. KEANE
The Bodhrán Makers

The first and best novel from one of Ireland's best-loved writers, a moving and telling portrayal of a rural community in the '50s, a poverty-stricken people who never lost their dignity.

"Furious, raging, passionate and very, very funny."
Boston Globe

"This powerful and poignant novel provides John B. Keane with a passport to the highest levels of Irish literature." *Irish Press*

"Sly, funny, heart-rending. . . Keane writes lyrically; recommended." *Library Journal*

ISBN 0 86322 300 1; paperback

JACK BARRY
Miss Katie Regrets

From the criminal underbelly of Celtic Tiger Dublin comes a gripping story of guns, drugs, prostitution and corruption.

A seemingly humdrum shooting leads a detective to an online male prostitution service and to hints of a link with a corrupt politician.

The plot moves between Dublin and Amsterdam, Manchester and British suburbia. At the centre of an apparent spider's web of intrigue sits the enigmatic figure of Miss Katie, a crabby Dublin transvestite who will, under pressure, kiss and tell. And, perhaps, kill.

ISBN 0 86322 354 0; paperback original

KEN BRUEN (ED)
Dublin Noir

Nineteen previously unpublished stories by acclaimed crime writers, each one set in Dublin

Brand new stories by Ray Banks, James O. Born, Ken Bruen, Reed Farrell Coleman, Eoin Colfer, Jim Fusilli, Patrick J. Lambe, Laura Lippman, Craig McDonald, Pat Mullan, Gary Phillips, John Rickards, Peter Spiegelman, Jason Starr, Olen Steinhauer, Charlie Stella, Duane Swierczynski, Sarah Weinman and Kevin Wignall.

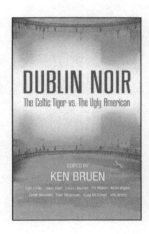

ISBN 0 86322 353 2; paperback original

SAM MILLAR
The Redemption Factory

"He writes well, with a certain raw energy, and he is not afraid to take risks with his fiction. The result is a novel that can sometimes be as shocking as it is original."
Irish Independent

A man is murdered, an anarchist suspected by his own group of being a police informer, but the killer has his doubts. Years later, in a deserted wood a corrupt businessman, Shank, silences a whistleblower. Lurking sometimes at the edge of the action, sometimes at the centre, is the deeply dysfunctional family of Shank and his two strange daughters, and their gruesome abattoir.

ISBN 0 86322 339 7; paperback original

SAM MILLAR
The Darkness of Bones

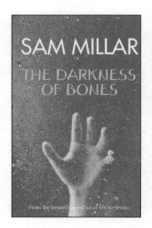

A tense tale of murder, betrayal, sexual abuse and revenge, and the corruption at the heart of the respectable establishment.

A young boy discovers a bone in a snow-covered forest. Initially, he thinks it could simply be that of an animal. But it belongs to a young girl who has been missing for three years. Meanwhile, in a derelict orphanage, a tramp discovers the sexually mutilated and decapitated corpse of its former head warden.

ISBN 0 86322 350 8; paperback original

KITTY FITZGERALD
Small Acts of Treachery

"Mystery and politics, a forbidden sexual attraction that turns into romance; Kitty Fitzgerald takes the reader on a gripping roller coaster through the recent past. In *Small Acts of Treachery* a woman of courage defies the power not only of the secret state but of sinister global elites. This is a story you can't stop reading, with an undertow which will give you cause to reflect." Sheila Rowbotham

"[It] is a super book with a fascinating story and great characters . . . all the more impressive because of the very sinister feeling I was left with that it is all too frighteningly possible." *Books Ireland*

ISBN 086322 297 8; paperback

KATE MCCAFFERTY
Testimony of an Irish Slave Girl

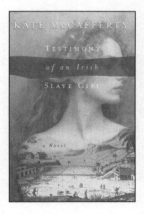

"McCafferty's haunting novel chronicles an overlooked chapter in the annals of human slavery . . . A meticulously researched piece of historical fiction that will keep readers both horrified and mesmerized." *Booklist*

"Thousands of Irish men, women and children were sold into slavery to work in the sugar-cane fields of Barbados in the 17th century . . . McCafferty has researched her theme well and, through Cot, shows us the terrible indignities and suffering endured." *Irish Independent*

ISBN 0 86322 314 1; hardback
ISBN 0 86322 338 9; paperback

KEN BRUEN

"Outstanding. . . . Ireland's version of Scotland's Ian Rankin."
Publishers Weekly

"Exhibits Ken Bruen's all-encompassing ability to depict the underbelly of the criminal world and still imbue it with a torrid fascination... carrying an adrenalin charge for those who like their thrillers rough, tough, mean and dirty." *The Irish Times*

ISBN 0 86322 302 8; paperback

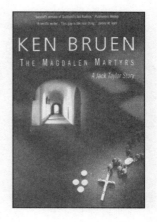

"Collectively, the Jack Taylor novels are Bruen's masterwork, and *The Dramatist* is the darkest and most profound installment of the series to date. A clean and sober Taylor – a man who has always been a danger to his friends – proves infinitely more destructive to those around him. The senseless death of a recurring character brings *The Dramatist* to a crushing conclusion. The novel's chilling final image of Taylor could serve as a dictionary illustration for noir. Readers who dare the journey will be days shaking this most haunting book out of their heads." *This Week*

ISBN 0 86322 319 2; paperback original

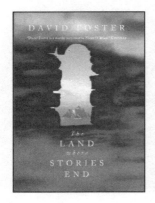

DAVID FOSTER
The Land Where Stories End

"Australia's most original and important living novelist." *Independent Monthly*

"A post-modern fable set in the dark ages of Ireland. . . [A] beautifully written humorous myth that is entirely original. The simplicity of language is perfectly complementary to the wry, occasionally laugh-out-loud humour and the captivating tale." *Irish World*

"I was taken by surprise and carried easily along by the amazing story and by the punchy clarity of the writing. . . This book is imaginative and fantastic. . . It is truly amazing." *Books Ireland*

ISBN 0 86322 311 7; hardback

CHET RAYMO
Valentine

"Such nebulous accounts [as we have] have been just waiting for someone to make a work of historical fiction out of them. American novelist and physicist Raymo has duly obliged with his recently published *Valentine: A Love Story*." *The Scotsman*

"[A] vivid and lively account of how Valentine's life may have unfolded… Raymo has produced an imaginative and enjoyable read, sprinkled with plenty of food for philosophical thought." *Sunday Tribune*

ISBN 0 86322 327 3; paperback original